Collins

D0267364

HarperCollins Publishers
Westerhill Rd, Bishopbriggs, Glasgow, G64 2QT

www.**fire**and**water**.com

First published 2001

Reprint 10 9 8 7 6 5 4 3 2 1 0

ISBN 0 00 710163 5

A catalogue reference for this book is available from The British Library

Photography: Angelo Gai
    With additional photography/material from: Ian Brooke, Sheila
        Ferguson, Ian and James Smart, The Printer's Devil
    Artville (pp 91, 92, 95, 96, 97, 99, 100, 102, 103, 104, 106, 107 108)
    The Anthony Blake Photo Library (pp 79, 83, 93[tl & br], 94[tr], 95[bl],
        96[bl], 97[br], 98[tl], 100[tl], 101[tl, bl], 102[tl], 103[bl], 104[tl],
        105[tr & br], 106[ml])
    Wine material: Andrea Gillies
    Map: Heather Moore
Layout & Origination: The Printer's Devil, Glasgow

Other titles in the Collins Language Survival Guide series:
    France (0 00 710161 9)
    Spain (0 00 710164 3)
    Germany (0 00 710162 7)
These titles are also published in a CD pack containing a 50-minute CD
and Language Survival Guide.

$$\frac{458}{1324323}$$

Printed in Italy by Amadeus SpA

CONTENTS

USEFUL WEBSITES

TOURIST INFORMATION SITES

Currency Converters
www.oanda.com
www.x-rates.com

Foreign Office Advice
www.fco.gov.uk/travel/
  countryadvice.asp

Passport Office
www.ukpa.gov.uk/

Health advice
www.thetraveldoctor.com
www.doh.gov.uk/traveladvice
www.doh.gov.uk/hat

Travel insurance
www.insurance.org.uk

Pets
www.maff.gov.uk/animalh/
  quarantine

Weather
www.skihotline.co.uk/reports

ITALIAN SITES

Hotel Listings
www.travel.it
www.italy-rome-hotel.com
www.italyhotel.com

Transport
www.fs-on-line.com (Italian
  railways)

Tourism
www.enit.it
www.initaly.com
www.italytour.com
www.itwg.com (Italian tourist web
  guide)
www.webtourist.net/travel/europe
  /italy
www.cybertour.it
www.romeguide.it
www.doge.it (Venice guide)
www.northernitaly.com
www.uffizi.firenze.it (Uffizi,
  Florence)

Internet Cafés
www.netcafes.com
www.ecs.net/cafe

Shopping
www.made-in-italy.com/index.html

Opera
www.operabase.com/en/

Newspapers
www.repubblica.it (La Repubblica
  online)
www.corriere.it (Corriere della Sera)
www.mega.it/mask (Florence's
  paper, La Maschera, with listings,
  maps, etc.)

INTRODUCTION

As technology sweeps across the world, travellers aren't just faced with the prospect of speaking a foreign language – they also have foreign machines to contend with. Machines for parking, for dispensing cash, for buying tickets and food. Often there is nobody about to ask how they work. *Collins Language Survival Guides* address this problem by showing photographically signs and situations you might come across.

The things that throw you are often the ones that look familiar – such as buses, trains or phones – but which operate slightly differently.

There are usually codes to how things operate, and though you might not think you are aware of them, you are probably using them every day: the colour-coding for roads (blue for motorways, green for major roads, yellow for temporary signs) or when buying milk (generally blue for whole milk, green for semi-skimmed and red for skimmed). It's when these familiar codes don't work in the same way, that you feel slightly at a loss and probably more unsure than you need be. By making a note of how these types of things work and knowing a few keywords, you will feel much more confident.

The unique combination of practical information, photos and phrases found in this book provides the key to hassle-free travel and the colour-coding below shows how information is presented and how to access it as quickly as possible.

i   *General, practical information which will provide useful tips on getting the best out of your trip*

destra
des-tra
right

sinistra
see-nees-tra
left

keywords

◀ **keywords**

these are words that are useful to know both when you see them written down or you hear them spoken

key talk ▶

short, simple phrases that you can change and adapt to suit your own situation

excuse me!
scusi!
skoo-zee

do you know where...?
sa dov'è...?
sa do-ve...

we're looking for...
cerchiamo...
cherk-ya-mo...

talking

The **Food Section** allows you to choose more easily from what is on offer, both for snacks and at restaurants.

The practical 5000-word, English-Italian and Italian-English **Dictionary** means that you will never be stuck for words.

SPEAKING ITALIAN

We've tried to make the pronunciation under the phrases as clear as possible. We've split up the words to make them easy to read, but don't pause too long between syllables. Italian isn't really hard to pronounce and once you learn a few basic rules, it shouldn't be too long before you can read straight from the Italian.

Longer words are usually stressed on the next to last syllable, but we show all stressed syllables in **heavy type**, so you won't be caught out by any exceptions.

The spellings **c** and **ch** might confuse you, because **c** is sometimes pronounced like English **ch** as in church, while the Italian **ch** is pronounced like the English **k**. (Look at the English for kilogram and the Italian **chilogramma**.) So **c'è** (there is) is pronounced like English check without the final **k** sound, while **che?** (what?) is pronounced **kay**. The rule to remember is that **c** followed by **e** or **i** makes it a soft **ch** sound. But **c** followed by **a**, **o** or **u** has a hard **k** sound. Try practising saying and reading the following words:

chiave *kee-a-vay* (key) **cibo** *chee-bo* (food)
chiesa *kee-ay-za* (church) **cena** *chay-na* (dinner)

The letter **g** behaves in a similar way. When followed by **a**, **o** or **u**, **g** will be hard. When followed by **e** or **i**, **g** will be soft. The word for lake is **lago**, for lakes the word is **laghi**. The **h** has been added to keep the **g** hard. So when you see a **ch** or **gh** combination in Italian, remember to make the **c** and **g** hard.

Sometimes Italian has two distinctive vowel sounds next to each other, in other words like **dei**, shown in the pronunciation as *day-ee*. These sounds merge with each other, so don't separate them with a long pause.

Finally, pronounce all **r**'s when you see them in Italian words.

Basic rules to remember are:

italian	sounds like	example	pronunciation
a	c**a**t	**pasta**	*pas-ta*
e	b**e**t/d**ay**	**letto/per**	*let-to/payr*
i	m**ee**t	**vino**	*vee-no*
o	g**o**t	**botta**	*bot-ta*
u	b**oo**t	**luna**	*loo-na*
gli	mi**lli**on	**figlio**	*feel-yo*
sc *(before **e/i**)*	**sh**op	**sci**	*shee*
sc *(before **a/o/u**)*	**sc**an	**scarpa**	*skar-pa*

EVERYDAY TALK

There are two forms of address in Italian, formal and informal. You should always stick with the formal until you are on a first-name basis. For the purposes of this book we will use the formal.

yes
sì
see

no
no
no

ok/that's fine
va bene
va be-nay

please
per favore
payr fa-vo-ray

thank you
grazie
grats-yay

thanks very much
grazie molto
grats-yay mol-to

don't mention it
prego
pray-go

that's very kind
molto gentile
mol-to jen-tee-lay

hello
buon giorno
bwon jor-no

goodbye
arrivederci
ar-ree-ve-der-chee

good evening
buona sera
bwo-na say-ra

good night
buona notte
bwo-na not-tay

see you later
a più tardi
a pyoo tar-dee

excuse me!
permesso!
per-mes-so

sorry!
scusi!
skoo-zee

I am sorry
mi dispiace
mee dees-pya-chay

I don't understand
non capisco
non ka-pees-ko

I don't know
non lo so
non lo so

Addressing people

Italians are quite formal when addressing each other. When greeting someone in the street or shop you can simply say *buon giorno, Signora* (for a woman) and *buon giorno, Signore* (for a man). If you are not sure how formal to be, a good alternative for hello is *salve* which you can use with anyone. Among young people and friends, you will hear *ciao*.

how are you?
come sta?
ko-may sta

fine thanks?
bene grazie
be-nay grat-see-ay

and you?
e lei?
e lay

hi, Michele
ciao Michele
chow mee-ke-le

bye, Luisa
ciao Luisa
chow loo-ee-za

piacere
nice to meet you
pya-cher-ay

*The simplest way to ask for something in a shop or bar is by naming what you want and adding **per favore**.*

keywords keywords keywords

1	**uno**
	oo-no

2	**due**
	doo-ay

3	**tre**
	tray

4	**quattro**
	kwat-ro

5	**cinque**
	cheen-kway

6	**sei**
	say

7	**sette**
	set-tay

8	**otto**
	ot-to

9	**nove**
	no-vay

10	**dieci**
	dee-ay-chee

a ... please
un/una ... per favore
oon/oo-na ... payr fa-vo-ray

a coffee please
un caffè per favore
oon kaf-fe payr fa-vo-ray

a beer please
una birra per favore
oo-na beer-ra payr fa-vo-ray

an ice cream and 2 beers please
un gelato e due birre per favore
oon jay-la-to ay doo-ay beer-ray payr fa-vo-ray

the *(singular)*
il/la
eel/la

the *(plural)*
i/le
ee/lay

the menu please
il menù per favore
eel me-noo payr fa-vo-ray

the bill please
il conto per favore
eel kon-to payr fa-vo-ray

another...
un altro/un' altra...
oon al-tro/oon al-tra...

more...
ancora...
an-ko-ra...

another beer
un'altra birra
oon al-tra beer-ra

another tea
un altro tè
oon al-tro te

2 more beers
ancora due birre
an-ko-ra doo-ay beer-ray

2 more coffees
ancora due caffè
an-ko-ra doo-ay kaf-fe

3 tickets
tre biglietti
tray beel-yet-tee

4 ice creams
quattro gelati
kwat-tro jay-la-tee

To catch someone's attention

The easiest way to catch someone's attention is by using *scusi*. If it is an older man or woman, it is polite to add *Signore* (for the man) and *Signora* (for the woman). If you are trying to get through a crowd, use *permesso*.

excuse me!
scusi, Signore/Signora!
skoo-zee seen-yo-ray/seen-yo-ra

can you help me?
può aiutarmi?
pwo a-yoo-tar-mee

do you know where... is?
sa dov'è...?
sa do-ve...

do you know how I get to...?
sa come si va a...?
sa ko-may see va a...

By combining key words and phrases you can build up your language and adapt the phrases to suit your own situation.

avete...?
do you have...?

do you have a map?
avete una cartina?
*a-**vay**-tay **oo**-na kar-**tee**-na*

do you have a room?
avete una camera?
*a-**vay**-tay **oo**-na **ka**-may-ra*

quanto costa?
how much?

how much is the wine?
quanto costa il vino?
*kwan-ta **kos**-ta eel **vee**-no*

how much is the trip?
quanto costa il viaggio?
*kwan-ta **kos**-ta eel vee-**ad**-jo*

vorrei...
I'd like...

I'd like a red wine
vorrei un vino rosso
*vor-**ray** oon **vee**-no **ros**-so*

I'd like an ice cream
vorrei un gelato
*vor-**ray** oon jay-**la**-to*

ho bisogno di...
I need...

I need a taxi
ho bisogno di un taxi
*o bee-**zon**-yo dee oon **tak**-see*

I need to go
ho bisogno di andare
*o bee-**zon**-yo dee an-**da**-ray*

quando?
when?

when does it open?
quando apre?
*kwan-do **a**-pray*

when does it close?
quando chiude?
*kwan-do kee-**oo**-day*

when does it leave?
quando parte?
*kwan-do **par**-tay*

when does it arrive?
quando arriva?
*kwan-do ar-**ree**-va*

dove?
where?

where is the bank?
dov'è la banca?
*do-**ve** la **ban**-ka*

where is the hotel?
dov'è l'albergo?
*do **ve** lal **ber**-go*

c'è...?
is there...?

is there a market?
c'è un mercato?
*che oon mer-**ka**-to*

where is there a market?
dove c'è un mercato?
*do-vay che oon mer-**ka**-to*

non c'è...
there is no...

there is no bread
non c'è pane
*non che pa-**nay***

is there no train?
non c'è un treno?
*non che oon **tray**-no*

posso...?
can I...?

can I go by train?
posso andare in treno?
*pos-so an-**da**-ray een **tray**-no*

can I smoke?
posso fumare?
*pos-so foo-**ma**-ray*

where can I buy milk?
dove posso comprare latte?
*do-vay **pos**-so kom-**pra**-ray **lat**-tay*

è...?
is it...?

is it near?
è vicino?
*e vee-**chee**-no*

is it far?
è lontano?
*e lon-**ta**-no*

mi piace...
I like...

I like wine
mi piace il vino
*mee pee-**a**-chay eel **vee**-no*

I don't like dancing
non mi piace ballare
*non mee **pya**-chay bal-**la**-ray*

These are a selection of small but very useful words to know.

grande
gran-day
large

piccolo
pee-ko-lo
small

un poco
oon po-ko
a little

basta
bas-ta
enough

più vicino
pyoo vee-chee-no
nearest

lontano
lon-ta-no
far

troppo caro
trop-po ka-ro
too expensive

pieno
pee-ay-no
full

libero
lee-bay-ro
free

e
ay
and

con/senza
kon/sent-sa
with/without

questo/quello
kwes-to/kwel-lo
this one/that one

subito
soo-bee-to
straightaway

più tardi
pyoo tar-dee
later

a large car
una macchina grande
oo-na mak-kee-na gran-day

a small house
una casa piccola
oo-na ka-za peek-ko-la

a little please
un poco per favore
oon po-ko payr fa-vo-ray

that's enough thanks
basta così grazie
bas-ta ko-zee grats-yay

where is the nearest chemist?
dov'è la farmacia più vicina?
do-ve la far-ma-chee-a pyoo vee-chee-na

is it far?
è lontano?
e lon-ta-no

it is too expensive
è troppo caro
e trop-po ka-ro

it is too small
è troppo piccolo
e trop-po peek-ko-lo

is it full?
e pieno?
e pee-ay-no

is it free (unoccupied)**?**
è libero?
e lee-bay-ro

a tea and 2 beers
un tè e due birre
oon te e doo-ay beer-ray

with sugar
con zucchero
kon tsook-kay-ro

with milk
col latte
kol lat-tay

without sugar
senza zucchero
sent-sa tsook-kay-ro

without milk
senza latte
sent-sa lat-tay

for me
per me
payr me

for her/for him
per lei/per lui
payr lay/per loo-ee

my passport
il mio passaporto
eel mee-o pas-sa-por-to

my keys
le mie chiavi
lay mee-ay kee-a-vee

I'd like this one
vorrei questo
vor-ray kwes-to

I'd like that one
vorrei quello
vor-ray kwel-lo

I need a taxi straightaway
ho bisogno di un taxi subito
o bee-zon-yo dee oon tak-see soo-bee-to

I'll call again later
richiamo più tardi
reek-ya-mo pyoo tar-dee

It is always good to be able to say a few words about yourself to break the ice, even if you won't be able to tell your life story.

my name is...
mi chiamo...
*mee kee-**a**-mo...*

I am from...
sono di...
so-nò dee...

I'm here on holiday
sono qui in vacanza
*so-no kwee een va-**kan**-za*

I'm here on business
sono qui per lavoro
*so-no kwee payr la-**vo**-ro*

I'm not married
non sono sposato/a
*non so-no spo-**za**-to/a*

I am married
sono sposato/a
*so-no spo-**za**-to/a*

I have a boyfriend
ho un ragazzo
*o oon rag-**at**-so*

I have a girlfriend
ho una ragazza
*o **oo**-na rag-**at**-sa*

I am a widow
sono vedova
*so-no **vay**-do-va*

I am a widower
sono vedovo
*so-no **vay**-do-vo*

I am divorced
sono divorziato/a
*so-no dee-vorts-**ya**-to/a*

I am separated
sono separato/a
*so-no sep-a-**ra**-to/a*

I have a son/daughter
ho un figlio/una figlia
*o oon **feel**-yo/**oo**-na **feel**-ya*

I have ... children
ho ... figli
*o ... **feel**-yee*

I work
lavoro
*la-**vo**-ro*

I am retired
sono in pensione
*so-no een pens-**yo**-nay*

I am a student
sono studente
*so-no stoo-**den**-tay*

Italy is very beautiful
l'Italia è molto bella
*lee-**tal**-ya e **mol**-to **bel**-la*

I love Italian food
mi piace molto la cucina italiana
*mee pee-a-chay **mol**-to la koo-**chee**-na ee-tal-**ya**-na*

Italian people are very kind
gli Italiani sono molto gentili
*lee ee-tal-**ya**-nee **so**-no **mol**-to jen-**tee**-lee*

I'd like to come back
vorrei ritornare
*vor-**ray** ree-**tor**-na-ray*

thank you very much for your kindness
grazie mille per la sua gentilezza
***grats**-yay **meel**-lay payr la **soo**-a jen-tee-**let**-sa*

I have enjoyed myself very much
mi sono divertito/a moltissimo
*mee so-no dee-ver-**tee**-to/a mol-**tees**-see-mo*

we will be back next year
ritorniamo l'anno prossimo
*ree-torn-**ya**-mo **lan**-no **pros**-see-mo*

can I have your address?
potrei avere il suo indirizzo?
*po-tray a-**vay**-ray eel **soo**-o een-dee-**reet**-so*

see you next year!
all'anno prossimo!
*al-**lan**-no **pros**-see-mo*

Although problems are not something anyone wants, you might come across the odd difficulty, and it is best to be armed with a few phrases to cope with the situation.

excuse me!
scusi!
skoo-zee

can you help me
può aiutarmi?
pwo a-yoo-tar-mee

I don't speak...
non parlo...
non par-lo...

I am sorry, I did not know
mi scusi, non lo sapevo
mee skoo-zee non lo sa-pay-vo

I am lost
mi sono smarrito/a
mee so-no smar-ree-to/a

we are lost
ci siamo persi
chee see-a-mo per-see

I have lost... | **my money** | **my tickets** | **my passport**
ho perso... | i soldi | i biglietti | il mio passaporto
ho payr-so... | *ee sol-dee* | *ee beel-yet-tee* | *eel mee-o pas-sa-por-to*

I have left...
ho lasciato...
o la-sha-to...

in the restaurant
nel ristorante
nel rees-to-ran-tay

on the train
sul treno
sool tray-no

I have missed... | **my flight** | **the train** | **the coach**
ho perso... | il volo | il treno | il pullman
ho per-so... | *eel vo-lo* | *eel tray-no* | *eel pool-man*

I need to get to...
devo andare a...
day-vo an-da-ray...

how can I get there today?
come ci posso arrivare oggi?
ko-may chee pos-so ar-ree-va-ray od-jee

my luggage hasn't arrived
il mio bagaglio non è arrivato
eel mee-o ba-gal-yo non e ar-ree-va-to

my case has been damaged
la mia valigia è stata danneggiata
la mee-a va-lee-ja e sta-ta dan-nay-ja-ta

my bag | **my purse** | **my camera**
la mia borsa | il mio portafoglio | la mia macchina fotografica
la mee-a bor-sa | *eel mee-o por-ta-fol-yo* | *la mee-a mak-kee-na fo-to-gra-fee-ka*

... has been stolen
... è stato rubato/a
... e sta-to roo-ba-to/a

you can get me at this address
mi trova a questo indirizzo
mee tro-va a kwes-to een-dee-reet-so

I have to go to hospital
devo andare in ospedale
day-vo an-da-ray een os-pay-da-lay

I have no money
non ho soldi
non o sol-dee

I can't find my son
non trovo mio figlio
non tro-vo mee-yo feel-yo

I can't find my daughter
non trovo mia figlia
non tro-vo mee-a feel-ya

go away!
se ne vada!
say nay va-da

that man is following me
quel uomo mi sta seguendo
kwel wo-mo mee sta seg-wen-do

Italians expect to receive good service and quality. They will complain when things are not to their liking.

there is no...
non c'è...
non che...

there is no soap
non c'è sapone
non che sa-po-nay

it is dirty
è sporco/a
e spor-ko/a

they are dirty
sono sporchi
so-no spor-kee

it is broken
è rotto/a
e rot-to/a

they are broken
sono rotti
so-no rot-tee

the ... does not work
il/la ... non funziona
eel/la ... non foonts-yo-na

the ... do not work
i/le ... non funzionano
ee/lay ... non foonts-yo-na-no

the window doesn't open
la finestra non apre
la fee-nes-tra non ap-ray

the window doesn't close
la finestra non chiude
la fee-nes-tra non kee-oo-day

there is too much noise
c'è troppo rumore
che trop-po roo-mor-ay

the room is too small
la camera è troppo piccola
la ka-may-ra e trop-po peek-ko-la

the room is too hot
la camera è troppo calda
la ka-may-ra e trop-po kal-da

the room is too cold
la camera è troppo fredda
la ka-may-ra e trop-po fred-da

it is too expensive
è troppo caro
e trop-po ka-ro

you are charging too much
lei mi chiede troppo
lay mee kyay-dee trop-po

I want to complain
voglio fare un reclamo
vol-yo fa-ray oon rek-la-mo

I want to speak to the manager
voglio parlare con il gerente
vol-yo par-la-ray kon eel jay-ren-tay

we want to order
vogliamo ordinare
vol-ya-mo or-dee-na-ray

the service is bad
il servizio è impossibile
eel ser-veets-yo e eem-pos-see-bee-lay

this food is cold
il cibo è freddo
eel chee-bo e fred-do

this cappuccino is cold
questo cappuccino è freddo
kwes-to kap-poo-chee-no e fred-do

there is a mistake
c'è un errore
che oon er-ro-ray

can we check the bill?
possiamo controllare il conto?
poss-ya-mo kon-trol-la-ray eel kon-to

I didn't order this
non ho ordinato questo
non o or-dee-na-to kwes-to

please take it off the bill
può toglierlo dal conto
pwo tol-yer-lo dal kon-to

The next four pages should give you an idea of the type of things you will come across in Italy.

▲ OPEN

CLOSED ▶

closing day Tuesday

▼ **OPENING HOURS**

mattino
morning

pomeriggio
afternoon

giorno di chiusura
day closed
Sun. & Mon.
afternoon

Shops are generally closed on Mon mornings but open in the afternoon. From Tue to Sat opening hours are generally 8.30 am to 1 pm and from about 4 pm to 7 pm. Shops are shut on Sun. except those in tourist areas which may open to sell holiday items.

Spingere ◀ PUSH

Tirare ◀ PULL

PAY HERE
pedestrian
entrance ▶

do you have...?	**stamps**	**phonecards**
avete...?	francobolli	schede telefoniche
a-vay-tay...	*fran-ko-**bol**-lee*	***skay**-day te-le-**fo**-nee-kay*
where can I get...?	**a newspaper**	**postcards**
dove posso comprare...?	un giornale	cartoline
*do-vay **pos**-so komp-**ra**-ray...*	*oon jor-**na**-lay*	*kar-to-**lee**-nay*

▲ IN SERVICE

FUORI SERVIZIO

▲ OUT OF SERVICE

— TOBACCONIST

▲ ENTRANCE

These are often attached to a bar and sell cigarettes, stamps, bus tickets, etc. You can also buy salt here – a legacy of the days when salt was a state monopoly.

▼ EMERGENCY EXIT

USCITA DI SICUREZZA

You will also see the word *uscita* used for exit on the motorway.

◀ There is an increasing number of automated machines. Instructions are often given in different languages.

Post boxes are red. The blue post box is for priority mail abroad.

▼

excuse me...
scusi...
skoo-zee...

how does this work?
come funziona?
ko-may foonts-yo-na

what do I have to do?
cosa devo fare?
ko-za day-vo fa-ray

what does this mean?
cosa significa?
ko-za seen-yee-fee-ka

▶ Service is usually included in a restaurant bill so tipping is discretionary. However, it is usual to leave a small tip. In busy bars, there will often be a saucer to leave coins.

NO FISHING
divieto means
forbidden

*from 1 April to
30 September*

divieto
di
pesca
dal 1 Aprile
al 30 Settembre

VIETATO FUMARE

▲ NO SMOKING

Smoking is still pretty popular in Italy and you are unlikely to find non-smoking areas in restaurants and bars. If people are smoking in a restaurant, they are also likely to light up in between courses (whether or not you have finished eating).

*no entry for
unauthorised
persons*

VIETATO
L'INGRESSO
AI NON ADDETTI
AI LAVORI

Vietato is another word
that means forbidden.

can I smoke?
posso fumare?
pos-so foo-*ma*-ray

I don't smoke
non fumo
non *foo*-mo

an ashtray
un portacenere
oon por-ta-*chen*-nay-ray

do you mind if I smoke?
le dà fastidio se fumo?
lay da fas-*teed*-yo say *foo*-mo

please don't smoke
le dipiace non fumare
lay deesp-*ya*-chay non foo-*ma*-ray

a smoking seat
un posto fumatore
oon *pos*-to foo-ma-*tor*-ay

There are toilets at railway stations, often with an attendant. Although you do not have to pay, you may see a plate for coins. The attendant may even hand out toilet paper. If you do come across a public toilet, it is unlikely to have toilet paper, so remember always to carry tissues. Bars and restaurants have toilets, but they will not look at you kindly if you use their facilities without buying something. Remember it is cheapest to buy a drink standing at the bar. Toilets are sometimes locked and you will have to ask for the key.

◀ Toilets are usually indicated with a pictogram.

▼ MEN

WOMEN ▼

UOMINI **DONNE**

Don't be fooled: *caldo* means hot, *freddo* means cold. ▶

Caldo

Freddo

NON-DRINKING
◀ WATER

excuse me! where is the toilet?
scusi! dov'è la toilette?
*skoo-zee do-**ve** la twa-**let***

excuse me! may I use the bathroom?
scusi! posso usare il bagno?
*skoo-zee **pos**-so oo-**za**-ray eel **ban**-yo*

do you have the key for the toilet?
avete la chiave per la toilette?
*a-**vay**-tay la kee-**a**-vay payr la twa-**let***

is there a disabled toilet?
ci sono le toilette per i disabili?
*chee so-no lay twa-**let** payr ee dee-**za**-bee-lee*

is there somewhere to change the baby?
c'è un posto per cambiare il bambino?
*che oon **pos**-to payr kamb-**ya**-ray eel bam-**bee**-no*

talking talking talking

Tourist offices provide free maps, usually with an English version. They are usually well-stocked with brochures and leaflets about attractions in the area. They can also help finding somewhere to stay.

Newer signs
▼ often carry pictograms.

town hall — municipio

local police — polizia municipale

information — informazioni

jetty (boarding for car ferry and hydrofoil) — imbarcadero

NAVIGARDA IMBARCHI

farmacia

chemist

Milano è Milano

EDIZIONE ITALIANA

A.P.T.

◀ You can usually get free maps (in English) from tourist offices.

excuse me!
scusi!
skoo-zee

do you know where...?
sa dov'è...?
sa do-ve...

how do I get to...?
per andare a...?
payr an-da-ray a...

is this the right way to...?
è la strada giusta per...?
e la stra-da joos-ta payr...

do you have a map of the town?
avete una piantina della città?
a-vay-tay oo-na pyan-tee-na del-la cheet-ta

can you show me on the map?
mi può indicare sulla piantina?
mee pwo een-dee-ka-ray sool-la pyan-tee-na

we're looking for...
cerchiamo...
cherk-ya-mo...

where is the tourist office?
dov'è l'ufficio turistico?
do-ve loof-fee-cho too-rees-tee-ko

is it far?
è lontano?
e lon-ta-no

a street directory
uno stradario
oo-no stra-dar-ee-o

*white signs indicate local destinations (green is for the **autostrada**, the motorway)*

blue signs indicate main routes

funicular railway

*brown signs indicate places of interest; **monumento ai caduti** is a war memorial.*

◀ **OTHER ROUTES**

altre direzioni

◀ *duomo means cathedral*

duomo-broletto

◀ *piazza means square*

piazza Nuova

name of the road

indicates one-way street

via Borsieri

centro — *centre*

parcheggio — *parking*

Santuario del Crocefisso — *Church of the Crucifix*

◀ **PEDESTRIAN AREA**
bicycles allowed

area pedonale

eccetto

a destra
a des-tra
to the right

a sinistra
a see-nees-tra
to the left

va
va
go

giri
jee-ree
turn

via
vee-a
road

piazza
pee-at-sa
square

semaforo
se-ma-fo-ro
traffic lights

chiesa
kee-ay-za
church

primo
pree-mo
first

secondo
se-kon-do
second

lontano
lon-ta-no
far

vicino a
vee-chee-no a
near to

accanto a
ak-kan-to a
next to

in faccia di
een fat-cha dee
opposite

fino a
fee-no a
until

keywords keywords keywords keywords keywords

BANKS & MONEY

Banks offer the best rate of exchange, though changing traveller's cheques can sometimes be quite lengthy. Remember to
take your passport with you and don't expect cashiers to speak
English. In smaller places banks tend to be shut in the afternoon, so
it is best to go in the mornings, when you can be sure that they are
open. Banking hours are generally 8.30 am to1.30 pm Monday to
Friday and in the afternoon for an hour from 2.45 to 3.45. But check
when you are there, as times vary from place to place. Credit cards
and switch payments are widely accepted.

◀ Italy has many regional banks
such as *Banco Popolare di
Sondrio*; nationwide banks
include **Credito Italiano** and
Banca Nazionale del Lavoro.

Some cash-
points are
located inside
the bank. Look
out for the
Bancomat sign.
◀

▲ Italian banks operate a
double-door or revolving-
door system with metal
detectors to check you
aren't armed. To enter you
press a button and wait for a
green light to show and let
you through.

Bureaus de Change are usually
open longer, but tend not to offer
◀ as good rates as banks.

◀ Most cash dispensers let you select the language for your transaction.

Italian money
The Italian currency is the Lira.
Coins: 50, 100, 200, 500, 1000, 2000.
Notes: 5000, 10,000, 20,000, 50,000, 100,000, 500,000
It is best to ask for notes of L.50,000.
The noughts can be very confusing, so always check what you are handing over and make sure you check the change.

carta di credito
kar-ta dee kray-dee-to
credit card

bancomat
ban-ko-mat
cashpoint

numero pin
noo-may-ro peen
pin number

spiccioli
speech-cho-lee
change

inserire
een-ser-ee-ray
insert

cambio
kamb-yo
exchange rate

banconote
ban-ko-no-tay
notes

contanti
kon-tan-tee
cash

In Jan. 2002 euro notes and coins (cents) will be introduced and both euros and the old national currency will be in circulation until end of Feb 2002. After that only euros will be in use.

where can I change money?
dove posso cambiare soldi?
do-vay pos-so kamb-ya-ray sol-dee

where is there a bureau de change
dove c'è un cambio
do-vay che oon kamb-yo

I want to change these traveller's cheques
vorrei cambiare questi travellers cheque
vor-ray kamb-ya-ray kwes-tee travellers cheques

the cashpoint has swallowed my card
il bancomat ha mangiato la mia carta
eel ban-ko-mat a man-ja-to la mee-a kar-ta

where is the nearest cashpoint?
dov'è il bancomat più vicino?
do-ve eel ban-ko-mat pyoo vee-chee-no

where is the bank?
dov'è la banca?
do-ve la ban-ka

small notes
biglietti piccoli
beel-yet-tee pee-ko-lee

Italy is one hour ahead of Great Britain apart from the last week of September when they have the same time.

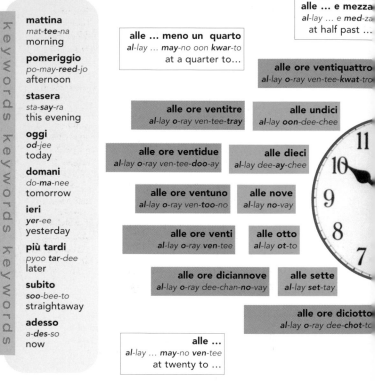

keywords keywords keywords keywords

mattina
mat-**tee**-na
morning

pomeriggio
po-may-**reed**-jo
afternoon

stasera
sta-**say**-ra
this evening

oggi
od-jee
today

domani
do-**ma**-nee
tomorrow

ieri
yer-ee
yesterday

più tardi
pyoo tar-dee
later

subito
soo-bee-to
straightaway

adesso
a-**des**-so
now

alle ... e mezza
al-lay ... e med-za
at half past ...

alle ... meno un quarto
al-lay ... may-no oon kwar-to
at a quarter to...

alle ore ventiquattro
al-lay o-ray ven-tee-kwat-tro

alle ore ventitre
al-lay o-ray ven-tee-tray

alle undici
al-lay oon-dee-chee

alle ore ventidue
al-lay o-ray ven-tee-doo-ay

alle dieci
al-lay dee-ay-chee

alle ore ventuno
al-lay o-ray ven-too-no

alle nove
al-lay no-vay

alle ore venti
al-lay o-ray ven-tee

alle otto
al-lay ot-to

alle ore diciannove
al-lay o-ray dee-chan-no-vay

alle sette
al-lay set-tay

alle ore diciotto
al-lay o-ray dee-chot-to

alle ...
al-lay ... may-no ven-tee
at twenty to ...

talking

when is the next...?	**train**	**boat**
quando c'è il prossimo...?	treno	battello
kwan-do che eel pros-see-mo...	*tray-no*	*bat-tel-lo*
what time is...?	**breakfast**	**dinner**
a che ora è...?	la prima colazione	la cena
a kay o-ra e...	*la pree-ma ko-lats-yo-nay*	*la chay-na*
when does it leave?	**when does it arrive?**	
quando parte?	quando arriva?	
kwan-do par-tay	*kwan-do ar-ree-va*	

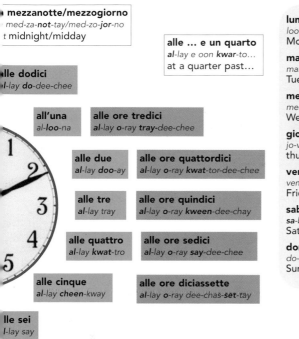

lunedì
loo-nay-dee
Monday

martedì
mar-tay-dee
Tuesday

mercoledì
mer-ko-lay-dee
Wednesday

giovedì
jo-vay-dee
thursday

venerdì
ven-er-dee
Friday

sabato
sa-ba-to
Saturday

domenica
do-me-nee-ka
Sunday

keywords keywords

mezzanotte/mezzogiorno
med-za-not-tay/med-zo-jor-no
t midnight/midday

alle dodici
l-lay do-dee-chee

alle ... e un quarto
al-lay e oon kwar-to...
at a quarter past...

all'una
al-loo-na

alle ore tredici
al-lay o-ray tray-dee-chee

alle due
al-lay doo-ay

alle ore quattordici
al-lay o-ray kwat-tor-dee-chee

alle tre
al-lay tray

alle ore quindici
al-lay o-ray kween-dee-chay

alle quattro
al-lay kwat-tro

alle ore sedici
al-lay o-ray say-dee-chee

alle cinque
al-lay cheen-kway

alle ore diciassette
al-lay o-ray dee-chas-set-tay

lle sei
l-lay say

alle ore diciotto e quarantacinque
al-lay o-ray dee-chot-to ay kwa-ran-ta-cheen-kway
at 18.45

what is the date?
qual è la data?
kwal e la da-ta

it is the 8th May
è il otto maggio
e eel ot-to mad-jo

16 September 2002
il sedici settembre duemilaedue
eel say-dee-chee set-tem-bray doo-ay-mee-la-ay-doo-ay

which day?
quale giorno?
kwa-lay jor-no

which month?
quale mese?
kwa-lay may-zay

talking

Timetables use the 24 hour clock. The Italian for timetable is **orario**. *There are winter (**invernale**) and summer (**estivo**) timetables.*

Train timetable ►

Fer = **feriale** weekdays Mon-Sat

operates until 23/12 from 7/1

	FS170 Ferrovie dello Stato Lecco-Molteno-Como													
	5124 Fer5 R	5126 Fer5 R	5128 Fer5 R	5020 Fer5 R **1**	5130 Fer5 R	5132 Fer5 R	5134 Fer5 R	5022 Fer5 R **2 4**	5136 Fer5 R	5138 Fer5 R	5012 Fer5 M **2**	5140 Fer5 R	5014 Fer5 M
Lecco		5.30	6.20	6.35		6.59		7.47	7.47	8.03	9.02	9.33	11.02	11.33
Valmadrera		5.35	6.25	6.40		7.05		7.53	7.53	8.14	9.07	9.43	11.07	11.43
Civate				6.43		7.07					9.10	9.46	11.10	11.46
Sala al Barro-Galbiate		5.39	6.29	6.46		7.10		7.57	7.57		9.13	9.49	11.13	11.49
Oggiono		5.45	6.34	6.51		7.19	7.42	8.06	8.11	8.22	9.19	9.55	11.19	11.55
Molteno	a	5.49	6.38	6.55		7.23	7.47	8.09	8.15	8.26	9.23		11.23	
Molteno					7.00				8.16					
Castello-Rogeno					7.04									
Molsina					7.07									
Merone					7.11				8.24					
Anzano del Parco					7.16									
Brenna-Alzate					7.20									
Cantù					7.25				8.35					
Attela Triscalo					7.29									
Albate-Camerlata	a				7.33				8.40					
Albate-Camerlata					7.34				8.41					
Como S. Giovanni	a				7.40				8.45					

1 Non sono ammesse le comitive nei giorni lavorativi escluso il sabato.
2 Si effetua fino al 23/12, dal 7/1.
3 Fino a Oggiono: si effetua il sabato.
4 Da Oggiono: si effetua nei giorni lavorativi.

no group travel during weekdays except Sat

up to Oggiono operates on Sat

from Oggiono operates on weekdays (Mon-Sat)

◄ *timetable from 26 June to 1 October 2000*

▲ *Night cruise*

keywords

orario
o-rar-yo
timetable

estivo
es-tee-vo
summer

invernale
een-ver-na-lay
winter

si effetua
see ef-fet-oo-a
operates

dalle/alle
dal-lay/al-lay
from/to

giorni
jor-nee
days

escluso
es-kloo-zo
except for

feriale
fer-ya-lay
Mon-Sat

festivo
fes-tee-vo
Sun and hols

Partenze ◄ DEPARTURES

Arrivi ◄ ARRIVALS

lun Mon
mar Tues
mer Wed
gio Thur
ven Fri
sab Sat
dom Sun

Bus timetable ▼

SPT (bus company)

number of bus service

Fes = **festivo**
Sun & hols

Fer = **feriale**
weekdays
Mon-Sat

services operating from there

Scol = **scolastici**
school term

p = square

v = street

uff. PT =
post office

monum. caduti
= war memorial

tickets must be bought on the ground (i.e. before boarding)

operates on school days except Sat

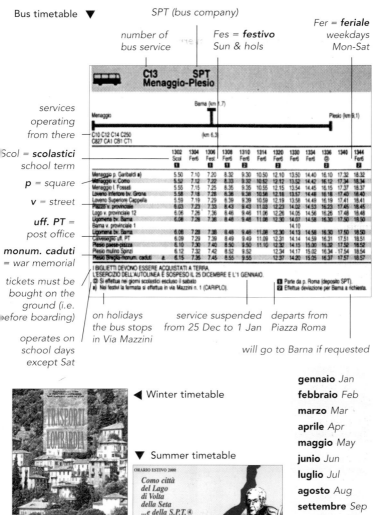

| | | | C13 | | SPT | | | | | | | |
| | | | | | Menaggio-Plesio | | | | | | | |

Barna (km 1.7)

Menaggio

Plesio (km 9.1)

C10 C12 C14 C250
C827 CA1 C81 CT1

(km 6.3)

	1302 Scol ❶	1304 Fer❶	1306 Fes ❶	1308 Feri ❶	1310 Feri ❷	1314 Feri❶	1320 Feri ❶	1330 Feri ❶	1334 Feri ❶	1336 Feri ❸	1340	1344 Feri❶
Menaggio p. Garibaldi a)	5.50	7.10	7.20	8.32	9.30	10.50	12.10	13.50	14.40	16.10	17.32	18.32
Menaggio v. Como	5.52	7.12	7.22	8.33	9.32	10.52	12.12	13.52	14.42	16.12	17.34	18.34
Menaggio l. Fossati	5.55	7.15	7.25	8.35	9.35	10.55	12.15	13.54	14.45	16.15	17.37	18.37
Loveno Inferiore bv. Grona	5.58	7.18	7.28	8.36	9.38	10.56	12.16	13.57	14.48	16.18	17.40	18.40
Loveno Superiore Cappella	5.59	7.19	7.29	8.39	9.39	10.59	12.19	13.58	14.49	16.19	17.41	18.41
Piazza v. provinciale	6.03	7.23	7.33	8.43	9.43	11.03	12.23	14.02	14.53	16.23	17.45	18.45
Logo v. provinciale 12	6.06	7.26	7.36	8.46	9.46	11.06	12.26	14.05	14.56	16.26	17.48	18.48
Ligomena bv. Barna	6.08	7.28	7.38	8.48	9.48	11.08	12.30	14.07	14.58	16.30	17.50	18.50
Barna v. provinciale 1								14.10				
Ligomena bv. Barna	6.08	7.28	7.38	8.48	9.48	11.08	12.30	14.13	14.58	16.30	17.50	18.50
Calvesaggio uff. PT	6.09	7.29	7.39	8.49	9.49	11.09	12.31	14.14	14.59	16.31	17.51	18.51
Plesio paese-piazza	6.10	7.30	7.40	8.50	9.50	11.10	12.32	14.15	15.00	16.32	17.52	18.52
Plesio mulino Sprizzi	6.12	7.32	7.42	8.52	9.52		12.34	14.17	15.02	16.34	17.54	18.54
Plesio Bregalo-monum. caduti a	6.15	7.35	7.45	8.55	9.55		12.37	14.20	15.05	16.37	17.57	18.57

I BIGLIETTI DEVONO ESSERE ACQUISTATI A TERRA.
L'ESERCIZIO DELL'AUTOLINEA È SOSPESO IL 25 DICEMBRE E L'1 GENNAIO.
❶ Si effettua nei giorni scolastici escluso il sabato
a) Nei festivi la fermata si effettua in via Mazzini n. 1 (CARIPLO).

❶ Parte da p. Roma (deposito SPT).
❷ Effettua deviazione per Barna a richiesta.

on holidays the bus stops in Via Mazzini

service suspended from 25 Dec to 1 Jan

departs from Piazza Roma

will go to Barna if requested

◀ Winter timetable

TRASPORTI LOMBARDIA

Como
Orario invernale 1999 / 2000

▼ Summer timetable

ORARIO ESTIVO 2000
Como città
del Lago
di Volta
della Seta
...e della S.P.T. ◀

TRASPORTI REGIONE LOMBARDIA

gennaio Jan
febbraio Feb
marzo Mar
aprile Apr
maggio May
junio Jun
luglio Jul
agosto Aug
settembre Sep
ottobre Oct
novembre Nov
dicembre Dec

do you have a timetable?
avete un orario?
a-**vay**-tay oon o-**rar**-yo

can you explain the timetable?
mi può spiegare l'orario?
mee pwo spyay-**ga**-ray lo-**rar**-yo

talk

TICKETS

Tickets for bus, metro and trains need to be validated, otherwise you can be fined. Bus tickets are validated on board the bus. Train and metro tickets are validated at the special orange machines in the stations.

There is an increasing number of self-service ticket machines. You can choose the language for ▼ your transaction.

tickets can be validated here

Bus ticket ▶ listing all the stops en route. The destination is punched.

Train ticket ▼

valid for 6 hours from validating | ticket valid for 2 months from date of issue | 2nd class | **Adulti** adults | **Ragazzi** children

Da From

A To

IC Intercity

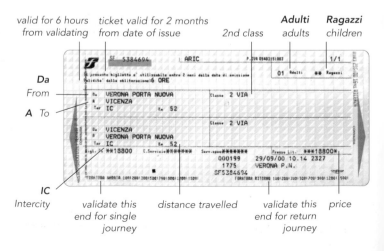

validate this end for single journey | distance travelled | validate this end for return journey | price

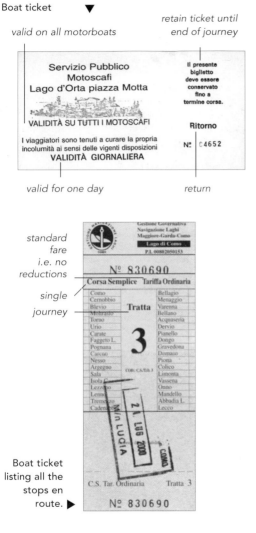

Boat ticket ▼

valid on all motorboats

retain ticket until end of journey

Servizio Pubblico
Motoscafi
Lago d'Orta piazza Motta

VALIDITÀ SU TUTTI I MOTOSCAFI

Il presente biglietto deve essere conservato fino a termine corsa.

Ritorno

I viaggiatori sono tenuti a curare la propria incolumità ai sensi delle vigenti disposizioni
VALIDITÀ GIORNALIERA

N° C4652

valid for one day

return

standard fare i.e. no reductions

single

journey

Gestione Governativa
Navigazione Laghi
Maggiore-Garda-Como
Lago di Como
P.I. 00802050153

N° 830690

Corsa Semplice Tariffa Ordinaria

Como	Bellagio
Cernobbio	Menaggio
Blevio	Varenna
Moltrasio	Bellano
Torno	Acquaseria
Urio	Dervio
Carate	Pianello
Faggeto L.	Dongo
Pognana	Gravedona
Careno	Domaso
Nesso	Piona
Argegno	Colico
Sala	Limonta
Isola C.	Vassena
Lezzeno	Onno
Lenno	Mandello
Tremezzo	Abbadia L.
Cadenabbia	Lecco

Tratta

3

COD. C.S./T.O.3

C.S. Tar. Ordinaria   Tratta 3

N° 830690

Boat ticket listing all the stops en route. ▶

City transport ticket ◀ which has been stamped

AZIENDA TRASPORTI MILANESI
2000
GIUBILEO
LINEE ORDINARIE URBANE
013   0498940

keywords keywords keywords keywords keywords

carnet 10 biglietti
kar-**nay** dee-**ay**-chee beel-**yet**-tee
book of 10 tickets

biglietto
beel-**yet**-to
ticket

riduzione
ree-doots-**yo**-nay
reduction

andata
an-**da**-ta
single

andata e ritorno
an-**da**-ta ay ree-**tor**-no
return

adulto
a-**dool**-to
adult

ragazzo
ra-**gat**-so
child

studente
stoo-**den**-tay
student

terza età
tert-za ay-**ta**
over 60s

disabile
dee-**za**-bee-lay
disabled

famiglia
fa-**meel**-ya
family

PUBLIC TRANSPORT

Most Italian cities operate an integrated transport system, which means that all the different kinds of transport are part of one network, and you can use any of them with your ticket. Bus tickets must be bought in advance and you can buy them at newsagents/kiosks and at tobacconists. In smaller places they will be sold at the shop or bar near to the bus stop. Look out for a sign stating that bus tickets are on sale. You validate the ticket in the machine at the back of the bus, or on long-distance buses there will be a conductor to check your ticket, not to sell you one.

◀ Tickets for Milan's integrated transport system

▲ City buses are generally orange. You enter from the back and validate your ticket at the machine as you enter.

Tram ▼

Sign showing bus tickets for sale – here, at the local butcher's. Shops like this shut from 12.30-3.30 pm, so you should buy tickets well in advance. ▼

Rural buses usually have a conductor. This does not mean you can buy a ticket on board – you still must buy it in advance.

◀ Bus station are generally located near train stations. It is the most likely place to find a public toilet.

City bus stop showing the different lines, services and which buses stop at metro ▼ stations (indicated by an M).

▶ Long-distance bus stop showing the different services and routes.

Italian airports are well served by buses. Tourist offices will have information. ▼

where does the bust to ... leave from?
da dove parte l'autobus per...?
da do-vay par-tay low-to-boos payr...

which bus goes to the centre?
quale autobus va al centro?
kwa-lay ow-to-boos va al chen-tro

which number goes to...?
quale linea va a...?
kwa-lay lee-nay-a va a...

when is the next bus to...?
quando c'è il prossimo autobus per...?
kwan-do che eel pros-see-mo ow-to-boos payr...

can you tell me when it is my stop
mi può dire quando è la mia fermata
pwo deer-mee kwan-do e la mee-a fer-ma-ta

is there a bus to...?
c'è un autobus per...?
che oon ow-to-boos payr...

does this bus go to...?
questo autobus va a...?
kwes-to ow-to-boos va a...

I want to get off!
voglio scendere!
vol-yo shen-day-ray

talking talking talking

Milan and Rome are the only two Italian cities to have metro systems. You can buy a carnet of 10 tickets which is cheaper than buying tickets individually. Tickets must be validated before you get on the train. You can also buy weekly tickets valid for 2 journeys per day 6 days a week. These are geared to commuters. There are also 24 and 48 hour tickets, which are ideal for tourists.

▲ Metro sign

Metro station ▶

Machine to validate tickets ▶
A single ticket is valid for 75 minutes from validating and can be used for one metro ride and any number of bus and tram journeys within that time limit.

tickets on sale at kiosk or from ticket machines

Kiosk selling metro tickets ▶
and parking tickets

The Milan underground has three colour-coded lines: MI is red, M2 is green and M3 yellow. There is also a fourth, blue line called the *passante ferroviario* ◀ linking with the main train stations.

a single ticket
un biglietto singolo
oon beel-yet-to seen-go-lo

a 24-hour ticket
un biglietto ventiquattro ore
oon beel-yet-to ven-tee-kwat-tro o-ray

a carnet of tickets
un carnet di biglietti
oon kar-nay dee beel-yet-tee

a 48-hour ticket
un biglietto quarantotto ore
oon beel-yet-to kwa-rant-ot-to o-ray

have you a map of the underground?
avete una piantina della metro?
a-vay-tay oo-na pyan-tee-na del-la met-ro

where is the nearest metro station?
dov'è la stazione della metropolitana più vicina?
do-ve la stats-yo-nay del-la met-ro-po-lee-ta-na pyoo vee-chee-na

I want to go to...
voglio andare a...
vol-yo an-da-ray a...

do I have to change?
devo cambiare?
day-vo kamb-ya-ray

where?
dove?
do-vay

which line do I take?
quale linea prendo?
kwa-lay lee-nay-a pren-do

in which direction?
per quale direzione?
payr kwa-lay dee-rets-yo-nay

which station is it for...?
qual è la stazione per...?
kwa-le la stats-yo-nay payr...

what is the next stop?
qual è la prossima fermata?
kwa-le la pros-see-ma fer-ma-ta

excuse me! I want to get off
permesso! voglio scendere
payr-mes-so vol-yo shen-day-ray

Italian trains are good value. Fares are charged according to the distance travelled, so buying a return does not make it any cheaper. Return tickets are valid only within 48 hours of outward journey, so it is not worth buying one if you are staying for a longer period. On Intercity trains you must pay a supplement when you purchase your ticket. If you do not, the train conductor can ask you to pay a surcharge that is more expensive than the supplement. On both Eurocity and Intercity trains, reservations are obligatory. Remember to validate your ticket before boarding the train.

DEPARTURES ▼

Tues 29 Aug

delay

destination   extra info.   class   timetable   platform

only 2nd class

for Lecco change at Molteno

only 2nd class

1st class at front Intercity

1st class at back Intercity

Additional General Information
Passengers are reminded that it is forbidden to walk across the tracks

2 singles to...
due andate per...
doo-ay an-da-tay payr...

2 returns to...
due andate e ritorno per...
doo-ay an-da-tay ay ree-tor-no payr...

I want to book...
voglio prenotare...
vol-yo pray-no-ta-ray...

2 seats
due posti
doo-ay pos-tee

a couchette
una cuccetta
oo-na koo-chet-ta

what time is the next train to...?
a che ora c'è il prossimo treno per...?
a kay o-ra che eel pros-see-mo tray-no payr...

which platform?
quale binario?
kwa-lay bee-nar-yo

is there a supplement to pay?
c'e un supplemento da pagare?
che oon soop-lay-men-to da pa-ga-ray

do I have to change?
devo cambiare?
day-vo kam-bee-a-ray

talking

stazione

▲ Station with rail logo

◀ Milan Central station information board

telephone booking collection

information desk

ticket office

Automated ticket
▼ machine

corsa semplice
kor-sa sem-plee-chay
one-way

andata e ritorno
an-da-ta ay ree-tor-no
return -

prima classe
pree-ma klas-say
first class

seconda classe
se-kon-da klas-say
second class

prezzo ridotto
pret-so ree-dot-to
reduced fare

prenotazione
pray-no-tats-yo-nay
reservation

carta d'argento
kar-ta dar-jen-to
over 60s pass

sportello
spor-tel-lo
ticket counter

tessera
tes-say-ra
pass

corridoio
ko-ree-doy-o
aisle

finestra
fee-nes-tra
window

fumatori
foo-ma-tor-ee
smoking

non fumatori
non foo-ma-tor-ee
non-smoking

keywords keywords keywords keywords keywords

Validating machines are usually situated at platform entrances and can easily be missed. ▼

does this train stop at...?
questo treno si ferma a...?
kwes-to tray-no see fer-ma a...

is this the train for...?
è questo il treno per...?
e kwes-to eel tray-no payr...

how long does the train stop for?
quanto tempo si ferma il treno?
kwan-to tem-po see fer-ma eel tray-no

this is my seat
questo è il mio posto
kwes-to e eel mee-o pos-to

talking

TAXI

The easiest place to find a taxi is at a railway station. Be sure to take an official taxi, yellow in Rome and white in most other places. In smaller places you can ask at the tourist office for the number of the local taxi. Tipping is normally 10-15% of the fare and you may be charged extra to go to or from the airport. Keep an eye on the change; it can get very confusing with all the noughts.

◀ Taxi sign
Two phone numbers are given, one for the town centre and one for the station.

▶

You can phone for a taxi. **Numero Verde** means free phone so you don't need any money to call.

Taxis are generally white (except in Rome).

This is a taxi stand at the railway station.

◀

▼ Roman taxis are yellow.

where is the nearest taxi stand?
dov'è il posteggio dei taxi più vicino
do-ve eel pos-ted-jo day tak-see pyoo vee-chee-no

to ... please
a ... per favore
a ... payr fa-vo-ray

how much is it to go to...?
quanto costa per andare a...?
kwan-to kos-ta payr an-da-ray a...

please order me a taxi
per favore, mi chiami un taxi
payr fa-vo-ray mee kee-a-mee oon tak-see

now
subito
soo-bee-to

for... o'clock
per le...
payr lay...

I need a receipt
ho bisogno di una ricevuta
o bee-zon-yo dee oo-na ree-chay-voo-ta

keep the change
tenga il resto
ten-ga eel res-to

is there a special rate for the airport?
c'è una tariffa speciale per l'aeroporto?
che oo-na ta-reef-fa spay-cha-lay payr lay-ro-por-to

CAR HIRE

You will find all the big car hire firms in Italy, but hiring a car on the spot can prove more expensive than arranging it before your trip. You have to be at least 21 and to have held a driving licence for over a year to hire a car. Drivers under 23 will be charged a daily surcharge.

◄ Most of the big hire firms operate in Italy
car hire

van hire

I want to hire a car
vorrei noleggiare una macchina
vor-ray nol-ed-ja-ray oo-na mak-kee-na

for one day
per un giorno
payr oon jor-no

for ... days
per ... giorni
payr ... jor-nee

I want...
vorrei...
vor-ray...

a small car
una macchina piccola
oo-na mak-kee-na peek-ko-la

a large car
una macchina grande
oo-na mak-kee-na gran-day

a people carrier
un monovolume
oon mo-no-vo-loo-may

an automatic car
un macchina con cambio automatico
oo-na mak-kee-na kon kam-bee-o ow-to-ma-teek-ko

how much is it?
quanto costa?
kwan-to kos-ta

is there a kilometre charge?
si paga per chilometro?
see pa-ga payr kee-lo-may-tro

I am ... old
ho ... anni
o ... an-nee

here is my driving licence
ecco la mia patente
ek-ko la mee-a pa-ten-tay

what is included in the insurance?
cos'è compreso nell'assicurazione?
ko-ze kom-pray-zo nel-las-see-koo-rats-yo-nay

how do the controls work?
come funzionano i comandi?
ko-may foonts-yo-na-no ee ko-man-dee

where are the documents?
dove sono i documenti?
do-vay so-no ee do-koo-men-tee

what do we do if...?
cosa si deve fare se...?
ko-za see day-vay fa-ray say...

when there is a breakdown
quando c'è un guasto
kwan-do che oon gwas-to

can we have a babyseat?
si può avere un seggiolino per il bambino?
see pwo a-vay-ray oon sed-jo-lee-no payr eel bam-bee-no

how is it fitted?
come si monta?
ko-may see mon-ta

talking talking talking talking talking

DRIVING

The minimum age for driving in Italy is 18. Italian drivers can sometimes be impatient and will often overtake dangerously. Zebra crossings show where you can cross the road but don't expect cars to stop for you. If you take your own car, you will need a green card from your insurance company which you may be asked to show at the border control. The **Polizia Stradale** look after the roads and their cars are equipped with speed-monitoring machines. You must carry your passport and car documents with you at all times and it is likely that the police will ask to look at these. If you are caught speeding they will fine you on the spot. If you break down, call 116 (ACI, the Italian equivalent to the AA). They operate 24 hours a day and have multilingual staff. They will need to know where you are, the type of car and the registration number.

Speed restrictions

built up area	50 km/h
main roads	90-110 km/h
motorway	130 km/h

▼ Direction indicators

NORTH **Nord**

EAST

Ovest **Est**

WEST

Sud **SOUTH**

◄ Danger

◄ Tunnel

▼ Italian car badge and number plate.

AE 563 XC

green indicates motorway (**autostrada**)

blue indicates main routes

centro centre

local signs are white

MILANO
CERNOBBIO
MENAGGIO

centro
MILANO - LECCO
VARESE

► One way street Late at night the amber light may be flashing. This means you can go through if nothing is coming.

◀ Take extra care at roundabouts.
Remember, you are driving on the right and traffic from the right has priority unless otherwise indicated.

pictograms on road signs indicate services available: Hospital, Post Office and police

◀ **CAUTION ELECTRONIC SPEED CONTROL**

No sounding ▶ horn

◀ **CAUTION LORRY EXIT**

local sites and route to the motorway (A9)

all routes, follow this sign if you are passing through

Voltiano temple & war memorial

funicular railway

SWITCH ON
▼ **LIGHTS**

we are going to...
andiamo a...
and-ya-mo a...

is it a good road?
è una buona strada?
e oo-na bwo-na stra-da

is the pass open?
il passo è aperto?
eel pas-so e a-payr-to

which is the best route?
qual è la strada migliore?
kwa-le la stra-da meel-yo-ray

can you show me on the map?
mi può indicare sulla cartina?
mee pwo een-dee-ka-ray sool-la kar-tee-na

do we need snow chains?
c'è bisogno delle catene per le gomme?
che bee-zon-yo del-lay ka-tay-nay payr lay gom-may

talking

*Italian motorways (**autostrada**) are often two-laned and cars can come up very fast in the outside lane. Italian drivers are apt to come up very close behind you and to flash their lights if they want you to get out of the way. On most of the motorways you have to pay a toll. The busiest times on Italian motorways are at the beginning and end of August when most offices and factories shut down for the annual summer break and Italians leave the cities for their country homes.*

◀ Entrance to motorway
Italian motorway signs are green.

PAY STATION COMING UP ▲

no hitch-hiking

toll to pay.

You must stop and pay unless you have a *Telepass*. This device, installed in the car, allows you to go through the automatic barrier.

▼

Motorway exit sign
Prossima Uscita on a motorway
▼ sign means next exit.

exit for
Malpensa
Airport

brown signs
are for places
of interest

SS 33 indicates a
Strada Statale,
a main road

CH indicates
border crossing
to Switzerland.

Viacards can be bought at newsagents and are useful if you use the motorway frequently.

Telepass, the in-car device

Pay with cash or by credit card. The amount will be lit up on the screen in front of you (on the passenger side if you are driving a left-hand drive).

There are ▶ different lanes for different methods of payment.

◀ SOS phones are every 2km on the motorway.

Service station ▶ in 500 m with facilities for the disabled and a cash point. Italian service stations offer hot and cold food.

If you break down on the motorway

If you break down on the motorway, first you should put on your warning lights and place the warning triangle about 30 m behind the car. There are SOS points every 2km. They are simple to use and instructions are in four languages. Simply press either the red cross button for ambulance assistance or the spanner button if you need breakdown recovery. The confirmation light (*lampada da conferma*) should light when your call has been acknowledged. You should then return to the car and wait for help to arrive.

my car has broken down
la mia macchina è in panne
*la **mee**-a **mak**-kee-na e een **pan**-nay*

what should I do?
cosa devo fare?
*ko-za **day**-vo **fa**-ray*

I'm a female on my own
sono da sola
*so-no da **so**-la*

my children are in the car
miei figli sono nella macchina
*mee-**yay feel**-yee **so**-no **nel**-la **mak**-kee-na*

the car is...
la macchina è...
*la **mak**-kee-na e...*

after exit...
dopo l'uscita...
*do-po loo-**shee**-ta...*

before exit...
prima dell'uscita...
***pree**-ma del-loo-**shee**-ta...*

it's a red Nissan
è un Nissan rosso
*e oon **nees**-san **ros**-so*

registration number...
targa numero...
***tar**-ga **noo**-may-ro...*

There are a number of different systems used for parking. More and more automated machines are being used and you will need coins (generally *L.1000* coins are very useful). Some machines will take banknotes but they must be in good condition. Some parking is with a parking disk (**disco orario**) and you can get these from petrol stations.

◀ Where you see this symbol there will be some kind of parking restriction.

DIVIETO di SOSTA — *no stopping*

riservato imbarco traghetto — *reserved for traffic boarding ferry*

▲ No parking outside authorised spaces

◀ Parking disk required. You must display it on the dash-board where it is visible.

maximum 60 minutes from 8 am–8 pm, holidays included

▶ You will be towed away if you park here

◀ Pay at the meter

Giorni feriali means Mon–Sat from 9 am–8 pm

Inizio means begins (i.e. parking restriction begins here).

▶ No parking at any time of the day (you will be towed away)

Parking ticket machine
Instructions on the right are
also in English.   ▶

orario (when payment applies)
00.00 to 24.00 (i.e. all the time)

tutti i giorni means every day

tariffe tariff
L.3000 per hour.
maximum stay allowed 3 hours
minimum payment L.1500
(30 minutes)

municipal
parking

pedestrian
entrance

Be careful: *libero*
means there are
◀ spaces, not that
parking is free.

libero

▲ PRIVATE PROPERTY

completo
◀ means
no spaces

completo

Multistorey car park ▼

◀ Free
parking

---

where is there a car park?
dove c'è un parcheggio?
*do-vay che oon par-**ked**-jo*

where's the best place to park?
dov'è il posto migliore per parcheggiare?
*do-**ve** eel **pos**-to meel-**yo**-ray payr par-**ked**-ja-ray*

I don't have a parking disc
non ho un disco orario
*non o oon deesk o-**rar**-yo*

can I park here?
posso parcheggiare qui?
***pos**-so par-**ked**-ja-ray kwee*

how long for?
per quanto tempo?
*payr **kwan**-to **tem**-po*

the ticket machine doesn't work
il parchimetro non funziona
*eel par-**kee**-may-tro non foonts-**yo**-na*

Petrol stations are generally follow shop hours and are closed between 12.30 and 3.30 pm. They stay open until 7.30 pm and are shut on Sundays. However, they usually have automatic pumps which accept L.10,000 and L.50,000 notes.

Senza Pb unleaded

Super 4-star

Gasolio diesel

◀ Many petrol stations have machines where you can select and pay for the petrol you want. Select the petrol, pay in advance and then the pump will release the petrol.

▲ Pumps in large petrol stations are generally numbered and you just need to tell the attendant the pump number.

where is the nearest petrol station?
dov'è la stazione di servizio più vicina?
do-ve la stats-yo-nay dee ser-veets-yo pyoo vee-chee-na

... worth of unleaded petrol
... di benzina senza piombo
... dee bent-see-na sent-sa pee-om-bo

can I get the car washed?
si può lavare la macchina?
see pwo la-va-ray la mak-kee-na

fill it up
il pieno
eel pee-ay-no

pump number
pompa numero
pom-pa noo-may-ro

talking

If you break down, phone 116 for assistance. Garages that do repairs are known as **Autofficina**.

◀ CAR WASH

car vacuum

I have broken down
sono in panne
*so-no een **pan**-nay*

the battery is flat
la batteria è scarica
*la bat-tay-**ree**-a e **ska**-ree-ka*

I need new tyres
ho bisogno delle gomme
*o bee-**zon**-yo **del**-lay **gom**-may*

I have run out of petrol
non ho più benzina
*non o pyoo bent-**see**-na*

the ... is not working
il/la ... non funziona
*eel/la ... non foonts-**yo**-na*

can you repair it?
può ripararlo?
*pwo ree-par-**ar**-lo*

when will it be ready?
quando sarà pronta?
*kwan-do sa-**ra pron**-ta*

can you replace the windscreen?
può cambiare il parabrezza?
*pwo kamb-**ya**-ray eel pa-ra-**bret**-sa*

the car won't start
la macchina non parte
*la **mak**-kee-na non **par**-tay*

I have a flat tyre
ho una foratura
*o **oo**-na fo-ra-**too**-ra*

where is the nearest garage?
dov'è l'autorimessa più vicina?
*do-**ve** low-to-ree-**mes**-sa pyoo vee-**chee**-na*

there is something wrong with...
c'è qualcosa che non va con...
*che kwal-**ko**-za kay non va kon...*

have you the parts?
avete i pezzi di ricambio?
*a-**vay**-tay ee **pet**-see dee ree-**kamb**-yo*

how long will it take?
quanto ci vuole?
*kwan-to chee **vwo**-lay*

how much will it cost?
quanto costerà?
*kwan-to kos-tay-**ra***

can you change...	**the oil**	**the water**	**the tyres**
mi può cambiare...	l'olio	l'acqua	le gomme
*mee pwo kamb-**ya**-ray...*	***lol**-yo*	***lak**-wa*	*lay **gom**-may*

talking talking talking talking talking talking talking

SHOPPING

Shops are generally shut on Monday mornings. Other days they are open in the mornings from 9 am to 1 pm and in the afternoons from 4 pm to 7.30 pm. Shops are shut on Sundays except for food shops selling bread which open in the mornings. Cake shops are also open on Sunday mornings.

When you buy something, you may notice the shop assistant is very insistent in handing you the receipt. You must take it with you: if you are stopped by the finance police within 100 m of the shop without it, both you and the shopkeeper will be fined. This measure was brought in to avoid tax evasion.

keywords keywords keywords

panificio
pa-nee-**fee**-cho
baker's

macelleria
ma-chel-lay-**ree**-a
butcher's

fruttivendola
froot-tee-**ven**-do-la
fruit shop

alimentari
a-lee-men-**ta**-ree
grocer's

pasticceria
pas-tee-cher-**ee**-a
cake shop

supermercato
soo-per-mer-**ka**-to
supermarket

pescheria
pes-kay-**ree**-a
fishmonger's

giornalaio
jor-nal-**a**-yo
newsagent's

▲ *Alimentari* is the grocer's, selling fresh bread, milk and other food. People will generally shop here daily for bread and milk. It tends to open early, about 8 am.

▲ Butcher & Pork products (e.g. ham, salami, sausage

newspapers

stationery

toys
gifts

An *enoteca* sells wine. ▶
Look out for local specialities.

◀

Pharmacies sell baby products such as
nappies and baby
food, but they cost
more than in supermarkets.

Supermarkets are generally open all day (until 8 pm) from Monday to Saturdays. They are generally shut on Sundays. You can find other services within supermarkets such as dry-cleaning and shoe repairs as well as a café serving fast food.

◀ Although Italians will still shop daily for bread, milk and other foods such as ham and cheese, they are now likely to do a large shop in a supermarket.

Giovedì e Venerdì aperto fino alle 22.00
Thu and Fri open until 10 pm

Fruit ▶ and veg must be weighed and stickered (the weighing machine has pictures so you can identify the produce) before getting to the checkout. The checkout assistant does not do this. You will also have to ask for and pay for plastic bags.

change machine at entrance

You need a L.500 coin for the trolley. ◀

pay for 2 ——
take 3 ——

paghi 2
prendi 3

where can I buy...?
dove posso comprare...?
*do-vay **pos**-so komp-**ra**-ray...*

do you have...?
avete...?
*a-**vay**-tay...*

I am looking for...
cerco...
***cher**-ko...*

can I pay with this card?
posso pagare con questa carta?
***pos**-so pa-**ga**-ray kon **kwes**-ta **kar**-ta*

batteries
pile
***pee**-lay*

how much is it?
quanto costa?
***kwan**-to **kos**-ta*

a present
un regalo
*oon ray-**ga**-lo*

4 plastic bags
quattro borse di plastica
***kwat**-tro **bor**-say dee **plas**-tee-ka*

a tin-opener
un apriscatole
*oon ap-ree-**ska**-to-lay*

a good wine
un buon vino
*oon bwon **vee**-no*

talking

*Quantities are expressed in kilos and grams. For those who are more used to pounds and ounces, 1 kilo is roughly equivalent to 2 lb, half a kilo is equivalent to 1 lb, 250 g is equivalent to a half pound and an ounce is equivalent to about 30 g. You will also hear the word **etto** used, which is 100 g. So 250 g could be expressed either **due cento cinquanta grammi** or **due etti e mezzo**, i.e. two and a half **etti**.*

Bread is sold by weight, or if you are buying ▶ rolls (*panini*) by number. Large wholemeal loaves are cut up and you can ask for a piece. Bread is bought fresh each day and eaten with meals. Italians don't usually put butter on their bread, so you won't find it on the dinner table. Italian butter is unsalted.

▲ Markets are held in the morning, either daily in large towns or weekly in smaller places. They generally have a great variety of stalls: cheese, bread, meat and fish. It is the best place to buy your fruit and vegetables. Markets will also have stalls selling hardware, clothes, shoes, etc. If you feel confident, in markets you can ask for a discount on anything other than food.

Ham is either cured, such as Parma ham, and known as *prosciutto crudo*. Cooked ham is *prosciutto cotto*. When you ask for *prosciutto*, you may hear the shop assistant asking whether you want *crudo* or *cotto*. It is sliced very finely. *Un etto di prosiutto* should generously fill a couple of bread rolls. ▼

talking

is there a market?
c'è un mercato?
*che oon mer-**ka**-to*

which day?
quale giorno?
*kwa-lay **jor**-no*

it's a bit too much
è un pò troppo caro
*e oon po **trop**-po **ka**-ro*

would you give me a discount?
mi fà uno sconto?
*mee fa **oo**-no **skon**-to*

da consumarsi entro
to be consumed by

▲ Milk is generally colour-coded. Here blue is for whole milk (*intero*), pink for semi-skimmed (*parzialmente scremato*). It is sold by the half litre (*mezzo litro*) or litre (*litro*).

Mineral water is sparkling (*frizzante*) or still (*naturale*). Look out for the colour coding: red for sparkling and blue/grey for still.

frozen foods ▶  **surgelati**

 SENZA COLORANTI ◀ *free of colouring*

SENZA ZUCCHERO

▲ *sugar-free*

integrale ◀ *wholemeal*

biologico

organic ▲

a piece of that cheese
un pezzo di quel formaggio
*oon **pet**-so dee kwel for-**mad**-jo*

a little more
ancora un pò
*an-**ko**-ra oon po*

a little less
un pò meno
*oon po **may**-no*

that's fine thanks
basta così grazie
*bas-ta ko-**zee** grats-yay*

8 slices of ham
otto fette di prosciutto
*ot-to **fet**-tay dee pro-**shoot**-to*

a litre of milk
un litro di latte
*oon **leet**-ro dee **lat**-tay*

a bottle of...
una bottiglia di...
*oo-na bot-**teel**-ya dee...*

mineral water
acqua minerale
*ak-wa mee-nay-**ra**-lay*

still
naturale
*na-too-**ra**-lay*

fizzy
gassata
*ga-**za**-ta*

a tin of...
una scatola di...
*oo-na **ska**-to-la dee...*

a jar of...
un vaso di...
*oon **va**-zo dee...*

a packet of...
un pacchetto di...
*oon pak-**ket**-to dee...*

that's everything thanks
è tutto grazie
*e toot-to **grats**-yay*

▼ Typical nutritional info per 100 g

energy
protein
carbohydrates
fat
calcium

talking talking talking talking talking talking talking

Here is a list of basic foodstuffs you might need.

Everyday Foods alimentari *a-lee-men-ta-ree*

biscuits	i biscotti *bees-**kot**-tee*
bread	il pane *pa-nay*
bread roll	il panino *pa-**nee**-no*
bread (sliced)	il pancarrè *pan-kar-**ray***
butter	il burro ***boor**-ro*
cereal	i cereali *chay-ray-**a**-lee*
cheese	il formaggio *for-**mad**-jo*
chicken	il pollo ***pol**-lo*
coffee	il caffè *kaf-**fe***
cream	la panna ***pan**-na*
crisps	le patatine *pat-a-**tee**-nay*
eggs	le uova ***wov**-a*
fish	il pesce ***pay**-shay*
flour	la farina *fa-**ree**-na*
fruit juice	il succo di frutta ***sook**-ko dee **froot**-ta*
ham (cooked)	il prosciutto cotto *pro-**shoot**-to **kot**-to*
ham (cured)	il prosciutto crudo *pro-**shoot**-to **kroo**-do*
herbal tea	la tisana *tee-**za**-na*
honey	il miele ***myay**-lay*
jam	la marmellata *mar-mel-**la**-ta*
margarine	la margarina *mar-ga-**ree**-na*
marmalade	la marmellata d'arance *mar-mel-**la**-ta da-**ran**-chay*
meat	la carne ***kar**-nay*
milk	il latte ***lat**-tay*
mustard	la senape ***sen**-a-pay*
oil	l'olio ***ol**-yo*
orange juice	il succo d'arancia ***sook**-ko da-**ran**-cha*
pasta	la pasta ***pas**-ta*
pepper	il pepe ***pep**-ay*
rice	il riso ***ree**-zo*
salt	il sale ***sa**-lay*
sausage	la salsiccia *sal-**see**-cha*
sugar	lo zucchero ***tsook**-kay-ro*
stock cube	i dadi da brodo ***da**-dee da **bro**-do*
tea	il tè *te*
tomatoes (tin)	i pelati *pay-**la**-tee*
tuna (tin)	il tonno ***ton**-no*
vinegar	l'aceto *a-**chay**-to*
yoghurt	lo yogurt ***yo**-goort*

The market is the best place to buy fresh fruit and vegetables.
*A greengrocer's is called **il fruttivendolo**.*

Fruit	frutta *froot-ta*
apples	le mele *may-lay*
apricots	le albicocche *al-bee-**kok**-kay*
bananas	le banane *ba-**na**-nay*
cherries	le ciliegie *cheel-**yay**-jay*
figs	i fichi *fee-kee*
grapefruit	il pompelmo *pom-**pel**-mo*
grapes	l'uva *oo-va*
lemon	il limone *lee-mo-nay*
melon	il melone *may-**lo**-nay*
nectarines	le pescanoci *pes-ka-**no**-chee*
oranges	le arance *a-ran-chay*
peaches	le pesche *pes-kay*
pears	le pere *pay-ray*
pineapple	l'ananas *a-na-nas*
plums	le prugne *proon-yay*
raspberries	i lamponi *lam-**po**-nee*
strawberries	le fragole *fra-go-lay*
watermelon	l'anguria *an-**goo**-ree-a*

Vegetables	verdura *ver-**doo**-ra*
artichokes	i carciofi *kar-**cho**-fee*
aubergines	le melanzane *may-lant-**sa**-nay*
asparagus	gli asparagi *as-**pa**-ra-jee*
carrots	le carote *ka-ro-tay*
cauliflower	il cavolfiore *ka-volf-**yor**-ay*
celery	il sedano *sed-a-no*
courgettes	le zucchine *tsook-**kee**-nay*
cucumber	il cetriolo *chay-tree-**yo**-lo*
french beans	i fagiolini *fa-jo-**lee**-nee*
garlic	l'aglio *al-yo*
leeks	i porri *por-ree*
lettuce	la lattuga *lat-**too**-ga*
mushrooms	i funghi *foong-ee*
onions	le cipolle *chee-**pol**-lay*
peas	i piselli *pee-**zel**-lee*
peppers	i peperoni *pay-pay-**ro**-nee*
potatoes	le patate *pa-**ta**-tay*
radishes	i ravanelli *ra-va-**nel**-lee*
spinach	gli spinaci *spee-**na**-chee*
spring onions	le cipolline *chee-pol-**lee**-nay*
tomatoes	i pomodori *po-mo-**do**-ree*
turnip	la rapa *ra-pa*

*Look out for **Upim** and **Standa**, Italy's two main chains of department stores. In Milan there is **Il Rinascente**. The stores are generally not open on Sundays.*

negozio
nay-**gots**-yo
shop

seminterrato
say-meen-ter-**ra**-to
basement

pianterreno
pee-an-ter-**ray**-no
ground floor

primo piano
pree-mo pee-**a**-no
first floor

reparto
ray-**par**-to
department

giocattoli
jo-**kat**-to-lee
toys

gioielleria
jo-yel-lay-**ree**-a
jewellery

donne
don-nay
ladies'

uomini
wo-mee-nee
men's

bambini
bam-**bee**-nee
children's

Italy is the land of style and you can find lots of small boutiques. ▼

sciarpe scarves   *pantaloni* trousers   *camicie* shirts

silk

Italians take their seasons very seriously. You may get a boiling-hot day in April, but this does not mean that you will see people stripping off into shorts and bare legs. Summer clothes won't be worn until the end of May.

You can get good bargains at the end of season sales (Aug/Sep (for summer and March for winter).

saldi fine stagione

on which floor can I find...?
a che piano si trova...?
*a kay pee-**a**-no see **tro**-va...*

lingerie
la biancheria intima
*la bee-an-kay-**ree**-a **een**-tee-ma*

swimsuits
costume da bagno
*kos-**too**-may da **ban**-yo*

shoes
le scarpe
*lay **skar**-pay*

Women's clothes sizes

UK/Australia	8	10	12	14	16	18	20	22
Europe	36	38	40	42	44	46	48	50
US/Canada	6	8	10	12	14	16	18	20

Men's clothes sizes (suits)

UK/US/Canada	36	38	40	42	44	46
Europe	46	48	50	52	54	56
Australia	92	97	102	107	112	117

Shoes

UK/Australia	2	3	4	5	6	7	8	9	10	11
Europe	35	36	37	38	39	41	42	43	45	46
US/Canada women	4	5	6	7	8	9	10	11	12	-
US/Canada men	3	4	5	6	7	8	9	10	11	12

Children's Shoes

UK/US/Canada	0	1	2	3	4	5	6	7	8	9	10	11
Europe	15	17	18	19	20	22	23	24	26	27	28	29

do you have this in my size?
c'è nella mia taglia?
che nel-la mee-a tal-ya

can I try this on?
posso provarlo?
po-so pro-var-lo

where are the changing rooms?
dove sono gli spogliatoi?
do-vay so-no lee spol-ya-toy-ee

I take size 44
la mia taglia è quarantaquattro
la mee-a tal-ya è kwa-ran-ta-kwat-tro

it is too big
è troppo grande
e trop-po gran-day

it is too small
è troppo piccolo
e trop-po peek-ko-lo

I need a larger/smaller size
ho bisogno di una taglia più grande/più piccola
o bee-zon-yo dee oo-na tal-ya pyoo gran-day/pyoo peek-ko-la

I take shoe size 39
io porto numero trentanove
ee-yo por-to noo-may-ro tren-ta-no-vay

do you have this in...?
c'è in...?
che een...

black/brown
nero/marrone
nay-ro/mar-ro-nay

other colours
altri colori
al-tree ko-lo-ree

talking talking talking

*Post offices are open 8.30 am–2 pm Monday to Friday. Main post offices in large towns will stay open all day until 7pm. On Saturdays they are open until 12 pm. Stamps can also be bought at **tabbacchi** or shops selling postcards.*

To ▶ ensure a fast, reliable delivery, you can pay extra and send your cards or letters *posta prioritaria*, priority mail, costing L.1200. Post letters and cards stamped *prioritaria* in the postbox with the blue sticker.

POSTA PRIORITARIA
Priority Mail

▲ Post Office

Post Office logo ▶

▼ Post Boxes are red.

The blue sticker indicates priority mail. In theory letters take 2 days to be delivered within Italy and 3 days for abroad. However, the Italian mail can sometimes be erratic. A stamp for a postcard to Europe is L.800.

talking talking

where is the post office?
dov'è la posta?
do-**ve** la **pos**-ta

do you have stamps?
avete dei francobolli?
a-**vay**-tay day fran-ko-**bol**-lee

10 stamps
dieci francobolli
dee-**ay**-chee fran-ko-**bol**-lee

for postcards
per cartoline
payr kar-to-**lee**-nay

for letters
per lettere
payr **let**-tay-ray

to Europe
per l'Europa
payr lay-oo-**ro**-pa

to America
per gli Stati Uniti
payr lee **sta**-tee oo-**nee**-tee

to Australia
per l'Australia
payr low-**stra**-lee-a

I want to send this registered
voglio spedire questo raccomandato
vol-yo spay-**dee**-ray **kwes**-to rak-ko-man-**da**-to

priority
posta prioritaria
pos-ta pree-o-ree-**tar**-ya

I want to send this parcel
voglio spedire questo pacco
vol-yo spay-**dee**-ray **kwes**-to **pak**-ko

surface
via normale
vee-a nor-**ma**-lay

airmail
via aerea
vee-a a-**ay**-ree-a

You can find photobooths at photo shops and stations. If you want to buy film, look out for 3 for 2 offers.

◀ Photographic shop

your photos ready in 30 minutes

VIETATO FOTOGRAFARE

◀ NO PHOTOGRAPHY

Photography is not allowed in art galleries, museums and churches.

◀ PHOTOGRAPHIC SERVICES AVAILABLE

where can I buy tapes for a videocamera?
dove posso comprare le cassette per la videocamera?
do-vay pos-so komp-ra-ray lay kas-set-tay payr la vee-day-o-ka-may-ra

a colour film	**24**	**36**	**exposures**
un rullino a colori	ventiquattro	trentasei	pose
oon rool-lee-no a ko-lo-ree	*ven-tee-kwat-tro*	*tren-ta-say*	*po-zay*

can you develop this film?
può svilupparmi questo rullino?
pwo svee-loop-par-mee kwes-to rool-lee-no

can we take pictures?
si può fare delle foto?
see pwo fa-ray del-lay fo-to

can you take a picture of us?
ci può fare una foto?
chee pwo fa-ray oo-na fo-to

talking

PHONES

*There is no shortage of public phones in Italy taking coins and phonecards (**scheda telefonica**) available from **tabacchi** and newsagents. Cheaper times to phone are between 10 pm and 8 am Monday-Saturday and all day Sunday. Italy is awash with mobile phones. If you take your own, ensure that you contact your service provider to enable you to use it abroad.*

► There are also machines selling phonecards.

◄ Phonecards will be on sale where you see the words *scheda telefonica*.

do you have phonecards?
avete delle schede telefoniche?
*a-**vay**-tay **del**-lay **skay**-day te-le-**fo**-nee-kay*

a phonecard
una scheda telefonica
*oo-na **skay**-da te-le-**fo**-nee-ka*

L.5000
cinquemila
***cheen**-kway-mee-la*

L.10,000
diecimila
*dee-ay-chee-**mee**-la*

L.15,000
quindicimila
***kween**-dee-chee-mee-la*

Signor Grandi please
Signor Grandi per favore
*seen-**yor gran**-dee payr fa-**vo**-ray*

extension number...
interno numero...
*een-**ter**-no **noo**-may-ro...*

can I speak to Paul?
posso parlare con Paul?
***pos**-so par-**la**-ray kon paul*

this is Caroline
qui è Caroline
kwee e caroline

can I have an outside line please?
posso avere la linea per favore
***pos**-so a-**vay**-ray la **lee**-nay-a payr fa-**vo**-ray*

hello
pronto
***pron**-to*

I'd like to make a reverse-charge call
vorrei fare una chiamata a carico destinatario
*vor-**ray** fa-ray **oo**-na kee-a-**ma**-ta a ka-**ree**-ko des-tee-na-**tar**-yo*

what is you phone number?
qual è il suo numero di telefono?
*kwal e eel **soo**-o **noo**-may-ro dee te-**le**-fo-no*

my phone number is...
il mio numero è...
*eel **mee**-o **noo**-may-ro e...*

Phonecards come in three prices: L.5000, L.10,000 and L.15,000. The euro price is given also.

To use phonecards you must tear off the perforated corner.

◀ Many payphones have instructions in English. Emergency numbers and dialling codes will be displayed in the phonebox.

scheda telefonica
skay-da te-le-fo-nee-ka
phonecard

cellulare
chel-loo-la-ray
mobile phone

prefisso
pray-fees-so
code

elenco telefonico
ay-len-ko te-le-fo-nee-ko
phonebook

pagine gialle
pa-jee-nay jal-lay
yellow pages

UK	00 44
USA	00 1
Australia	00 61

▲ International dialling codes from Italy

◀
Numero verde literally means green number. It is freephone, so no money is needed.

I'll call back...
richiamo...
reek-ya-mo...

later
più tardi
pyoo tar-dee

tomorrow
domani
do-ma-nee

do you have a mobile phone?
ha un telefonino?
a oon te-le-fo-nee-no

is it switched on?
è acceso
e ach-ay-zo

what is your mobile number?
cos'è il suo numero di cellulare
ko-ze eel soo-o noo-may-ro dee che-loo-la-ray

If you want to check your e-mail messages, internet cafés are becoming more and more widespread. If you know where you are going to be staying in Italy, check in advance at www.cyberia.net/cyberia/guide/ccafe.htm if there is a local internet café nearby.

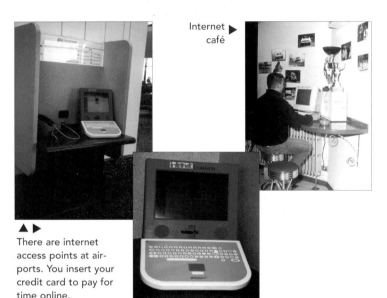

Internet ▶ café

▲ ▶

There are internet access points at airports. You insert your credit card to pay for time online.

talking talking talking

what is your e-mail address?
cos'è il suo indirizzo e-mail?
*ko-**ze** eel **soo**-o een-dee-**reet**-so ee-mail*

my e-mail address is...
il mio indirizzo e-mail è...
*eel **mee**-o een-dee-**reet**-so e...*

caroline.smith@anycompany.co.uk
caroline punto smith chiocciola anycompany punto co punto uk
*caroline **poon**-to smith chee-**och**-lo-la anycompany **poon**-to co **poon**-to uk*

can I send an e-mail?
posso mandare un e-mail?
*po-so man-**da**-ray oon ee-mail*

did you get my e-mail?
ha ricevuto il mio e-mail?
*a ree-chay-**voo**-to eel **mee**-o ee-mail*

can you send it by e-mail?
può mandarlo via e-mail?
*pwo man-**dar**-lo **vee**-a ee-mail*

as an attachment
allegato
*al-lay-**ga**-to*

how much does an hour of netsurfing cost?
quanto costa un hora in internet
*kwan-to **kos**-ta oon **o**-ra een **een**-ter-net*

◀ Here you can photocopy and send faxes.

National and local tourist and what's-on information can be accessed via the internet.

▼

I want to send a fax
voglio mandare un fax
vol-yo man-da-ray oon faks

do you have a fax?
avete un fax?
a-vay-tay oon faks

can I send a fax from here?
posso mandare un fax da qui?
pos-so man-da-ray oon faks da kwee

can I receive a fax here?
posso ricevere un fax qui?
pos-so ree-chev-ay-ray oon faks kwee

how much is it to send a fax?
quanto costa per mandare un fax?
kwan-to kos-ta payr man-da-ray oon faks

it has ... pages
ha ... pagine
a ... pa-jee-nay

what is your fax number?
cos'è il suo numero di fax?
ko-ze eel soo-o noo-may-ro dee faks

can you confirm the number
può confirmare il numero
pwo kon-feer-ma-ray eel noo-may-ro

did you get my fax?
ha ricevuto il mio fax?
a ree-chay-voo-to eel mee-o faks

talking talking

OUT & ABOUT

Local tourist offices have free maps and brochures. They can generally help with booking accommodations and advise on local attractions and excursions. Museum opening hours are very variable so it is best to check before you visit. If you are visiting churches or religious sites you should remember that these are primarily places of worship, so dress appropriately: no shorts or bare shoulders.

▲ Most Italian cities, towns and small villages have a tourist information office, known officially as *l'Azienda di Promozione Turistica*, but they can usually be identified with the *i* sign. ▼

Places of interest such as museums and art galleries are ▼ signposted in brown.

▲ Churches are signposted in yellow. Opening hours can vary, particularly in smaller places. Churches are places of worship and visitors should take care to dress appropriately. If a Mass is taking place, you should disturb worshippers as little as possible.

Muncipal art collection

Archeological museum

Medieval museum

National Art Gallery

Industrial Heritage Museum

Piazza means square, *Duomo* means cathedral. ▼

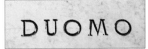

◀ Entrance ticket
entrance fee
*to the Palazzina and
the Forestiera*
single ticket L.10,000

An international
student card will get
reductions into many ◀
museums and sites.

scenic walk —
public beach —

The opera season in
cities runs Oct–June
(though the season
at *La Scala* starts in
Dec). Theatre performances in Italy generally start
at 9 pm. Concert tickets are sold in music stores,
kiosks or at the place of performance, prior to it.

keywords keywords keywords

spettacolo
*spet-***ta***-ko-lo*
show

esposizione
*es-po-zeets-***yo***-nay*
exhibition

passeggiata
pas-sed-ja-ta
walk

divertimenti
*dee-ver-tee-***men***-tee*
attractions

fiera
*fee-***ay***-ra*
fair

chiesa
*kee-***ay***-za*
church

duomo
dwo-mo*
cathedral

isola
*ee-***zo***-la*
island

municipio
*moo-nee-***cheep***-yo*
town hall

talking talking talking

excuse me, where is the tourist office?
scusi, dov'è l'ufficio turistico?
*skoo-zee do-***ve*** loof-***fee***-cho too-***rees***-tee-ko*

do you have...?
avete...?
*a-***vay***-tay...*

a town guide
una guida della città
*oo-na **gwee**-da **del**-la cheet-**ta***

leaflets
degli opuscoli
*del-yee o-***poos***-ko-lee*

we want to visit...
vogliamo visitare...
*vol-***ya***-mo vee-zee-***ta***-ray...*

are there any excursions?
ci sono delle gite?
*chee **so**-no **del**-lay **jee**-tay*

when can we visit the...?
quando si può visitare...?
*kwan-do see pwo vee-zee-***ta***-ray...*

when does it close?
quando chiude?
*kwan-do kee-***oo***-day*

how much is it to get in?
quanto costa l'ingresso?
*kwan-to **kos**-ta leen-**gres**-so*

is there a guided tour?
c'è una visita guidata?
*che **oo**-na **vee**-zee-ta gwee-**da**-ta*

Many beaches in Italy are private or attached to a hotel and you will have to pay to hire a sunbed and sunshade.

sports centre

swimming pool

▲ It is obligatory to wear a swimming cap in pools. Check locally for pool times.

◀ **SPORTS CENTRE**

ice rink

pool – solarium

gym

The local tourist office will have brochures on many sporting and leisure activities. If you are interested in hiking, ask for brochures on any local hikes. ▶

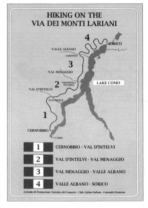

HIKING ON THE
VIA DEI MONTI LARIANI

1	CERNOBBIO - VAL D'INTELVI
2	VAL D'INTELVI - VAL MENAGGIO
3	VAL MENAGGIO - VALLE ALBANO
4	VALLE ALBANO - SORICO

Azienda di Promozione Turistica del Comasco - Club Alpino Italiano - Comunità Montane

talking talking

where can we...?
dove si può...?
do-vay see pwo...

how much is it...?
quanto costa...?
kwan-to kos-ta...

go riding
andare a cavallo
an-da-ray a ka-val-lo

is there a swimming pool?
c'è una piscina?
che oo-na pee-shee-na

where can we go...?
dove si può...?
do-vay see pwo...

play tennis
giocare a tennis
jo-ka-ray a ten-nees

to hire bikes
noleggiare le bici
no-led-ja-ray lay bee-chee

per hour/day
all'ora/al giorno
al-lo-ra/al jor-no

is dangerous to swim here?
è pericoloso nuotare qui?
e pay-ree-ko-lo-zo nwo-ta-ray kwee

windsurfing
fare del windsurfing
fa-ray del windsurfing

play golf
giocare a golf
jo-ka-ray a golf

to fish
pescare
pes-ka-ray

waterskiing
fare lo sci nautico
fa-ray lo shee now-tee-ko

how do we hire a beach umbrella?
come si noleggia un ombrellone?
ko-may see no-led-ja oon om-brel-lo-nay

◀ The football season in Italy runs from end Aug to early June. Games are usually played on Sun afternoons. Italians are passionate about the game.

STADIUM ▶
If you do go to a match, be prepared for fireworks being set off (it may be worth worth wearing a scarf to cover your mouth).

main stand seats L.65.000 ——

reductions L.45.000
disabled-military-retired
children born from 1982 to 1988

Tickets to football matches can be bought at the stadiums. ▼

TRIBUNA L. 65.000
CENTRALE

RIDOTTI L. 45.000
INVALIDI-MILITARI-PENSIONATI
RAGAZZI NATI DAL 1982 AL 1988
RAGAZZI NATI DAL 1989 ENTRANO GRATIS IN TUTTI I SETTORI

▲ Football ground prices

—— Curva seats are at each end of the ground. The most expensive tickets are Tribuna in the main stand.

we'd like to see a football match
ci piacerebbe vedere una partita di calcio
*chee pee-a-chay-**reb**-bay ved-**ay**-ray **oo**-na par-**tee**-ta dee **kal**-cho*

where can we get tickets?
dove si prendono i biglietti?
*do-vay see **pren**-do-no ee beel-**yet**-tee*

how much are they?
quanto costano?
*kwan-to **kos**-ta-no*

how do we get to the stadium?
come si arriva allo stadio?
*ko-may see ar-**ree**-va **al**-lo **stad**-yo*

what time is the match?
quando comincia la partita?
*kwan-do ko-**meen**-cha la par-**tee**-ta*

talking

Hotels are classified one to five stars. One star is generally quite basic, with shared facilities. Two star might have en suite facilities. Three star will have en suite facilities and perhaps a pool. Four star will probably be down to the location. And five star is luxury, either because its location or the type of building it occupies.

◀ Italian hotels are star rated

The Italian word for hotel is *albergo*, but you will often find the word hotel. ▶

Booking in advance

You can phone up the hotel of your choice and book a room. They generally require a fax to confirm the booking and your credit card number. Smaller places generally don't take bookings very far in advance, particularly if there is perhaps a trade fair on, when they are likely to be busy.

I would like to book a room
vorrei prenotare una camera
vor-**ray** pray-no-**ta**-ray oo-na **ka**-may-ra

single/double
singola/doppia
seen-go-la/**dop**-pya

for ... nights
per ... notti
payr ... **not**-tee

from ... to ...
dal ... al ...
dal ... al ...

my name is...
il mio nome è...
eel **mee**-o **no**-may e...

I'll fax to confirm
confermo con un fax
kon-**fer**-mo kon oon faks

my credit card number is ...
il numero della mia carta di credito è...
eel **noo**-may-ro **del**-la **mee**-a **kar**-ta dee **kray**-dee-to e...

expiry date...
data di scadenza...
da-ta dee ska-**dent**-sa...

Hotels are generally signposted. ▶
The busiest time outside the
cities is August, particularly the
weekend nearest 15 August,
known as *ferragosto*.

There is little difference
between a *pensione* and a 1-
or 2-star hotel. Many retired
Italians spend the winter
months in hotels or *pensioni*
by the seaside. ▼

Locanda

▲ A *locanda* is a basic guesthouse,
generally with shared facilities, though
there will be a sink in the room. No
food is provided. Smaller city estab-
lishments may shut in August.

PENSIONE

do you have a room?
avete una camera?
*a-**vay**-tay **oo**-na **ka**-may-ra*

a single/double room
una camera singola/doppia
*oo-na **ka**-may-ra **seen**-go-la/**dop**-pya*

a family room
una camera per una famiglia
*oo-na **ka**-may-ra payr **oo**-na fa-**meel**-ya*

with ensuite bath
con bagno
*kon **ban**-yo*

with shower
con doccia
*kon **doch**-cha*

for tonight
per stanotte
*payr sta-**not**-tay*

for just one night
per una notte sola
*payr **oo**-na **not**-tay **so**-la*

for ... nights
per ... notti
*payr ... **not**-tee*

how much is it?
quanto costa?
*kwan-to **kos**-ta*

is breakfast included?
comprende la colazione?
*com-**pren**-day la ko-lats-**yo**-nay*

how much is half board?
quanto costa mezza pensione?
*kwan-to **kos**-ta **med**-za pens-**yo**-nay*

full board
la pensione completa
*la pens-**yo**-nay kom-**play**-ta*

I would like to see the room
vorrei vedere la camera
*vor-**ray** ved-**ay**-ray la **ka**-may-ra*

talking talking talking talking

To stay at a youth hostel in Italy you generally have to be a member of the International Youth Hostelling Association. You can join on the spot or simply pay a supplement. In the summer you will have to book in advance as they are often full.

◀ Signs for a youth hostel
▼

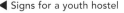

Ostello per la gioventù

Paper recyling bank
You will also come across
bottle banks. In smaller
villages there is a refuse
point where you leave
your rubbish. The times
of the collection will be
posted next to it. ▶

RACCOLTA   CARTA

◀ Italian plugs are two-pin and you
should take an adapter with you if
you are taking any of your own
electrical appliances such as hairdryer or iron. The electric current is
220 v.

how do we get to the youth hostel?
come si arriva all'ostello per la gioventù
*ko-may see ar-**ree**-va al-**los**-tel-lo payr la jov-en-**too***

how much is it to become a member?
quanto costa diventare socio?
***kwan**-to **kos**-ta dee-ven-**ta**-ray so-cho*

talking

◀ Local tourist offices provide annual guides to self-catering, hotel and and camping accommodation in their area. They should also be able to assist you with booking.

Camere ◀ ROOMS

FULL UP ▶ **COMPLETO**

keywords keywords keywords

detersivo per i piatti
day-ter-see-vo payr ee pee-a-tee
washing-up liquid

carta igienica
kar-ta ee-jay-nee-ka
toilet paper

sapone
sa-po-nay
soap

apriscatole
ap-ree-ska-to-lay
tin-opener

candele
kan-day-lay
candles

fiammiferi
fee-am-mee-fay-ree
matches

bombola del gas
bom-bo-la del gaz
gas cylinder

---

there is/are no...
non c'è/non ci sono...
non che/chee so-no...

can you show us how it works?
può farci vedere come funziona?
pwo far-chee ved-ay-ray ko-may foonts-yo-na

how does ... work?
come funziona...
ko-may foonts-yo-na...

the cooker
la cucina
la koo-chee-na

the dishwasher
la lavastoviglia
la la-va-sto-veel-ya

the washing machine
la lavatrice
la la-va-tree-chay

the microwave
il forno a microonde
eel for-no a mee-kro-on-day

who do I contact if there is a problem?
con chi parlo se c'è un problema?
kon kee par-lo say che oon prob-lay-ma

when is the rubbish collected?
quando passano gli spazzini?
kwan-do pas-sa-no lee spats-see-nee

where do we leave the rubbish?
dove mettiamo la spazzatura?
do-vay met-ya-mo la spats-sa-too-ra

can we have another key?
possiamo avere un'altra chiave?
poss-ya-mo a-vay-ray oon-alt-ra kee-a-vay

talking talking talking

The local tourist office will provide information about local campsites. Off-site camping is only allowed in Italy provided you have the permission of the landowner on whose land you are camping – otherwise it is illegal. Official campsites are open mainly from April to September and are well equipped.

◀ **CAMPSITE**
The local tourist information office will provide a list of sites.

no parking from 1 Jun to 30 Sep for lorries and camping vans —

dal 1 giugno
al 30 settembre
per autocarri
e camper

◀ Campsites display
their prices. You generally pay per person, per place plus extra for hot water and electricity.

A car towing a caravan or trailer must not exceed 50 kph in built-up areas, 70 kph outside built-up areas and 80 kph on motorways.

is there a campsite near here?
c'è un campeggio qui vicino?
*che oon kam-**ped**-jo kwee vee-**chee**-no*

have you any vacancies?
avete dei posti?
*a-**vay**-tay day **pos**-tee*

we want to stay for ... nights
vogliamo restare per ... notti
*vol-**ya**-mo res-**ta**-ray payr ... **jor**-nee*

how much is it...?
quanto costa...
kwan-to kos-ta...

per tent
per tenda
payr ten-da

per caravan
per roulotte
*pary roo-**lot***

where are...?
dove sono...?
do-vay so-no...

the showers
le doccie
lay doch-chay

the toilets
le toilette
lay twa-let

is there a restaurant on the campsite?
c'è un ristorante nel campeggio?
*che oon rees-to-**ran**-tay nel kam-**ped**-jo*

is there a more sheltered site?
c'è un posto più riparato?
*che oon **pos**-to pyoo ree-pa-**ra**-to*

talking talking

DRY-CLEANERS ▶

trousers
skirts
jackets
coats
jumpers

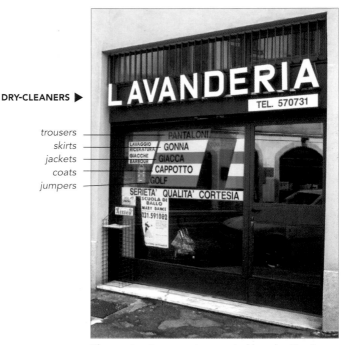

There are not many coin-operated launderettes in Italy. Large supermarkets have cleaning services which take 1 to 2 hours and are good value. At the dry-cleaners it will take a day, but it is generally better value and service.

is there a launderette?
c'è una lavanderia automatica?
*che oon la-van-day-**ree**-a ow-to-**ma**-tee-ka*

where can I do some washing?
dove posso lavare questi panni?
***do**-vay **pos**-so la-**va**-ray **kwes**-tee **pan**-nee*

is there a laundry service?
c'è il servizio lavanderia?
*che eel ser-**veets**-yo la-van-day-**ree**-a*

where is the nearest dry-cleaner's?
dov'è la tintoria più vicina?
*do-**ve** la teen-to-**ree**-a pyoo vee-**chee**-na*

is there an iron
c'è un ferro da stiro?
*che oon **fer**-ro da **stee**-ro*

when will my things be ready?
quando saranno pronti?
***kwan**-do sa-**ran**-no **pron**-tee*

talking talking talking

Disabled facilities are gradually improving in Italy with some museums and churches providing wheelchair-accessible entrances.

◀ Disabled parking is usually available and indicated by the yellow wheelchair sign. The space is reserved for disabled parking only.

Some service ▶ stations offer facilities for the disabled.

◀ Trains marked with this blue disabled badge are equipped to carry wheelchairs. These are mainly the newer intercity trains.

are there any toilets for the disabled?
ci sono le toilette per i disabili?
chee so-no lay twa-let payr ee dee-za-bee-lee

is there an entrance for wheelchair?
c'è l'accesso per la sedia a rotelle?
che la-ches-so payr la sed-ya a ro-tel-lay

is it possible to visit ... with a wheelchair?
si può visitare ... con la sedie a rotelle?
see pwo vee-zee-ta-ray ... kon la sed-ya a ro-tel-lay

is there a reduction for the disabled?
c'è una riduzione per i disabili?
che oo-na ree-doots-yo-nay payr ee dee-za-bee-lee

I need a bedroom on the ground floor
ho bisogno di una camera al pian terreno
o bee-zon-yo dee oo-na ka-may-ra al pee-an ter-ray-no

can I take the train to ... with a wheelchair?
si può prendere il treno per ... con la sedia a rotelle?
see pwo pren-day-ray eel tray-no payr ... kon la sed-ya a ro-tel-lay

I'm a wheelchair
sono in una sedia a rotelle
so-no een oo-na sed-ya a ro-tel-lay

is there a lift?
c'è un ascensore?
che oon a-shen-so-ray

WITH KIDS

Despite Italy's reputed love of children, northern Italy has the lowest birth rate in Europe. In some restaurants you might find it quite difficult to find a highchair.

```
GESTIONE
12363 / 106
ONE GOVERNATIVA NAVIGAZIONE LAGHI

        Navigazione Lago di Como
            P.IVA 00802050153

        Biglietteria di Menaggio

21-07-00 | 17:35 |  36841  |  22/ 1

Da MENAGGIO          a TREMEZZO

A -->

1 - ORDINARIO BATTELLO
Vale giorni 1

L. 11.800      = Euro 6,09

Adulti 2  Ragazzi 1

Non sono ammesse fermate intermedie
```

◄ On most public transport children under 4 travel free. Between 4 and 12 years old they can get a 50% discount on their ticket.

2 adults, 1 child

keywords keywords keywords

bambino/a
bam-bee-no/a
child

seggiolino
sed-jo-lee-no
baby seat

seggiolone
sed-jo-lo-nay
high chair

lettino
let-tee-no
cot

parco giocchi
par-ko jok-kee
play park

panolini
pa-no-lee-nee
nappies

what is there for children to do?
cosa c'è da fare per i bambini?
ko-za che da fa-ray payr ee bam-bee-nee

where can I change the baby?
dove posso cambiare il bambino?
do-vay pos-so kamb-ya-ray eel bam-bee-no

do you have...?	**a high chair**	**a cot**
avete...?	un seggiolone	un lettino
a-vay-tay...	*oon sed-jo-lo-nay*	*oon let-tee-no*

nappies	**baby wipes**	**baby food**
panolini	salviettine	alimenti per bambini
pa-no-lee-nee	*sal-vyet-tee-nay*	*a-lee-men-tee payr bam-bee-nee*

is there a children's menu?	**a half portion**
c'è un menù per bambini?	una meta porzione
che oon me-noo payr bam-bee-nee	*oo-na may-ta ports-yo-nay*

is there a play park near here?
c'è un parco giocchi qui vicino?
che oon par-ko jo-kee kwee vee-chee-no

talking talking talking

You should fill in an E111 form before you leave. They are available from post offices and should be stamped by them. The form entitles you to free medical emergency treatment. If you have to have treatment, take the form to any Italian USL office and obtain a certicate of entitlement. Ask for the list of practitioners you can visit and then take the certificate to one of them, who will charge you a fee which you can claim on your return (you should will have to send your E11 form and original bills, prescriptions and receipts to the address listed in the Health Advice Brochure which you get with the form). For prescribed medicines you will be charged a standard fee which is not refundable.

Pharmacies are open during shopping hours. If you are feeling unwell (and it is not an emergency), your first point of call should be the pharmacy, especially if you have an idea of what is wrong. They are usually helpful and know which products would suit.

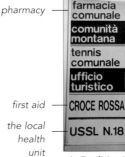

pharmacy

first aid

the local health unit

▲ Facilities in towns are usually well signposted.

Each pharmacy must display the list of duty chemists open at night ◀ or on Sunday.

---

where is there a chemist?
dove c'è una farmacia?
do-vay che oo-na far-ma-chee-a

have you something for...?
avete qualcosa per...?
a-vay-tay kwal-ko-za payr...

indigestion
l'indigestione
leen-dee-jest-yo-nay

sunburn
la scottatura solare
la skot-ta-too-ra so-la-ray

diarrhoea
la diarrea
la dee-a-ray-a

a cough
la tosse
la tos-say

I need...
ho bisogno di...
o bee-zon-yo dee...

a painkiller
un analgesico
oon a-nal-jay-zee-ko

antibiotics
antibiotici
an-tee-bee-o-tee-chee

talking

OSPEDALE di MENAGGIO →

▲ Sign to local hospital

▶
You are entering a hospital zone in 150 m

zona ospedaliera
150 m

I am not well
mi sento male
*mee **sen**-to **ma**-lay*

... doesn't feel well
... si sente male
*... see **sen**-tay **ma**-lay*

I need a doctor
ho bisogno di un dottore
*o bee-**zon**-yo dee oon dot-**to**-ray*

please call the doctor
mi chiami il dottore
*mee kee-**a**-mee eel dot-**to**-ray*

my son/my daughter is ill
mio figlio/mai figlia sta male
*mee-o **feel**-yo/mee-a **feel**-ya sta ma-lay*

I have a pain here
ho un dolore qui
*o oon do-**lor**-ay kwee*

I am on this medication
sto prendendo queste medicine
*sto pren-**den**-do **kwes**-tay may-dee-**chee**-nay*

I'm pregnant
sono incinta
*so-no een-**cheen**-ta*

I am on the pill
prendo la pillola
***pren**-do la **peel**-lo-la*

I'm breastfeeding
sto allattando al seno
*sto al lat-**tan**-do al **say**-no*

I have cystitis
ho la cistite
*o la chees-**tee**-tay*

I'm diabetic
sono diabetico/a
*so-no dee-a-**bet**-ee-ko*

I am allergic to...
sono allergico/a a...
*so-no al-**ler**-jee-ko a...*

I have high blood pressure
ho la pressione alta
*o la pres-**yo**-nay **al**-ta*

my blood group is...
il mio gruppo sanguigno è...
*eel **mee**-yo **groop**-po san-**gween**-yo e...*

can I have a receipt for my insurance
mi dà una ricevuta per l'assicurazione
*mee da **oo**-na ree-chay-**voo**-ta payr las-see-koo-rats-**yo**-nay*

I need a dentist
ho bisogno di un dentista
*o bee-**zon**-yo dee oon den-**tees**-ta*

I have toothache
ho mal di denti
*o mal dee **den**-tee*

I need a temporary filling
ho bisogno di un'otturazione provvisoria
*o bee-**zon**-yo dee oon ot-too-rats-**yo**-nay prov-vee-**sor**-ya*

can your repair my dentures?
può riparare la mia dentiera?
*pwo ree-pa-ra-ray la mee-a dent-**yer**-a*

my filling has come out
è uscita l'otturazione
*e oo-**shee**-ta lot-too-rats-**yo**-nay*

talking talking talking talking talking

*If you need emergency treatment, you should go directly to the **Pronto Soccorso** (A & E) in the nearest hospital. You should present them with your E111 form and your passport.*

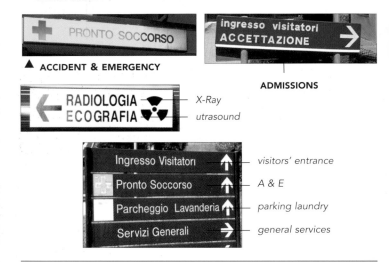

PRONTO SOCCORSO

▲ **ACCIDENT & EMERGENCY**

ingresso visitatori
ACCETTAZIONE →

ADMISSIONS

← RADIOLOGIA
ECOGRAFIA — *X-Ray*
— *utrasound*

Ingresso Visitatori ↑ — *visitors' entrance*

Pronto Soccorso ↑ — *A & E*

Parcheggio Lavanderia ↑ — *parking laundry*

Servizi Generali → — *general services*

If you need to go to hospital

will he/she have to go to hospital?
deve andare all'ospedale?
day-vay an-da-ray al-los-ped-a-lay

where is the hospital?
dov'è l'ospedale
do-ve los-ped-a-lay

where is the nearest A & E department?
dov'è il pronto soccorso più vicino?
do-ve eel pron-to sok-kor-so pyoo vee-chee-no

please take me to the hospital
per favore mi porti all'ospedale
payr fa-vo-ray mee por-tee al-los-ped-a-lay

I need to go to casualty
devo andare al pronto soccorso
day-vo an-da-ray al pron-to sok-kor-so

when are visiting hours?
quando sono le ore di visite?
kwan-do so-no lay o-ray dee vee-zee-tay

which ward?
quale reparto?
kwa-lay ray-par-to

can you explain what is the matter?
può spiegare cos'è il problema?
pwo spyay-ga-ray ko-ze eel prob-lay-ma

EMERGENCY

*If you are robbed or suffer a crime, you should make a report to the police (either **Polizia** or **Carabinieri**, both perform more or less the same function) at the police station, **Questura**. You will need a copy of the report to present to your insurance company if you want to make a claim. All the emergency services can be called on 113 though each has its own number: Police, 112; Medical emergency 118; Fire brigade 115.*

◀ Address of the local police

Police car ▶

help!
aiuto!
a-**yoo**-to

can you help me!
può aiutarmi?
pwo a-yoo-**tar**-mee

please call...
per favore chiamate...
payr fa-**vo**-ray kee-a-**ma**-tay...

the police
la polizia
la po-leet-**see**-a

an ambulance
un'ambulanza
oon am-boo-**lant**-sa

help! Fire!
aiuto! Fuoco!
a-**yoo**-to fwo-ko

please call the fire brigade!
per favore chiamate i vigili del fuoco!
payr fa-**vo**-ray kee-a-**ma**-tay ee **vee**-jee-lee del **fwo**-ko

my ... has been stolen
mi hanno rubato...
mee **an**-no roo-**ba**-to...

I want to report a theft
voglio denunciare un furto
vol-yo den-oon-**cha**-ray oon **foor**-to

here are my insurance details
ecco i dati della mia assicurazione
ek-ko ee **da**-tee **del**-la **mee**-a as-see-koo-rats-**yo**-nay

please give me your insurance details
mi dia i vostri dati di assicurazione
mee **dee**-a ee **vos**-tree **da**-tee dee as-see-koo-rats-**yo**-nay

where is the police station?
dov'è la questura?
do-**ve** la kwes-**too**-ra

I would like to phone...
vorrei telefonare...
vor-**ray** te-le-fo-**na**-ray...

my car has been broken into
hanno svaligiato la mia macchina
an-no sva-lee-**ja**-to la **mee**-a **mak**-kee-na

I need a report for my insurance
ho bisogno di un verbale per la mia assicurazione
o bee-**zon**-yo dee oon ver-**ba**-lay payr la **mee**-a as-see-koo-rats-**yo**-nay

talking talking talking talking talking

FOOD AND DRINK

ITALIAN FOOD

Italians enjoy good food and to do this they make sure that they cook with the best ingredients available.

In the north of Italy traditionally the main meal of the day is lunch, *il pranzo*. In the south of Italy, because of the heat, it is dinner, *la cena*. However with working habits changing and people working further away from their homes, a large lunch is not always possible except at weekends.

La prima colazione (breakfast) is often eaten standing at a bar and is usually an **espresso** (small strong black coffee) or **cappuccino** and **brioche** (sweet bun). Otherwise at home it is generally milky coffee and biscuits. However, cereals are becoming more common.

A traditional full Italian meal consists of **antipasto** (often finely sliced ham, salami, and other cold meats), **primo** (pasta or risotto) and **secondo** (meat or fish) served with a salad or French fries or vegetables. Cheese and a dessert normally follow.

Many bars and *caffès* ▶ serve food: generally salads, sandwiches, pasta dishes and pizzas. Check where the bar is situated: if it is in a very touristy area, it may be expensive. It is worth checking side streets to see if you can find a quieter bar. If Italians are eating there, take that as a recommendation.

MENÙ TURISTICO

▲ Many restaurants offer set price meals (sometimes including wine). Although generally good value, the food is aimed mainly at the tourist market.

A *rosticceria* sells spit-roasted chicken and food to be eaten there (generally standing) or to take away. The food should be good and well-worth sampling. ▶

As well as a tobacconist, a *tabbacaio* is often a bar and may serve meals. There are no frills, but the food will be good. ▼

▲ Italians are more interested in their food than the decor, so most restaurants are quite similar, with crisp linen tablecloths and unfussy surroundings.

Traditionally, a *trattoria* is a family-run restaurant, usually with less choice than a restaurant. There may be no menu and you will be told what is available that day. Again, it is somewhere well worth trying. ▼

Trattoria

Hamburger chains are appearing in Italy, but with a slight Italian flavour in that Italians don't like queuing, so you may find them trying to sneak ahead! ▼

▲ Self-service type restaurant; good for a quick meal.

cucina caslinga ◀ HOME COOKING

where can we get a snack?
dove possiamo trovare uno spuntino?
do-vay pos-ya-mo tro-va-ray oo-no spoon-tee-no

can you recommend a good restaurant?
ci può consigliare un buon ristorante?
chee pwo kon-seel-ya-ray oon bwon rees-to-ran-tay

are there any vegetarian restaurants?
ci sono dei ristoranti vegetariani?
chee so-no day rees-to-ran-tee vay-jay-tar-ya-nee

do we need to book a table?
dobbiamo prenotare un tavolo?
dob-ya-mo pray-no-ta-ray oon ta-vo-lo

what do you recommend?
che cosa ci consiglia?
kay ko-za chee kon-seel-ya

how do we get to the restaurant?
come ci si arriva a questo ristorante?
ko-may chee see ar-ree-va a kwes-to rees-to-ran-tay

talking talking talking

*If you want a snack rather than a full meal, bars generally have things such as **pizza**, **toast** (toasted sandwiches) and **panini** (sandwiches). They may also serve pasta dishes such as **spaghetti**, **lasagne**, etc.*

keywords

formaggio
for-**mad**-jo
cheese

prosciutto
pro-**shoot**-to
ham

pomodoro
po-mo-**do**-ro
tomato

farcito
far-**chee**-to
stuffed with
titbits

liscio
lee-sho
plain

various sandwiches
made with Italian
bread rolls

sandwiches
(generally made
with flatter bread)

toasted sandwiches
with extra filling e.g.
gherkin or tomato

pizza

chips

PANÌNI MÌSTÌ
SANDWÌCHES
TOAST FARCÌTÌ
PÌZZA
PATATÌNE FRÌTTE
VÌNO-WÌNE-BEER
CAFFÈ-CAPPUCCÌO

tramezzini

These are sandwiches made with *ciabatta*
◀ bread.

talking

I'd like … please
vorrei … per favore
vor-**ray** … payr fa-**vo**-ray

a cappuccino
un cappuccino
oon kap-poo-**chee**-no

a large black coffee
un caffè americano
oon kaf-**fe** a-mer-ee-**ka**-no

decaffeinated
decaffeinato
day-kaf-fay-**na**-to

a hot chocolate
una cioccolata calda
oo-na chok-ko-**la**-ta **kal**-da

a tea with milk
un tè al latte
oon te al **lat**-tay

an orange juice
un succo d'arance
oon **sook**-ko da-**ran**-chay

an peach juice
un succo di pesca
oon **sook**-ko dee **pes**-ka

a red wine
un vino rosso
oon **vee**-no **ros**-so

a white wine
un vino bianco
oon **vee**-no bee-**an**-ko

a lager
una birra
oo-na **beer**-ra

a bottle of mineral water
una bottiglia di acqua minerale
oo-na bot-**teel**-ya dee **ak**-wa mee-nay-**ra**-lay

fizzy
gassata
gas-**sa**-ta

still
naturale
na-too-**ra**-lay

Paninoteca

SANDWICH
◀ **SHOP**

THE — tea
CAFFÈ — coffee
CIOCCOLATA — hot chocolate
GELATI — ice creams

▲ A *gelateria* is a bar selling ice cream where you can also get drinks. Italy has a mouth-watering variety of ice creams which can be almost a meal in themselves.

bibite

▲ **SOFT DRINKS**

▲ If you buy a cone, *un cono*, you might be asked if you want one scoop (*una pallina*) or two scoops (*due palline*). If you prefer it in a tub, ask for *una coppa*. The word for flavour is *gusto*.

Ice-creams at ▶
L.3000

ICE-CREAM

chocolate — CIOCCOLATO
vanilla — VANIGLIA
hazelnut — NOCCIOLA
lemon — LIMONE
strawberry — FRAGOLA
banana — BANANA
apricot — ALBICOCCA

can we eat here?
si può mangiare qui?
see pwo man-ja-ray kwee

what can we eat?
cosa si può mangiare?
ko-za see pwo man-ja-ray

is there a dish of the day?
c'è un piatto del giorno?
che oon pee-at-to del jor-no

what is the dish of the day?
qual è il piatto del giorno?
kwal e eel pee-at-to del jor-no

what sandwiches do you have?
quali panini avete?
kwa-lee pa-nee-nee a-vay-tay

I'd like an ice-cream
vorrei un gelato
vor-ray oon jay-la-to

what flavours do you have?
che gusti ci sono?
kay goos-tee chee so-no

talking

Italy is the home of the pizza. They are thin based and cooked in wood-fired ovens. You won't find the wide range of deep-pan options that originated in America. Nor will you find combinations such as ham and pineapple, though new additions are gradually finding their way into the classic pizza repertoire.

PIZZE

tomato, mozzarella, oregano —
Margherita
(pom, mozz, origano)

Siciliana
(pom, acciughe, olive, origano) — tomato, anchovies, olives, oregano

tomato, mozzarella, onion, olives
Pugliese
(pom, mozz, cipolle, olive)

Marinara
(pom, aglio, origano) — tomato, garlic, oregano

tomato, mozzarella, anchovies
Napoletana
(pom, mozz, acciughe)
tomato, mozzarella, anchovies, capers, olives

tomato, mozzarella, ham
Romana
(pom, mozz, acciughe, capperi, olive)

Prosciutto
(pom, mozz, prosciutto)

tomato, mozzarella, mushroom
Prosciutto e Funghi
(pom, mozz, prosciutto, funghi) — tomato, mozzarella, ham, mushroom

Funghi
(pom, mozz, funghi)

with 4 cheeses: mozzarella, fontina, gorgonzola, gruyère
Gorgonzola — blue-veined Gorgonzola cheese

Ai 4 Formaggi

Ai Frutti di Mare — seafood

tomato, mozzarella, in-season vegetables
Quattro Stagioni — 4-section (or season) pizza: with tomato, ham, onion, pepper, artichokes & whatever is available

Capricciosa
(pom, mozz, capricci di verdure)

tomato, mozzarella, spicy salami
Diavola
(pom, mozz, salame piccante)

Al Tonno
(pom, mozz, tonno, cipolla)

tomato, mozzarella, tuna, onion

tomato, mozzarella, grilled vegetables
Vegetariana
(pom, mozz, verdure grigliate)

tomato, wild mushroom
Rustica
(pom, mozz, speck) — tomato, mozzarella & a type of bacon

Funghi Porcini

folded-over pizza with tomato, mozzarella, ham, mushroom & vegetables in olive oil
Calzone liscio
(pom, mozz, prosciutto)
folded-over pizza with tomato, mozzarella, ham

Calzone farcito
(pom, mozz, prosciutto, funghi, farcitura)

one pizza please
una pizza per favore
oo-na peet-sa payr fa-vo-ray

2 pizzas please
due pizze per favore
doo-ay peet-say payr fa-vo-ray

I'd like a pizza
vorrei una pizza
vor-ray oo-na peet-sa

what is there to drink?
cosa c'è da bere?
ko-za che da ber-ay

*When you ask for a **birra** in Italy, you will be served lager. If you want an ale or bitter, you should ask for **birra scura** or **birra rossa**. Draught beer will come either **piccola** (half pint approx.) or **media** (just under a pint). If you want to drink beer, look out for bars which call themselves pubs. They may be quite expensive.*

half a pint of lager
una birra piccola
oo-na beer-ra peek-ko-la

a pint of lager
una birra media
oo-na beer-ra med-ya

draught
alla spina
al-la spee-na

an Italian lager
una birra nazionale
oo-na beer-ra nats-yo-na-lay

do you have any ales?
avete delle birre rosse?
a-vay-tay del-lay beer-ray ros-say

t a l k i n g

Restaurants tend to shut one day a week. As a rule, eating places (including restaurants) have a menu with prices outside, so you will be prepared for the cost before going in.

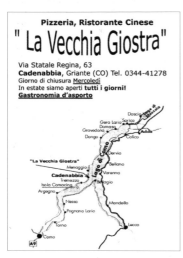

Pizzeria, Ristorante Cinese

" La Vecchia Giostra "

Via Statale Regina, 63
Cadenabbia, Griante (CO) Tel. 0344-41278
Giorno di chiusura <u>Mercoledì</u>
In estate siamo aperti **tutti i giorni!**
<u>Gastronomia d'asporto</u>

◀ Menu of combined pizzeria and Chinese restaurant
Italians are conservative in their eating habits so you will not find a great variety of foreign restaurants as you do in London, for instance. However, Chinese and Indian restaurants are gradually appearing.

A pizza is often a cheaper option than a full meal. ▶

I would like to book a table
vorrei prenotare un tavolo
vor-**ray** pray-no-**ta**-ray oon **ta**-vo-lo

for tonight
per stasera
payr sta-**say**-ra

for lunch
per pranzo
payr **prant**-so

for 7.30
per le sette e mezza
payr lay **set**-tay ay **med**-za

a non-smoking area
un posto non fumatore
oon **pos**-to non foo-mat-**or**-ay

for 4 people
per quattro persone
payr **kwat**-tro per-**so**-nay

for tomorrow night
per domani sera
payr do-**ma**-nee **say**-ra

for 12.30
per le dodici e mezza
payr lay **do**-dee-chee e **med**-za

for 8 o'clock
per le otto
payr lay **ot**-to

in the name of...
a nome di...
a **no**-may dee...

In the countryside there is a type of rustic restaurant known as a *crotto*. These serve the real traditional food of the region, often homegrown and prepared. At harvest time (around the start of September) there are festivals, *sagre*, where you can sample the produce of the harvest.

▼

Crotto del Merlo

The typical Italian dining table will have a basket of bread rolls, *grissini* (breadsticks), salt and pepper, toothpicks, oil and vinegar to dress your salad, a jug or ◀ bottle of wine and mineral water.

OUR OWN CHEESE ▶ formaggio nostrano

the menu please
il menù per favore
*eel me-**noo** payr fa-**vo**-ray*

the wine list please
la lista dei vini per favore
*la **lees**-ta day **vee**-nee payr fa-**vo**-ray*

is there a set-price menu?
c'è un menù turistico?
*che oon me-**noo** too-**rees**-tee-ko*

for a starter I will have...
per antipasto prendo...
*payr an-tee-**pas**-to **pren**-do...*

for a main dish I will have...
per secondo prendo...
*payr se-**kon**-do **pren**-do...*

do you have any vegetarian dishes?
avete dei piatti vegetariani?
*a-**vay**-tay day **pyat**-tee ve-jay-ta-ree-**a**-nee*

what desserts do you have?
cosa c'è per il dolce?
*ko-za che payr eel **dol**-chay*

a glass of water
un bicchiere di acqua semplice
*oon beek-**yer**-ay dee **ak**-wa **semp**-lee-chay*

some more bread
ancora un pò di pane
*an-**ko**-ra oon po dee **pa**-nay*

the bill please
il conto per favore
*eel **kon**-to payr fa-**vo**-ray*

we'd like separate bills
ci fà il conto separato
*chee fa eel kon-to sep-a-**ra**-to*

*Most restaurants charge **pane e coperto** (cover charge). Service is generally 10% and is often automatically charged. If not, tipping of 10% is an acceptable amount.*

Restaurant bill listing ▶
exactly what has
been consumed.

*receipt for fiscal
purposes*

bill/invoice

information about client

firm

*residence or
home address*

VAT

number of people
bread & cover charge
wine
other drinks
starter
first course
main course
vegetables
cheeses
sweet
fruit
coffee
liqueurs

RICEVUTA FISCALE - FATTURA (Legge 30 Dicembre 19991 n. 413)		
taverna antico agnello s.r.l. ristorante via olina n. 18 28016 Orta S. Giulio (no) tel. 0322 90259 partita i.v.a. 01130970039		
☐ RICEVUTA FISCALE ☐ FATTURA - RICEVUTA FISCALE	N. ATTRIBUTO	
DATA 02.03.00	XNR N° 04079 /2000	
Dati identificativi del Cliente		
DITTA		
Residenza o domicilio		
P. IVA		
Per N. 1 pasti		
Pane - Coperto		4000
Vino		4000
Altre bevande		4000
Antipasti		14000
Primi		21000
Secondi		
Contorni		
Formaggi		9000
Dolce		
Frutta		
Caffè		3000
Liquori		

ALIQ. IVA	IMPONIBILE	IMPOSTA	CORRISPETTIVO PAGATO	59000
%			CORRISPETTIVO NON PAGATO	
TOTALE			TOTALE DOCUMENTO	

☐ PAGATO _____ A TITOLO DI: ☐ ANTICIPO ☐ ACCONTO

☐ R.F. EMESSA ALL'ATTO DELLA PRESTAZIONE O CONSEGNA (CORRISPETTIVO GIÀ SALDATO ANTICIPATAMENTE)

☐ SALDO DI R.F. GIÀ EMESSA ☐ RIFERIM. PREC. DOCUM. R.F. _____ DEL _____

Tipolitografia Esperia snc - Novara - Autorizzazione del Ministero delle Finanze VI-12-1095/94 del 31-01-94

▲ You must take your bill with you because the law states that if you are found within 100 m of a bar, restaurant or shop without the receipt, both you and the owner will be fined.

**Menù a prezzo fisso
(solo pranzo)
£ 18.000**

◀ FIXED PRICE MENU
(ONLY LUNCH)
L.18.000

You don't have to have all the courses, you could skip the **antipasto** *and just have the first and second courses. Or you could have* **antipasto** *and the second course.*

MENU *menu*

ANTIPASTI *starters*
antipasto misto *sliced ham, salami and other sliced meats*
prosciutto e melone *Parma ham and melon*

PRIMI *first courses*
pasta *different types of pasta dishes*
  al pomodoro *with a tomato sauce*
  al ragù *with a Bolognese sauce*
  all'arrabbiata *with a tomato and chilli pepper sauce*
  alla carbonara *with a bacon and egg sauce*
  alla puttanesca *with a tomato, chilli pepper and anchovy sauce*
  al pesto *with a basil, pine nut and pecorino sauce*
  in brodo *in broth (generally ravioli or other stuffed pasta)*
risotto *rice cooked in stock*
minestra *vegetable and pasta soup*

SECONDI *main dishes*
carne *meat*
  vitello *veal*
  manzo *beef*
  maiale *pork*
  pollo *chicken*
  agnello *lamb*
pesce *fish*

CONTORNI *vegetables*

FORMAGGI *cheeses*

DOLCI *sweets*

FRUTTA *fruit*

---

enjoy your meal!
buon appetito!
*bwon ap-pay-**tee**-to*

thanks, and you too!
grazie, e altrettanto!
***grats**-yay ay al-tret-**tan**-to*

talk

WINE

> *The classic Italian wine is a red, made for food, light, cherryish, dry, sharp. But things are changing. Not only are better, richer white wines emerging now, but fruitier, deeper-flavoured, more international reds. The best of them still retain that signature Italian twist, a hint of cherrystone and of herb dryness perhaps, rather than conforming to dull New World prototype.*

Italian classification of wine is a rough guide to quality but there are bad and good wines in every grade. ▼

vintage

Vino da Tavola (table wine) is the lowest class; rustic, usually rough-edged, rarely quaffable without food.

Rosso red

Alcoholic content 13% makes for quite a heavy wine.

◀ DOC (*Denominazione di Origine Controllata*) operates like AC in France, with tight controls on wine production. The higher classification of DOCG does not necessarily promise a better wine, despite its adding of **Garantita** (guaranteed). Some DOC quality wines can also appear as IGT (*Indicazione Geograficha Tipica*; see p. 87).

Indicazione Geograficha Tipica is the equivalent of French *vin de pays*; it can be rustic, can be superb.

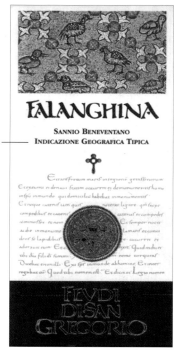

bianco
bee-an-ko
white

rosso
ros-so
red

rosato
ro-za-to
rosé

secco
sek-ko
dry

dolce
dol-chay
sweet

un quarto
oon kwar-to
a quarter litre

un mezzo
oon med-so
half a litre

un litro
oon leet-ro
a litre

the wine list please
la lista dei vini per favore
la lees-ta day vee-nee payr fa-vo-ray

what wines do you have?
quali vini avete?
kwa-lee vee-nee a-vay-tay

is there a local wine?
c'è un vino locale?
che oon vee-no lo-ka-lay

can you recommend a good wine?
ci può consigliare un buon vino?
chee pwo kon-seel-ya-ray oon bwon vee-no

a glass of red wine
un bicchiere di vino rosso
oon beek-yer-ay dee vee-no ros-so

a quarter litre of white wine
un quarto di vino bianco
oon kwar-to dee vee-no bee-an-ko

a bottle of wine
una bottiglia di vino
oo-na bot-teel-ya dee vee-no

red
rosso
ros-so

white
bianco
bee-an-ko

a half litre of wine
un mezzo litro di vino
oon med-zo leet-ro dee vee-no

a litre of wine
un litro di vino
oon leet-ro dee vee-no

FLAVOURS OF ITALY

burrida
famous Genoese fish soup
pesto
*sauce made from basil, olive oil,
pecorino and pine-nuts*
focaccia
*flat bread brushed with garlic, salt
and olive oil*
cappon magro
cold seafood and vegetable salad

baccalà alla milanese
Milanese salt cod fritters, served with lem
cotoletta alla milanese
fried veal cutlet dressed in breadcrumb
risotto alla milanese
rich saffron-coloured risotto
ossobucco
shin of veal cooked in tomato sauce
wines: Sassella, Grumello, Inferno

acqua cotta
*traditional soup made from
onions, peppers, celery and
tomato. Beaten eggs and
parmesan are added on serving.*
bistecca alla fiorentina
large thick grilled T-bone steak
stracotto
braised beef cooked in red wine
trippa
tripe with tomatoes and onions
fagioli all'uccelletto
*haricot beans in tomato, garlic
and sage*
**wines: Chianti, Vernaccia,
Brunello di Montalcino**

abbacchio
suckling pig
coda alla vaccinara
oxtail stewed with tomatoes and herbs
spaghetti all'amatriciana
spaghetti in a tomato and bacon sauce
gnocchi alla romana
*oven-baked dumplings made from
semolina, butter and parmesan*
carciofi alla Giudia
flattened, deep-fried globe artichokes
saltimbocca alla romana
finely sliced veal with ham and sage
wines: frascati, Est! Est! Est!

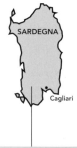

bottarga
*preserved tuna or mullet roes,
served in thin slices as a starter*
cinghiale
wild boar
porceddu
suckling pig

apples
risi e bisati
rice cooked with eel
risotto alle seppie
risotto cooked with squid
fegato alla veneziana
calf's liver slices fried in butter with onions
baccalà alla vicentina
salt cod simmered in milk
polenta
corn or maize meal porridge
wines: Soave, Valpolicella, Bardolino

pasta
*fresh pasta: tagliatelle, pap-
pardelle, ravioli, etc*
bolognese sauce
*finely minced steak and
tomato sauce served with
pasta and in lasagne and
cannelloni*
parmigiano
*parmesan cheese, grated
over pasta dishes*
parma ham
*cured ham which is finely
sliced*
cotechino
*spicy pork sausage often
served with lentils*
**wines: Sangiovese,
Trebbiano**

agnello
*lamb is a main
ingredient*

pizza
Naples is the home of the pizza
parmigiana di melanzane
*layers of finely sliced aubergines
cooked in the oven with olive oil,
tomato and parmesan*
**wines: Greco di Tufo, Taurasi,
Limoncello**
(lemon liqueur served as an aperitif)

**CAMPANIA, BASILICATA &
CALABRIA**
mozzarella di bufala
*mozzarella made from buffalo milk
and stored in a buttermilk bath*

pescespada
grilled mozzarella and herb-stuffed swordfish
triglie alla siciliana
red mullet cooked in white wine and orange peel
caponata
aubergines cooked in a sweet and sour sauce
farsu magru
veal stuffed and rolled up, cooked in wine
cannoli
*fried pastries stuffed with ricotta, candied fruits
and dark chocolate*
wines: Marsala *(dark dessert wine)*

There are times when you cannot eat some things. It is as well to warn the waiter before making your choice.

I'm vegetarian
sono vegetariano/a
so-no ve-jay-ta-ree-ya-no/a

I don't eat meat/pork
non mangio carne/carne di maiale
non man-jo kar-nay/kar-nay dee ma-ya-lay

I don't eat fish/shellfish
non mangio pesce/i frutti di mare
non man-jo pay-shay/ee froot-tee dee ma-ray

I'm allergic to shellfish
sono allergico/a ai frutti di mare
so-no al-ler-jee-ko/a a-ee froot-tee dee ma-ray

I am allergic to peanuts
sono allergico/a alle arachidi
so-no al-ler-jee-ko/a al-lay a-ra-kee-dee

I can't eat raw eggs
non posso mangiare le uova non cotte
non pos-so man-ja-ray lay wo-va non kot-tay

I can't eat liver
non posso mangiare il fegato
non pos-so man-ja-ray eel fay-ga-to

I am on a diet
sono a dieta
so-no a dee-ay-ta

I don't drink alcohol
non bevo l'alcool
non bay-vo lal-kol

what is in this?
cosa c'è dentro?
ko-za che den-tro

is it raw?
è crudo?
e kroo-do

is it made with unpasteurised milk?
è fatto con latte non pastorizzato?
e fat-to kon lat-tay non pas-to-reed-za-to

fritto
freet-to
fried

bollito
bol-lee-to
boiled

alla brace
al-la bra-chay
barbecued

arrosto
ar-ros-to
roast

allo spiedo
al-lo spyay-do
on a spit

ripieno
ree-pyay-no
stuffed

alla griglia
al-la greel-ya
grilled

affumicato
af-foo-mee-ka-to
smoked

al sangue
al sang-way
rare

cotto
kot-to
cooked

crudo
kroo-do
raw

al dente
al den-tay
firm

al forno
al for-no
baked

brasato
bra-za-to
cooked in wine

MENU READER

A

abbacchio suckling or milk-fed
lamb, usually eaten at Easter.
Roasted with garlic and
rosemary
  abbacchio alla cacciatora lamb
cooked in olive oil, garlic and
rosemary

acciughe anchovies: fresh, salted
or in olive oil
  acciughe ripiene fresh
anchovies filled with fillets of
salted anchovies and cream
cheese and fried in oil

aceto vinegar
  aceto balsamico balsamic
vinegar, the best comes from
Modena

acqua brillante tonic water

acqua cotta literally 'cooked
water', a traditional Tuscan soup
made from onions,
peppers, celery and tomato.
Beaten eggs and parmesan are
added just before serving

acqua minerale mineral water;
this can be still (**naturale**), with
gas (**effervescente**), or with
artificial gas (**gassata**)

affettato misto selection of
cold meats: ham, salami,
mortadella, etc

affogato poached
  affogato al caffè vanilla ice
cream with hot espresso coffee
poured over it

affumicato smoked

aglio

albicocche

aglio garlic
  aglio, olio e peperoncino garlic,
olive oil and hot chilli sauce

agnello lamb
  agnello al forno roast lamb
with vegetables
  agnello all'arrabbiata lamb
cooked in a tomato and chilli
sauce
  agnello arrosto roast lamb

agnollotti pasta squares filled
with white meat and cheese,
usually served with bolognese
sauce

agoni small fish from Italian lakes,
usually marinated in vinegar and
herbs

agrodolce sweet and sour sauce
made from sugar, water, vinegar,
wine, pine-nuts and sultanas,
often served with vegetables or
meat such as rabbit or duck

ai ferri grilled

a, al, alla etc means with, or in
the style of: eg **pasta al sugo** is
pasta with tomato sauce, and
pollo alla cacciatora is chicken
hunter-style

albicocche apricots
  albicocche ripiene stuffed
apricots

alici anchovies, often served
dipped in flour and fried

alloro bayleaf

amarene dark morello cherries

amaretti macaroons, biscuits with a strong almond flavour

Amaretto di Saronno almond liqueur

amaro bitter liqueur drunk as a *digestivo* (to aid digestion)

amatriciana, ...all' bacon, tomato and onion sauce

analcolico non-alcoholic, slightly bitter drink served as an aperitif

ananas pineapple

anatra duck
  anatra di Palmina duck cooked in wine
  anatra in porchetta roast duck stuffed with its liver and ham

anguille eel
  anguille alla comácchio stewed eel
  anguille carpionate fried eels
  anguille in umido eel stewed in tomato sauce

anguria watermelon

anguria

anice aniseed liqueur

anisetta powerful aniseed liqueur

annelletti baked squid or cuttle-fish rings

antipasto starters/appetizers
  antipasto misto selection of cold starters such as ham, salami, russian salad and pickles

aperitivo aperitif

Aperol aperitif made with the essence of various plants

aragosta crayfish
  aragosta allo spiedo crayfish cooked kebab-style

arance oranges

aranciata orangeade

arancini di riso rice croquettes filled with minced veal and peas

arrabbiata, ...all' tomato sauce with bacon, tomatoes, onion and hot chillies

arrosto roast meat, usually cooked in casserole with wine and herbs
  arrosto di maiale roast pork
  arrosto di manzo roast beef
  arrosto di vitello roast veal

asparagi asparagus
  asparagi alla parmigiana lightly

asparagi

boiled asparagus baked with parmesan

astice lobster

B

baccalà salt cod, popular in Italy
  baccalà alla fiorentina salt cod cooked in tomato sauce
  baccalà alla vicentina salt cod cooked in milk with anchovies, onion, garlic, parsley and herbs
  baccalà alla livornese salt cod cooked in a tomato sauce
  baccalà alla milanese Milanese salt cod fritters, served with lemon

bagna cauda hot garlic and anchovy dip. Literally it means 'hot bath' because raw vegetables such as pepper, celery and artichokes are dipped into it

banana banana

basilico basil

Bel Paese soft creamy mild cheese

baccalà alla fiorentina

ben cotto well done

besciamella béchamel sauce

bianco, in literally it means white, pasta or rice served with melted butter, garlic, sage and parmesan

bietola beetroot

birra beer; draught beer (*birra alla spina*) is also available

biscotti biscuits

bistecca steak
  bistecca alla fiorentina thickly cut, charcoal-grilled steak
  bistecca alla pizzaiola fried steak in a tomato and herb sauce

bistecchini di cinghiale wild boar steaks in a sweet and sour sauce

bitter non-alcoholic, bitter drink served as an aperitif

bocconcini di vitello little pieces of veal cooked in wine and butter

bollito boiled
  bollito misto different kinds of meat and vegetables cooked together. There are many regional variations

bolognese, ...alla with tomato and minced meat sauce, served with parmesan

bomba doughnut with custard filling

bonet chocolate pudding with caramel

borlotti dried red haricot beans

boscaiola, ...alla with mushroom and ham sauce

bottarga preserved tuna or mullet roes, served in thin slices as a starter (speciality from Sardinia)

brace, ...alla grilled

braciola rib steak/chop
  braciole al ragù chops cooked in tomato sauce

brasato beef stew

bresaola dried cured beef, cut very finely and served with black pepper and olive oil

broccoletti leafy green vegetable similar to turnip tops

broccoli broccoli

brodetto di pesce a substantial fish soup made with different kinds of fish

brodo bouillon or broth often served with meat-stuffed pasta such as ravioli (*in brodo*)

bruschetta thickly-sliced bread rubbed with garlic and olive oil, often served topped with cheese and tomato

bucatini a type of pasta like thick spaghetti with a hole running through it

budino a blancmange-type pudding
  budino di ricotta pudding made from ricotta cheese

bistecca alla fiorentina

buridda famous Genoese fish soup using a variety of fish

burrini a creamy cheese from Basilicata

burro butter
burro, ...al fried in butter, usually wih garlic and sage
burro e salvia butter and sage sauce

busecca rich tripe and cheese soup

C

cacciatora, ...alla meat or game, hunter-style, meaning cooked with tomato, herbs, garlic and wine

cachi persimmons

caciocavallo cow's cheese which is quite strong when mature

caffè coffee – if you ask for *un caffè* you'll be served *un espresso* (small, strong and black)
caffè americano black filter coffee
caffè corretto coffee laced with *grappa* (strong spirit)
caffè doppio a large coffee (twice the normal size)
caffèllatte milky coffee

calamaretti imbottiti baby squid stuffed with breadcrumbs and anchovies

calamari squid
calamari fritti squid rings dipped in batter and fried

calzone folded over pizza with filling. There are lots of local variations

camomilla camomile tea

Campari bitter-tasting aperitif made with herbs and fruit

canederli tirolesi Tyrolean dumplings made with bacon and sausage

cannella cinnamon

cannellini small white beans

cannelloni meat-filled tubes of pasta covered with béchamel sauce and baked until golden

caponata

brown. Vegetarian options are usually filled with spinach and ricotta

cannoli fried pastries stuffed with ricotta, candied fruit and bitter chocolate from Sicily

cantucci nutty biscuits

capocello smoked salami preserved in olive oil

caponata Sicilian dish of aubergines cooked in a sweet and sour sauce

cappelletti literally 'little hats' filled with ricotta cheese, can be served with bolognese meat sauce

capperi capers

cappon magro an elaborate cold seafood and cooked vegetable salad

cappuccino frothy white coffee

caprese tomato and mozzarella salad with basil

capretto baby goat (kid)
capretto arrosto kid roasted in the oven with vegetables and wine

caprino soft goat's cheese, usually eaten with a sprinkling of olive oil and freshly ground black pepper

caramelle sweets

carbonade beef cooked in wine; the classic accompaniment is polenta

carbonara, ...alla smoked bacon, egg, cream and parmesan

carciofi globe artichokes

carciofi alla Giudia young globe artichokes, flattened and deep-fried

carciofi alla romana globe artichokes stuffed with breadcrumbs, parsley and anchovies

carciofi ripieni artichokes stuffed with mozarella, parmesan and anchovies

carciofina artichoke hearts

cardi cardoons (vegetable similar to fennel)

carciofina

carne meat

carote carrots

carpaccio raw sliced lean beef eaten with lemon juice, olive oil and thickly grated parmesan cheese

carpione carp

carpione, in pickled in vinegar, wine and lemon juice. Fish is often served this way and fried

casalinga, ...alla home-made

cassata layers of ice cream with candied fruits

carpaccio

cassata siciliana sponge dessert with ricotta and candied fruits

cassoeula substantial pork and vegetable casserole

castagnaccio chestnut cake

castagne chestnuts

cavolatte rich custard pudding

cavolfiore cauliflower

cavolo cabbage

ceci chickpeas

céfalo grey mullet

cena dinner

Centerbe herbal liqueur

cervelle calves' brains usually fried

cetriolo cucumber

China bitter liqueur

chinotto fizzy soft drink with taste of bitter orange

cialzons alla carnia pasta squares filled with spinach, chocolate and cinnamon

ciambella ring-shaped fruit cake

ciambellini ring-shaped aniseed biscuits

cicoria chicory

ciliege cherries

cinghiale wild boar

Cinzano popular aperitif

ciliege

cioccolata calda rich hot chocolate, often served with cream

cioccolatini chocolates

cioccolato chocolate

ciociara, ...alla with mushroom, cream and ham sauce

cipolle onions
  cipolle ripiene stuffed onions
coccio a yeast cake with dried fruit
cocco coconut
cocomero watermelon
coda di bue oxtail
  coda alla vaccinara famous Roman dish, consisting of oxtail stewed with tomatoes and herbs
conchiglie shell-shaped pasta
confetti sugared almonds
congelato frozen
coniglio rabbit
  coniglio all'ischitana rabbit stewed in wine
  coniglio in umido rabbit stew
contorni vegetable side dishes
cornetto a croissant filled with jam, custard or chocolate
cosciotto d'agnello
  all'abruzzese braised lamb with garlic, rosemary, tomatoes and wine
cotechino spicy pork sausage usually cooked with lentils
cotoletta cutlet/chop

cotechino

cotoletta al prosciutto veal cutlet with a slice of Parma ham
cotoletta alla bolognese veal cutlet topped with ham and cheese
cotoletta alla milanese veal cutlet dipped in egg and breadcrumbs then fried. Served with lemon wedges
cotoletta alla valdostana breaded veal chop stuffed with cheese
cotoletta di vitello veal cutlet
cotolette di abbacchio lamb chops
cotolette di agnello alla brace marinated, grilled lamb chops
cotto cooked
cozze mussels
  cozze arraganate grilled mussels
crema di... cream soup or sauce/custard
crêpe pancake
crespolina stuffed pancake
crocchette di patate potato croquettes
crodino slightly bitter, non-alcoholic aperitif
crostata tart which is usually filled with fruit and glazed
  crostata di frutta fruit tart
crostini di fegatini chicken liver pâté on toast
crudo raw
Cynar bitter aperitif (made from artichokes)

D

dente, ...al pasta cooked so that it is still quite firm to the bite
déntice sea bream
digestivo slightly bitter, herb-flavoured liqueur to help digestion
dolce dessert
dolcelatte soft, creamy blue cheese
dragoncello tarragon

E

entrecote steak

F

fagiano pheasant
  fagiano con funghi pheasant with porcini mushrooms
  fagiano in salmì pheasant stewed in wine
fagioli type of bean
  fagioli al tonno haricot beans with tuna fish in olive oil
  fagioli con cotiche bean stew with pork
  fagioli nel fiasco haricot beans cooked in a flask
fagiolini runner beans
faraona guinea fowl
farcito stuffed
farfalle butterfly-shaped pasta
farsu magru veal stuffed and rolled up, cooked in wine (Sicilian speciality)
fave broad beans
  fave al guanciale broad beans cooked with bacon and onion
fegatini di pollo chicken livers
fegato liver (mainly calves')
  fegato alla veneziana calves' liver fried in butter and onion
ferri, ...ai grilled without oil
fettuccine fresh ribbon pasta
ficatu all'agru e duci calves' liver in sweet and sour sauce
fichi figs
  fichi d'India prickly pears
filetto fillet steak
  filetto di tacchino alla bolognese turkey breast served with a slice of ham and cheese

fichi

Filu Ferru very strong liqueur from Sardinia
finanziera, ...alla with chicken livers, mushrooms and wine sauce
finocchio fennel
fiori di zucchini courgette flowers fried in batter
focaccia flat bread brushed with garlic, salt and olive oil, sprinkled with herbs or onions. There are many variations
fonduta al parmigiano cheese fondue made with Fontina cheese, eggs, butter and truf-

focaccia

fles. Eaten with crusty bread
fontina mild to strong cow's milk cheese from northern Italy
formaggio cheese
forno, ...al cooked in the oven
fragole strawberries
frittata omelette, usually with different ingredients

fritto misto di mare

fritto fried
  fritto misto platter of deep-fried food including different kinds of meat and vegetables
  fritto misto di mare fried/grilled selection of seafood
frullato di fruta milk shake made with fruits
frutta fruit
frutti di mare shellfish/seafood
funghi mushrooms – very popular and varied in Italy. In autumn many Italians take to the woods in search of the prized porcini
  funghi trifolati sliced mushrooms fried with garlic and parsley
Fuoco dell'Etna very strong liqueur from Sicily
fusilli spiral-shaped pasta

G

gamberi prawns
gamberoni giant prawns
gazzosa fizzy bottled lemonade
gelato ice cream
  gelato misto a selection of different flavoured ice creams
gioddu yoghurt
girasole sunflower

gnocchi small dumplings made from potato and flour, can be made with spinach. Boiled and served with tomato sauce or ragù
  gnocchi alla romana dumplings made from semolina, butter and parmesan, baked in the oven
  gnocchi verdi spinach and cheeese dumplings, usually cooked in melted butter, garlic and sage
Gorgonzola a strong blue cheese made from cows' milk
granchio crab
grana hard cows' milk cheese; generic name given to Parmesan cheese
granita flavoured crushed ice drink
  granita di caffè coffee drink with crushed ice and cream
  granita di limone lemon drink with crushed ice
granseola large crab
grappa strong spirit from grape pressings, often added to coffee
grattugiato grated
griglia, ...alla grilled
grigliata di cervo grilled venison steaks
grigliata mista mixed grill consisting of various barbecued meats
grissini breadsticks provided along with bread on the table
guanciale streaky bacon made from pig's cheek
gulasch spicy beef stew

I

impepata di cozze peppery mussels
insalata salad
  insalata caprese tomato, basil and mozarella salad
  insalata di mare mixed seafood salad
  insalata di pomodori tomato salad
  insalata di riso rice salad

insalata mista mixed salad
insalata russa cold diced cooked vegetables served with mayonnaise
insalata verde green salad
involtini rolls of veal or pork stuffed with chicken liver, pork sausage and parmesan
italiana, ...alla platters with mixed cured meats/cheeses, olives and savouries like anchovies and pickles

L

lamponi raspberries
lasagne layers of pasta with bolognese and béchamel sauces, baked until golden

limone

lombata di maiale pork chop
lonza type of salami
luccio pike
lumache snails

M

maccheroni macaroni
maccheroni ai quattro formaggi pasta with four cheeses
maccheroni alla chitarra square-shaped pasta often served with lamb in chilli and tomato sauce
macedonia (con panna) fresh fruit salad (with cream)
macinata mince
magro, di a meatless dish (often a fish alternative)
maiale pork
maionese mayonnaise
mandorle almonds
manzo beef
marmellata jam
Marsala dark dessert wine from Sicily
Martini famous Italian aperitif
mascarpone rich cream cheese used in desserts such as tiramisù
mela apple
melanzane aubergines – found in a great variety of regional dishes
melanzane alla Parmigiana layers of aubergine baked with tomato or meat sauce, parma ham and grated parmesan cheese

lamponi

lasagne verdi layers of green (spinach) pasta filled with bolognese and béchamel sauces. May be made with ricotta filling
latte milk
lattuga lettuce
lemonsoda fizzy drink with taste of real lemons
lenticchie lentils usually cooked with pork sausage
lepre hare
lepre in salmì hare stewed in wine
latte milk
lesso boiled
limonata bottled lemon drink
limone lemon
limoncello lemon liqueur
lingua tongue
linguine thin strips of pasta

melanzane

melanzane ripiene stuffed aubergines

melograno pomegranate

melone melon

menta mint

merengata meringue and ice cream dessert

merluzzo cod

miele honey

milanese, ...alla normally applied to veal cutlets which are dipped in egg and breadcrumbs before frying

minestra soup
  minestra calanchina vegetable and rice soup served with cheese

minestrone thick vegetable, bean and pasta soup with many regional variations
  minestrone al pesto minestrone flavoured with pesto

melograno

sauce

missultitt grilled dried fish from Lake Como, often eaten with *polenta*

misto di funghi mushroom stew

more blackberries

mortadella type of salami

mostarda fruit pickled in syrup and mustard sauce. Served with *bollito* (boiled meats)

mozzarella cheese traditionally made from buffalo milk but increasingly made from cow's milk. Usually preserved in liquid and used on pizza
  mozzarella in carozza mozarella sandwiched between slices of bread dipped in egg and bread-crumbs and then fried

mugnaia, ...alla usually applies to fish dusted in flour then fried in butter

N

nocciole hazelnuts

nocciole d'agnello noisette of lamb

nocepesca nectarine

noci walnuts

norma, ...alla a sauce from Sicily, with tomatoes and aubergines

O

olio oil
  olio d'oliva olive oil

olive olives

orecchiette ear-shaped pasta
  orecchiette ai broccoli pasta with broccoli

origano cool, milky drink made from barley

orzata milk

ossobucco marrow-bone veal steak cooked in tomato and wine sauce

ostriche oysters

P

paglia e fieno literally 'straw and grass', a combination of green and plain ribbon pasta cooked

ossobucco

with mushrooms, sausage and cream

pan pepato sweet loaf with mixed nuts

pancetta streaky bacon

pandoro a large yeast cake rich in butter and eggs, traditionally eaten at Christmas

pane bread
  pane e coperto cover charge
  pane integrale wholemeal bread

panettone a large cork-shaped yeast cake with dried fruit, rich in eggs and butter. Traditionally eaten at Christmas

panforte a hard, dried-fruit and nut cake

panino bread roll or sandwich

panna cream

pansôti (di Rapallo) literally 'pot-bellied', pasta squares filled with spinach and egg and served in a walnut and parmesan sauce

panzerotti ravioli stuffed with mozzarella, salami and ham, usually fried

paparelle e fegatini chicken livers with pasta

pappardelle wide ribbon-shaped pasta
  pappardelle al sugo di lepre wide ribbon pasta with hare, wine and tomato sauce

parmigiana, ...alla with parmesan cheese

parmigiana di melanzane layers of aubergine cooked in the oven with tomato sauce and parmesan cheese

parmigiano parmesan cheese. A hard cow's milk cheese used extensively in Italian cooking. It is always best to use freshly grated parmesan

pasta the dry variety takes between 10 and 15 minutes to cook. The fresh variety just 3 or 4 minutes
  pasta al forno pasta baked with minced meat, eggs, tomato and cheese
  pasta all'uovo fresh pasta made from flour and eggs
  pasta asciutta pasta served with a sauce such as *spaghetti al sugo* and not in a soup form such as *ravioli in brodo* (ravioli in bouillon)
  pasta con le sarde a baked dish of layers of pasta and fried sardines
  pasta e fagioli pasta with beans
  pasta fresca fresh pasta

pasticcio pie

pastina in brodo pasta pieces in clear broth

panettone

patate potatoes
  patate fritte chips
patatine crisps
  patatine fritte chips
pecorino hard tangy cheese
  made from ewe's milk, used in
  pesto
penne quill-shaped pasta
  penne rigate ribbed quill-
  shaped pasta
pepe pepper
peperonata sweet peppers
  cooked with tomatoes and olive
  oil
peperoncino hot chilli pepper
peperoni peppers
  peperoni ripieni stuffed
  peppers (the filling depends on
  the region)
pere pears
pesca peach
pesce fish
  pesce arrosto baked fish
  pesce persico perch

patate

pesce spada swordfish, often
  grilled or served in a tomato
  sauce
pesce spada alla siciliana
  swordfish cooked with orange
  and lemon juice
pesto sauce traditionally made
  from fresh young basil leaves
  pounded with garlic, pine-nuts,
  olive oil and pecorino cheese
petto di pollo chicken breast
pezzenta variety of salad
piatto dish
  piatto del giorno dish of the
  day
  piatti tipici regional dishes
piccatine al limone tender thinly
  sliced veal in butter and lemon
pietanze main courses
pinoli pine nuts
piselli peas
pistacchio pistachio
pizza originally from Naples and
  cooked in wood-burning ovens.
  The most basic is *pizza
  margherita* with tomato, basil
  and mozarella
  pizza ai funghi mushroom pizza
  pizza alla Siciliana pizza with
  tomato, anchovy, black olives
  and capers
  pizza capricciosa pizza with baby
  artichoke, ham and egg
  pizza cardinale pizza with ham
  and olives
  pizza frutti di mare pizza with
  seafood

pizza margherita named after the first queen of a united Italy and symbolising the colours of the Italian flag: red (tomatoes), green (basil) and white (mozarella)

pizza marinara tomato and garlic pizza

pizza Napoli/Napoletana pizza with tomato, cheese, anchovy, olive oil and oregano

pizza quattro formaggi a pizza divided into four sections, each with a different type of cheese topping

pizza quattro stagioni literally means four seasons: the pizza is divided into four sections with a selection of toppings on each section

pizzaiola, ...alla cooked with tomatoes, garlic and herbs

pizzetta small cheese and tomato pizza

pizzoccheri pasta noodles made from buckwheat flour and cooked in the oven with cabbage, potatoes and melted cheese

polenta coarse corn or maize meal porridge which solidifies and can be cut into slices. Considered rather bland by those who have not grown up with it, it is a perfect accompaniment to stews. Can be dipped in egg, breadcrumbs, grated parmesan and then fried

polenta e osei polenta with song birds. Not for the squeamish

polenta uncia polenta cooked with butter, garlic and Fontina cheese

pollame poultry/fowl

pollo chicken

pollo alla diavola chicken grilled with herbs and chilli pepper

pollo alla marengo chicken cooked in wine, served with eggs and prawns

pollo alla romana chicken with tomatoes and peppers

pollo arrosto roast chicken

polpette meatballs made from minced lean beef with grated parmesan and parsley

polpo octopus, served in salad (cold) or tomato sauce

polpo affogato octopus cooked in tomato sauce

pomodoro tomato

pomodoro, ...al classic tomato sauce (same as *sugo*)

pomodori da sugo plum tomatoes

polenta e peperoni

pomodori

pomodori ripieni stuffed tomatoes

pompelmo grapefruit

porceddu suckling pig

porchetta roast suckling pig

porcini prized cep mushrooms which are often dried

porri leeks
pranzo lunch
prezzemolo parsley
prima colazione breakfast
primo first course
prosciutto ham
  prosciutto cotto boiled ham
  prosciutto crudo cured Parma ham which is sliced off the bone
  prosciutto di cinghiale cured ham made from wild boar
  prosciutto e melone Parma ham and melon slices
Prosecco sparkling dry white wine
provolone creamy cow's milk cheese, mild to strong
prugne plums
puttanesca, ...alla tomato, garlic, hot chilli, anchovies and capers

Q

quaglie quails

R

radicchio red-leaf lettuce
ragù, ...al minced meat, tomato and garlic (same as *bolognese*)
rana pescatrice monkfish
rane frogs' legs
ravioli pasta cushions filled with meat or cheese and spinach
ribes blackcurrants
riccio di mare sea urchin
ricotta soft white cheese used as filling for pasta as well as in desserts
rigatoni ribbed tubes of pasta
ripieno stuffed
risi e bisati rice cooked with eel, a traditional Venetian dish
risi e bisi thick rice and pea soup (almost liquid risotto) cooked with bacon
riso rice
  riso alla pilota rice cooked with sausage, nutmeg and cinnamon
risotto rice cooked in broth with different ingredients added

risotto alla milanese

risotto ai funghi risotto with porcini mushrooms
risotto al nero di seppie risotto made with cuttlefish and its ink
risotto alla milanese rich yellow risotto flavoured with saffron, parmesan and butter. It is cooked in meat broth
risotto alla pescatora seafood rice
risotto alle seppie Venetian speciality, risotto cooked with squid. Its ink turns the rice black
risotto con le quaglie quails with risotto
robiola creamy cheese with a mild taste
rognone kidney

rosmarino

rosmarino rosemary
rospo monkfish

S

salame salami (there are many types)
sale salt
salmone salmon
salsa sauce
  salsa verde sauce made of olive oil, breadcrumbs, anchovies, hard boiled egg and parsley, usually served with boiled meat or fish
salsicce sausages: there are many regional variations but they are mainly thick pork sausages which can be boiled or grilled
saltimbocca alla romana veal cooked in white wine with parma ham
salvia sage
Sambuca aniseed liqueur, served with coffee beans and set alight
sampiero John Dory (type of fish)
sangue, ...al rare
sarde sardines
  sarde e beccafico sardines stuffed with breadcrumbs, anchovies, sultanas and pine-nuts
  sarde in saour sardines marinated in vinegar, sultanas and pine nuts
sartù di riso rice and meat timbale (rather like a pie)
scaloppine veal escalopes
  scaloppine al limone veal escalopes cooked in lemon juice
  scaloppine al marsala veal escalopes cooked in marsala
  scaloppine alla milanese veal escalopes dipped in egg, breadcrumbs and fried in butter, served with wedges of lemon
scamorza a cheese similar to mozzarella but smoked
scampi scampi
secondo main dish, usually meat or fish

scaloppine al marsala

sedano celery
selz soda water
semifreddo chilled dessert made with ice cream
senape mustard
seppie coi piselli squid cooked with peas
servizio compreso service included
sfogliatelle frolle puff pastry cakes filled with ricotta cheese
sgavecio fried fish served cold with vinegar and seasonings
sgombro mackerel
soffritto pig's offal with tomatoes and spices

scaloppine alla milanese

sogliola sole

sopa cauda soup made from bread and pigeon meat

soppressata type of salami, with pistachio

sott'oglio in olive oil

spaghetti spaghetti

  spaghetti aglio, olio e peperoncino spaghetti with garlic, chilli pepper and olive oil sauce

  spaghetti all'amatriciana spaghetti with bacon, onion and tomato sauce

  spaghetti alle vongole spaghetti with clams

  spaghettini aromatici very fine spaghetti cooked in a sauce of anchovies, garlic, black olives and capers

speck bacon

spaghetti alle vongole

spezzatino stew, usually with tomato sauce

spiedini meat kebabs

spiedo, ...allo spit-roasted, or on skewer, kebab-style

spinaci spinach

  spinaci alla piemontese spinach cooked with anchovies and garlic

spremuta freshly squeezed fruit juice

  spremuta di pompelmo fresh grapefruit juice

spumante sparkling wine

stoccafisso stoccafisso (*bacalà*, as opposed to *baccalà*) is dried, not salted cod and needs still more soaking before cooking

stracciatella consommé with egg stirred in and grated parmesan

stracotto braised beef which is cooked with vegetables for over three hours so that the meat becomes very tender. Often served with polenta

Strega strong herb-flavoured liqueur

succo di fruta bottled fruit juice

sugo sauce, often refers to the basic tomato, basil and garlic sauce (same as *al pomodoro*)

surgelato frozen

T

tacchino turkey

tagliatelle ribbon-like pasta often served in cream sauce

Taleggio soft, creamy cheese similar to Camembert

tartine canapés

tartufo truffles: both white (*bianco*) and black (*nero*) used extensively in risotto and game dishes

  tartufo di cioccolato a rich chocolate ice cream shaped like a truffle

tè tea. It is not very popular in Italy and normally served with lemon (*al limone*). If you want it with milk you must ask for **tè al latte**

teglia earthenware casserole dish

tiella di sardine baked sardines with cheese

timballo a baked dish
timballo di melanzane baked dish of aubergines, egg, cheese and parma ham

timo thyme

tinche tench

tiramisù dessert made with mascarpone, sponge, coffee and marsala

tónica tonic water

tonno tuna fish
tonno, ...al with a sauce made of tuna fish and tomatoes
tonno e fagioli tuna and bean salad

torrone nougat, traditionally eaten at Christmas

torta cake/flan/tart

tortellini meat-filled pasta cushions reputedly modelled on Venus's navel
tortellini panna e prosciutto tortellini cooked with cream and ham

tortine al tartufo little savoury tarts with truffles

tramezzini ready-made sliced white bread with mixed fillings

trenette long thin strips of pasta, traditionally served with pesto sauce

triglie red mullet
triglie alla livornese red mullet fried with chillies in tomato sauce
triglie alla siciliana a Sicilian dish of red mullet cooked in white wine and orange peel

trippa tripe, often cooked with tomatoes and onions

trota trout
trote alla panna acida trout in soured cream

U

ucelli scappati pork kebabs

umido, in stewed

uova eggs

uva

uova alla fiorentina poached eggs on spinach tarts

uva grapes

uva passa raisins

V

vaniglia vanilla

Vecchia Romagna Italian cognac

verdure vegetables

vermicelli very thin pasta

Vermut very popular aperitif made from herbs and wine

verza Savoy (green) cabbage

vino wine
vin bianco white wine
vin dulce sweet wine
vin rosato rosé wine
vin rosso red wine
vin secco dry wine

vitello veal

vongole clams
vongole, ...alle clam, parsley, garlic and olive oil

W

wurstel Frankfurter sausages

Y

yogurt yoghurt

Z

zabaglione frothy dessert made with egg yolks and sugar beaten with marsala over heat

zafferano saffron, used in *risotto alla milanese*

zampone spicy sausage in the shape of a pig's trotter, sliced and served hot

zucca marrow

zucchero sugar

zucchini courgettes

zuccotto rich cream and nut pudding in the shape of a pumpkin

zuppa soup

  zuppa di cozze mussel and tomato soup

zuppa di fagioli bean soup

zuppa di pesce seafood soup with many delicious regional variations

zuppa inglese dessert similar to trifle

zuppa pavese a bread soup with broth and poached eggs, topped with grated cheese

zucchini

DICTIONARY

english–italian

italian–english

A

a(n) un/una/uno
abbey l'abbazia *(f)*
able: to be able (to) essere capace (di)
abortion l'aborto *(m)*
about su ; circa
  a book about... un libro su...
  about ten o'clock circa le dieci
above sopra
abroad l'estero *(m)*
  to go abroad andare all'estero
abscess l'ascesso *(m)*
accelerator l'acceleratore *(m)*
accent l'accento *(m)*
to accept accettare
access l'accesso *(m)*
  wheelchair access l'accesso per disabili
accident l'incidente *(m)*
accident & emergency department il pronto soccorso
accommodation l'alloggio *(m)*
to accompany accompagnare
account *(bill)* il conto
  (in bank) il conto in banca
account number il numero del conto
to ache fare male
  it aches fa male
acid l'acido *(m)*
actor *(m/f)* l'attore/l'attrice
adaptor *(electrical appliance)* il riduttore
address l'indirizzo *(m)*
  what is the address? qual è l'indirizzo?
address book la rubrica
admission charge/fee il biglietto d'ingresso
to admit *(to hospital)* ricoverare
adult l'adulto(a)
  for adults per adulti
advance: in advance in anticipo
advertisement la pubblicità
  (in newspaper) l'annuncio *(m)*
to advise consigliare
A&E il pronto soccorso
aeroplane l'aeroplano *(m)*
aerosol l'aerosol *(m)*
afraid: to be afraid avere paura
after dopo
afternoon il pomeriggio
  this afternoon oggi pomeriggio
  tomorrow afternoon domani

pomeriggio
  in the afternoon di pomeriggio
aftershave il dopobarba
again ancora ; di nuovo
against contro
age l'età *(f)*
agency l'agenzia *(f)*
ago fa
  a week ago una settimana fa
to agree essere d'accordo
agreement l'accordo *(m)*
AIDS l'AIDS *(m)*
airbag l'airbag *(m)*
airbed il matarassino gonfiabile
air-conditioning l'aria condizionata *(f)*
air freshener il deodorante per l'ambiente
airline la linea aerea
air mail: by air mail per via aerea
airplane l'aeroplano *(m)*
airport l'aeroporto *(m)*
airport bus l'autobus per l'aeroporto *(m)*
air ticket il biglietto d'aereo *(m)*
aisle il corridoio
alarm l'allarme *(m)*
alarm clock la sveglia
alcohol l'alcool *(m)*
alcohol-free analcolico(a)
alcoholic alcolico(a)
all tutto(a)
allergic to allergico(a) a
  I'm allergic to... sono allergico(a) a...
allergy l'allergia *(f)*
to allow permettere
all right *(agreed)* va bene
  are you all right? sta bene?
almost quasi
alone solo(a)
Alps le Alpi
already già
also anche
altar l'altare *(m)*
aluminium foil la carta stagnola
always sempre
a.m. del mattino
am: I am sono
amber *(light)* il giallo
ambulance l'ambulanza *(f)*
America l'America *(f)*
American americano(a)
anaesthetic l'anestetico *(m)*
  local anaesthetic l'anestetico locale
  general anaesthetic l'anestetico generale

1

anchor l'ancora (f)
ancient antico(a)
and e
angina l'angina pectoris (f)
angry arrabbiato(a)
animal l'animale (m)
ankle la caviglia
anniversary l'anniversario (m)
to announce annunciare
announcement l'annuncio (m)
annual annuale
another un altro/un'altra
  another beer un'altra birra
  another coffee un altro caffè
answer la risposta
to answer rispondere
answerphone la segreteria telefonica
antacid l'antiacido (m)
antibiotic l'antibiotico (m)
antifreeze l'antigelo (m)
antihistamine l'antistaminico (m)
antiques i pezzi d'antiquariato
antique shop il negozio d'antiquariato
antiseptic l'antisettico (m)
any dei/delle/degli (di)
  I haven't any money non ho soldi
  have you any apples? ha delle mele?
anyone qualcuno
anything qualcosa
anywhere da qualche parte
apartment l'appartamento (m)
appendicitis l'appendicite (f)
apple la mela
application form il modulo di domanda
appointment l'appuntamento (m)
  I have an appointment ho un
  appuntamento
approximately circa
April aprile
architect m/f l'architetto
architecture l'architettura (f)
are sono
arm il braccio
armbands (swimming) i braccioli
armchair la poltrona
to arrange sistemare
to arrest arrestare
arrivals (plane, train) gli arrivi
to arrive arrivare
art l'arte (f)
art gallery la galleria d'arte ; la
  pinacoteca
arthritis l'artrite (f)
artificial finto(a)

artist m/f l'artista
ashtray il portacenere
to ask (question) domandare
  (for something) chiedere
asleep: he/she is asleep dorme
aspirin l'aspirina (f)
asthma l'asma (f)
  I have asthma ho l'asma
at a
  at home a casa
  at 8 o'clock alle otto
  at once subito
  at night di notte
to attack aggredire
attractive attraente
auction l'asta (f)
audience il pubblico
August agosto
aunt la zia
au pair la ragazza alla pari
Australia l'Australia (f)
Australian australiano(a)
author m/f l'autore/l'autrice
automatic automatico(a)
automatic car la macchina con cambio
  automatico
auto-teller (cashpoint) il Bancomat®
autumn l'autunno (m)
available disponibile
avalanche la valanga
avenue il viale
average medio(a)
to avoid evitare
awake: to be awake essere sveglio(a)
away via
awful terribile
axle (car) l'asse (m)

B

baby il/la bambino(a)
baby food gli alimenti per bambini
baby milk il latte per bambini
baby wipes le salviettine per bambini
baby's bottle il biberon
babyseat (in car) il seggiolino per
  bambini
babysitter il/la babysitter
back (of body) la schiena
backpack lo zaino
bacon la pancetta

bad *(food)* andato(a) a male
  (weather, news) brutto(a)
badminton il badminton
bag la borsa
baggage i bagagli
baggage allowance il peso consentito di bagaglio
baggage reclaim il ritiro bagagli
bait *(for fishing)* l'esca *(m)*
baked al forno
baker's la panetteria ; il panificio
balcony il balcone
bald *(person)* calvo(a)
  (tyre) liscio(a)
ball *(large: football, etc)* il pallone
  (small: golf, tennis, etc) la pallina
ballet il balletto
balloon il palloncino
banana la banana
band *(musical)* la banda
bandage la benda
bank la banca
  (river) la riva
bank account il conto in banca
banknote la banconota
bankrupt fallito(a)
bar il bar
bar of chocolate la tavoletta di cioccolato
barbecue il barbecue
  to have a barbecue fare il barbecue
barber il barbiere
to bark abbaiare
barn il granaio
barrel *(wine/beer)* il barile
basement il seminterrato
basil il basilico
basket il cestino
basketball il basket
bat *(baseball, etc)* la mazza
bath il bagno
  to have a bath fare un bagno
bathing cap la cuffia
bathroom il bagno
  with bathroom con bagno
battery *(radio, camera, etc)* la pila
  (car) la batteria
bay *(along coast)* la baia
B&B la pensione familiare
to be essere
beach la spiaggia
  private beach la spiaggia privata

sandy beach la spiaggia con sabbia
nudist beach la spiaggia di nudisti
beach hut la cabina
bean il fagiolo
beard la barba
beautiful bello(a)
beauty salon l'istituto di bellezza *(m)*
because perché
to become diventare
bed il letto
  double bed il letto matrimoniale
  single bed il letto a una piazza
  sofa bed il divano letto
  twin beds i letti gemelli
bed and breakfast la pensione familiare
bed clothes le coperte e lenzuola
bedroom la camera da letto
bee l'ape *(f)*
beef il manzo
beer la birra
  draught beer la birra alla spina
before prima di
  before breakfast prima di colazione
to begin cominciare
behind dietro di
beige beige
to believe credere
bell *(church)* la campana
  (doorbell) il campanello
to belong to appartenere a
  it belongs to... appartiene a...
below sotto
belt la cintura
bend *(in road)* la curva
berth *(train, ship)* la cuccetta
beside *(next to)* accanto a
  beside the bank accanto alla banca
best: the best il/la migliore
bet la scommessa
to bet scommettere
better (than) meglio (di)
between fra
to beware of stare attento(a) a
beyond oltre
bib *(baby's)* il bavaglino
bicycle la bicicletta ; la bici
  by bicycle in bicicletta
bicycle repair kit il kit per riparare la bici
bidet il bidet
big grande
  bigger (than) più grande (di)
bike *(pushbike)* la bici
  (motorbike) la moto

3 **bike lock** il lucchetto della bici
bikini il bikini
bill *(in hotel, restaurant)* il conto
(for work done) la fattura
(gas, telephone) la bolletta
bin *(dustbin)* il bidone
bin liner la borsa della spazzatura
binoculars il binocolo
bird l'uccello *(m)*
biro la biro
birth la nascita
birth certificate il certificato di nascita
birthday il compleanno
happy birthday! auguri! buon compleanno
my birthday is on... il mio compleanno è il...
birthday card il biglietto d'auguri di compleanno
birthday present il regalo di compleanno
biscuits i biscotti
bit il pezzo
a bit un po'
bite *(of insect)* la puntura
(of dog) la morsicatura
a bite to eat qualcosa da mangiare
to bite *(animal)* mordere
(insect) morsicare
bitten morso(a)
(by insect) morsicato(a)
bitter *(taste)* amaro(a)
black nero(a)
black ice il ghiaccio sulla strada
blanket la coperta
bleach la candeggina
to bleed sanguinare
blender il frullatore
blind *(person)* cieco(a)
blind *(for window)* l'avvolgibile *(f)*
blister la vescica
block of flats il palazzo
blocked *(pipe, sink)* ingorgato(a)
(road) bloccato(a)
blond *(person)* biondo(a)
blood il sangue
blood group il gruppo sanguigno
blood pressure la pressione sanguigna
blood test l'analisi del sangue *(f)*
blouse la camicetta
to blow-dry asciugare con il fon
blue *(light)* azzurro(a)
dark blue blu scuro
light blue azzurro(a)
blunt *(knife, blade)* non taglia

boar il cinghiale
to board *(plain, train, etc)* imbarcarsi su
boarding card/pass la carta d'imbarco
boarding house la pensione
boat la barca ; il battello
(rowing) la barca a remi
boat trip la gita in battello
body il corpo
(dead) il cadavere
to boil bollire
boiler la caldaia
boiled bollito(a)
bomb la bomba
bone l'osso *(m)*
fish bone la spina di pesce
bonfire il falò
bonnet *(car)* il cofano
book il libro
book of tickets il blocchetto di biglietti
to book prenotare
booking la prenotazione
booking office *(train)* la biglietteria
bookshop la libreria
boot *(of car)* il bagagliaio
boots *(long)* gli stivali
(ankle) gli stivaletti
border *(of country)* la frontiera
boring noioso(a)
born: to be born essere nato(a)
to borrow prendere in prestito
boss il capo
both tutti e due
bottle la bottiglia
a bottle of wine una bottiglia di vino
a half-bottle una mezza bottiglia
bottle opener l'apribottiglie *(m)*
bowl *(for cereal, soup)* la scodella
bow tie la cravatta a farfalla
box la scatola
box office il botteghino
boxer shorts i boxer
boy *(young child)* il bambino
(teenage) il ragazzo
boyfriend il ragazzo
bra il reggiseno
bracelet il braccialetto
brain il cervello
to brake frenare
brake fluid il liquido dei freni
brake light il fanalino dello stop

brake pads le pastiglie dei freni
brakes i freni
branch *(of tree)* il ramo
  (of bank, etc) la succursale
brand *(make)* la marca
brass l'ottone *(m)*
brave coraggioso(a)
bread il pane
  brown bread il pane integrale
  French bread il filoncino
  sliced bread il pancarré
bread roll il panino
to break rompere
breakable fragile
breakdown *(car)* il guasto
  (nervous) l'esaurimento nervoso *(m)*
breakdown van il carro attrezzi
breakfast la (prima) colazione
breast il seno
to breast-feed allattare
to breathe respirare
brick il mattone
bride la sposa
bridegroom lo sposo
bridge il ponte
briefcase la cartella
Brillo-pad la paglietta
to bring portare
Britain la Gran Bretagna
British britannico(a)
broccoli i broccoli
brochure l'opuscolo *(m)*
broken rotto(a)
broken down *(car, etc)* guasto(a)
bronchitis la bronchite
bronze il bronzo
brooch la spilla
broom *(brush)* la scopa
brother il fratello
brother-in-law il cognato
brown marrone
bruise il livido
brush la spazzola
bubble bath il bagnoschiuma
bucket il secchiello
buffet car il vagone ristorante
to build costruire
building l'edificio *(m)*
bulb *(lightbulb)* la lampadina
bumbag il marsupio
bumper *(on car)* il paraurti

bunch *(of flowers)* il mazzo di fiori
  (of grapes) il grappolo d'uva
bungee jumping il bungee jumping
bureau de change l'agenzia di
  cambio *(f)*
burger l'hamburger *(m)*
burglar il/la ladro(a)
burglar alarm l'antifurto *(m)*
to burn bruciare
bus l'autobus *(m)*
bus pass la tessera dell'autobus
bus station la stazione delle autolinee
bus stop la fermata (dell'autobus)
bus ticket il biglietto d'autobus
business gli affari
  on business per affari
business card il biglietto da visita
business class la business class
businessman/woman l'uomo/la donna
  d'affari
business trip il viaggio d'affari
busy occupato(a) ; impegnato(a)
but ma ; però
butcher's il macellaio
butter il burro
button il bottone
to buy comprare
by *(next to)* accanto a
  (via) via
  by bus in autobus
  by car in macchina
  by train in treno
  by ship in battello
bypass *(road)* la circonvallazione

C

cab *(taxi)* il taxi
cabaret il cabaret
cabin *(on boat)* la cabina
cabin crew l'equipaggio di bordo *(m)*
cablecar la funivia
café il bar
  internet café il cyber-café
cafetière la caffettiera
cake *(big)* la torta
  (small) il pasticcino
cake shop la pasticceria
calculator la calcolatrice
calendar il calendario
call *(telephone call)* la chiamata
to call chiamare
  (phone) chiamare per telefono
calm calmo(a)
camcorder la videocamera

camera la macchina fotografica
camera case la custodia della macchina fotografica
to camp campeggiare
camping gas il camping gas
camping stove il fornellino da campeggio
campsite il campeggio
can il barattolo ; la scatola
to can *(to be able)* potere
  I can posso
  we can possiamo
  I cannot non posso
  we cannot non possiamo
  can I...? posso...?
  can we...? possiamo...?
Canada il Canada
Canadian canadese
canal il canale
to cancel cancellare ; annullare
cancellation la cancellazione
cancer il cancro
candle la candela
canoe la canoa
to canoe andare in canoa
can opener l'apriscatole *(m)*
cap *(hat)* il berretto
  (diaphragm) il diaframma
capital *(city)* la capitale
car la macchina
car alarm l'antifurto *(m)*
car ferry il traghetto
car hire l'autonoleggio *(m)*
car insurance l'assicurazione della macchina *(f)*
car keys le chiavi della macchina
car park il parcheggio
car parts i pezzi di ricambio
car radio l'autoradio *(f)*
car seat *(for children)* il seggiolino per bambini
carwash l'autolavaggio *(m)*
carafe la caraffa
caravan la roulotte
carburettor il carburatore
card *(greetings)* il biglietto d'auguri
  (business) il biglietto da visita
  (playing cards) le carte da gioco
cardboard il cartone
cardigan il cardigan
careful attento(a)
  to be careful fare attenzione
carpet *(fitted)* la moquette
  (rug) il tappeto
carriage *(railway)* il vagone

carrots le carote
to carry portare
carton il cartone
case *(suitcase)* la valigia
cash i contanti
to cash *(cheque)* incassare
cash desk la cassa
cash dispenser *(autoteller)* il Bancomat®
cashier il/la cassiere(a)
cashpoint il Bancomat®
casino il casinò
casserole dish la casseruola
cassette la cassetta
cassette player il registratore
castle il castello
casualty department il pronto soccorso
cat il gatto
cat food il cibo per gatti
catacombs le catacombe
catalogue il catalogo
to catch *(bus, train, etc)* prendere
cathedral il duomo
Catholic cattolico(a)
cave la grotta
cavity *(in tooth)* la cavità
CD il CD
CD player il lettore CD
ceiling il soffitto
cellar la cantina
cellphone il cellulare
cemetery il cimitero
centimetre il centimetro
central centrale
central heating il riscaldamento
central locking *(car)* la chiusura centralizzata
centre il centro
century il secolo
ceramics la ceramica
cereal *(for breakfast)* i cereali
certificate il certificato
chain la catena
chair la sedia
chairlift la seggiovia
chalet lo chalet
challenge la sfida
chambermaid la cameriera

Champagne lo Champagne
change il cambio
  (small coins) gli spiccioli
  (money returned) il resto
to change: *to change money* cambiare
  soldi
  to change clothes cambiarsi
  to change train cambiare treno
changing room lo spogliatoio
Channel *(English)* la Manica
chapel la cappella
charcoal il carbone
charge *(fee)* la tariffa
to charge chiedere
  please charge it to my account lo
  metta sul mio conto, per favore
charger *(for battery)* il caricabatterie
charter flight il volo charter
cheap economico(a)
  cheaper più economico(a)
cheap rate *(phone)* la tariffa economica
to check controllare
to check in *(airport)* fare il check-in
  (at hotel) firmare il registro
check-in il check-in
cheek la guancia
cheers! salute! ; cin-cin!
cheese il formaggio
chef il cuoco
chemist's la farmacia
cheque l'assegno *(m)*
cheque book il libretto degli assegni
cheque card la carta assegni
cherries le ciliegie
chess gli scacchi
chest *(of body)* il petto
chewing gum la cicca
chicken il pollo
chicken breast il petto di pollo
chickenpox la varicella
child il/la bambino(a)
children *(small)* i bambini
  (older children) i ragazzi
  for chidren per bambini
child safety seat *(car)* il seggiolino di
  sicurezza per bambini
chimney il camino
chin il mento
china la porcellana
chips *(french fries)* le patatine fritte
chocolate la cioccolata
chocolates i cioccolatini

choir il coro
choice la scelta
to choose scegliere
chop *(meat)* la costoletta
chopping board il tagliere
christening il battesimo
Christian name il nome di battesimo
Christmas il Natale
  Merry Christmas! Buon Natale!
Christmas card il biglietto d'auguri
  natalizi
Christmas Eve la vigilia di Natale
church la chiesa
cigar il sigaro
cigarette la sigaretta
cigarette lighter l'accendino *(m)*
cigarette papers le cartine
cinema il cinema
circle *(theatre)* la galleria
circuit breaker il salvavita
circus il circo
cistern la cisterna
  (of toilet) il serbatoio dell'acqua
city la città
city centre il centro città
class: *first class* prima classe
  second class seconda classe
clean pulito(a)
to clean pulire
cleaner *(person)* l'addetto(a) alle pulizie
cleanser *(for face)* il detergente
clear chiaro(a)
client il/la cliente
cliff *(along coast)* la scogliera
  (mountain) la rupe
to climb scalare
climbing l'alpinismo *(m)*
climbing boots gli scarponi da
  montagna
Clingfilm® la pellicola per alimenti
clinic la clinica
cloakroom il guardaroba
clock l'orologio *(m)*
to close chiudere
closed *(shop, etc)* chiuso(a)
cloth il panno
clothes i vestiti
clothes peg la molletta
clothes shop il negozio d'abbigliamento
cloudy nuvoloso(a)
club il club
clutch *(car)* la frizione
coach il pullman

coach station la stazione dei pullman
coach trip la gita in pullman
coal il carbone
coast la costa
coastguard il guardacoste
coat il cappotto
coat hanger la gruccia
cockroach lo scarafaggio
cocktail il cocktail
cocoa il cacao
code il codice
coffee *(espresso)* il caffè
  black coffee il caffè americano
  white coffee il caffellatte
  cappuccino il cappuccino
  decaffeinated coffee il decaffeinato
coil *(IUD)* la spirale
coin la moneta
Coke® la Coca®
colander lo scolapasta
cold freddo(a)
  I'm cold ho freddo
  it's cold fa freddo
cold *(illness)* il raffreddore
  I have a cold ho il raffreddore
cold sore l'herpes *(m)*
Coliseum il Colosseo
collar il colletto
collar bone la clavicola
colleague il/la collega
to collect raccogliere
  (to collect someone) andare a prendere
collection *(of stamps)* la collezione
  (of letters) la levata
  (of rubbish) la rimozione
colour il colore
colour-blind daltonico(a)
colour film *(for camera)* la pellicola a colori
comb il pettine
to come venire
  (to arrive) arrivare
to come back tornare
to come in entrare
  come in! avanti!
comedy la commedia
comfortable comodo(a)
company *(firm)* la ditta
compartment lo scompartimento
compass la bussola
to complain fare un reclamo
complaint il reclamo
complete completo(a)
to complete *(piece of work)* finire
  (form) riempire

compulsory obbligatorio(a)
computer il computer
computer disk *(floppy)* il dischetto
computer game il videogioco
computer program il programma di computer
concert il concerto
concert hall la sala da concerti
concession la riduzione
concussion la commozione cerebrale
condensed milk il latte condensato
conditioner il balsamo
condoms i preservativi
conductor *(on bus)* il bigliettaio
cone il cono
conference il congresso
to confirm confermare
confirmation *(of flight, etc)* la conferma
confused confuso(a)
congratulations le congratulazioni
connection *(train, etc)* la coincidenza
constipated stitico(a)
consulate il consolato
to consult consultare
to contact mettersi in contatto con
contact lens cleaner il liquido per lenti a contatto
contact lenses le lenti a contatto
to continue continuare
contraceptive l'anticoncezionale *(m)*
contract il contratto
convenient: is it convenient? va bene?
convulsions le convulsioni
to cook cucinare
cooked cotto(a)
cooker la cucina
cookies i biscotti
cool fresco(a)
cool-box *(picnic)* la borsa termica
copper il rame
copy la copia
to copy copiare
cork il tappo
corkscrew il cavatappi
corner l'angolo *(m)*
cornflakes i cornflakes
corridor il corridoio
cosmetics i cosmetici
to cost costare
  how much does it cost? quanto costa?

c/d eng-italian

costume *(swimming)* il costume da bagno
cot il lettino
cottage il cottage
cotton il cotone
cotton bud il cotton fioc®
cotton wool il cotone idrofilo
couchette la cuccetta
cough la tosse
to cough tossire
cough mixture lo sciroppo per la tosse
cough sweets le pasticche per la tosse
counter *(in shop, bar, etc)* il banco
country *(not town)* la campagna
(nation) il paese
countryside la campagna
couple *(two people)* la coppia
a couple of... un paio di...
courgettes le zucchine
courier service il corriere
course *(of meal)* il piatto
(of study) il corso
cousin il/la cugino(a)
cover charge il coperto
cow la mucca
crafts l'artigianato *(m)*
craftsperson l'artigiano(a)
cramps i crampi
crash *(car)* lo scontro
to crash *(car)* avere un incidente
crash helmet il casco
cream *(lotion)* la crema
(dairy) la panna
soured cream la panna acida
whipped cream la panna montata
credit card la carta di credito
crime il reato
crisps le patatine
croissant la brioche
to cross *(road)* attraversare
cross la croce
cross-country skiing lo sci di fondo
crossing *(sea, lake)* la traversata
crossroads l'incrocio *(m)*
crossword puzzle il cruciverba
crowd la folla
crowded affollato(a)
crown la corona
cruise la crociera
crutches le grucce

to cry *(weep)* piangere
crystal *(made of)* di cristallo
cucumber il cetriolo
cufflinks i gemelli
cul-de-sac il vicolo cieco
cup la tazza
cupboard l'armadio *(m)*
curlers i bigodini
currant la sultanina
currency: *(foreign) currency* la valuta (estera)
current *(electric, water)* la corrente
curtain la tenda
cushion il cuscino
custom *(tradition)* il costume
customer il/la cliente
customs *(duty)* la dogana
cut il taglio
to cut tagliare
cutlery le posate
to cycle andare in bicicletta
cycle track la pista ciclabile
cycling il ciclismo
cyst la cisti
cystitis la cistite

D

daily *(each day)* ogni giorno ; quotidiano(a)
dairy produce i latticini
dam la diga
damage il danno
damp umido(a)
dance il ballo
to dance ballare
danger il pericolo
dangerous pericoloso(a)
dark *(colour)* scuro(a)
(night) buio(a)
after dark a notte fatta
date la data
date of birth la data di nascita
daughter la figlia
daughter-in-law la nuora
dawn l'alba *(f)*
day il giorno
per day al giorno
every day ogni giorno
(span of time la giornata
dead morto(a)
deaf sordo(a)
dear caro(a)

9 **debts** i debiti

decaffeinated decaffeinato(a)
have you decaffeinated coffee? ha del decaffeinato?

December dicembre

deckchair la sedia a sdraio

to declare dichiarare
nothing to declare niente da dichiarare

deep profondo(a)

deep freeze il surgelatore

deer il cervo

to defrost scongelare

to de-ice sbrinare

delay il ritardo
how long is the delay? di quant'è il ritardo?

delayed: to be delayed *(flight)* subire un ritardo

delicatessen il negozio di specialità gastronomiche

delicious delizioso(a)

demonstration la manifestazione

dental floss il filo interdentale

dentist il/la dentista

dentures la dentiera

deodorant il deodorante

to depart partire

department il reparto

department store il grande magazzino

departure la partenza

departure lounge la sala partenze

deposit il deposito

to describe descrivere

description la descrizione

desk la scrivania
(information, etc) il banco

dessert il dolce

details i dettagli

detergent il detersivo

detour la deviazione

to develop *(photos)* sviluppare

diabetes il diabete

diabetic diabetico(a)
I'm diabetic sono diabetico(a)

to dial fare il numero

dialect il dialetto

dialling code il prefisso telefonico

dialling tone il segnale di libero

diamond il diamante

diapers i pannolini

diaphragm il diaframma

diarrhoea la diarrea

diary l'agenda *(f)*

dice il dado

dictionary il dizionario ; il vocabolario

to die morire

diesel il gasolio

diet la dieta
I'm on a diet sono a dieta
special diet una dieta specifica

different diverso(a)

difficult difficile

to dilute diluire

dinghy *(rubber)* il canotto

dining room la sala da pranzo

dinner *(evening meal)* la cena
to have dinner cenare

dinner jacket lo smoking

direct *(train, etc)* diretto(a)

directions le indicazioni
to ask for directions chiedere la strada

directory *(telephone)* l'elenco telefonico *(m)*

directory enquiries il servizio informazioni

dirty sporco(a)

disability il handicap

disabled *(person)* disabile ; handicappato(a)

to disagree non essere d'accordo

to disappear scomparire

disaster il disastro

disco la discoteca

discount lo sconto

to discover scoprire

disease la malattia

dishtowel lo strofinaccio dei piatti

dishwasher la lavastoviglie

disinfectant il disinfettante

disk *(floppy disk)* il disco

to dislocate *(joint)* lussarsi

disposable *(camera)* usa e getta

distance la distanza

distilled water l'acqua distillata *(f)*

district *(of town)* il quartiere

to disturb disturbare

to dive tuffarsi

diversion la deviazione

diving i tuffi

divorced divorziato(a)

DIY shop il negozio di bricolage

dizzy: to be dizzy avere il capogiro

to do fare

doctor il medico/la dottoressa
documents i documenti
dog il cane
dog food il cibo per cani
dog lead il guinzaglio
doll la bambola
dollars i dollari
domestic *(flight)* nazionale
donor card la tessera dell'A.I.D.O.
door la porta
doorbell il campanello
double doppio(a)
double bed il letto matrimoniale
double room la camera doppia
down: *to go down* scendere
downstairs giù ; dabbasso
drain lo scarico
draught *(of air)* la corrente (d'aria)
   there's a draught c'è corrente
draught lager la birra alla spina
drawer il cassetto
drawing il disegno
dress il vestito
to dress *(to get dressed)* vestirsi
dressing *(for food)* il condimento
   (for wound) la fasciatura
dressing gown la vestaglia
drill *(tool)* il trapano
drink *(soft)* la bibita
to drink bere
drinking water l'acqua potabile *(f)*
to drive guidare
driver *(of car)* l'autista *(m/f)*
driving licence la patente
drought la siccità
to drown affogare
drug *(medicine)* il farmaco
   (narcotics) la droga
drunk ubriaco(a)
dry secco(a) ; asciutto(a)
to dry asciugare
dry-cleaner's la tintoria ; il lavasecco
dummy *(for baby)* la tettarella
during durante
dust la polvere
duster lo straccio
dustpan and brush lo scopino e la
   paletta
duty-free esente da dogana
duvet il piumino

duvet cover il copripiumone
dye la tinta
dynamo la dinamo

E

each ogni
ear l'orecchio *(m)*
earache il mal d'orecchi
earlier più presto
early presto
to earn guadagnare
earphones le cuffie
earplugs i tappi per le orecchie
earrings gli orecchini
earth la terra
earthquake il terremoto
east l'est *(m)*
Easter la Pasqua
   Happy Easter! Buona Pasqua!
easy facile
to eat mangiare
economy *(class)* la classe turistica
egg l'uovo *(m)*
   eggs le uova
   fried egg l'uovo fritto
   hard-boiled egg l'uovo sodo
   scrambled eggs le uova strapazzate
   soft-boiled egg l'uovo alla coque
either ... or o ... o
elastic band l'elastico *(m)*
Elastoplast il cerotto
elbow il gomito
electric elettrico(a)
electric blanket la coperta elettrica
electrician *m/f* l'elettricista
electricity l'elettricità *(f)*
electricity meter il contatore
   dell'elettricità
electric razor il rasoio elettrico
electric shock la scossa
elevator l'ascensore *(m)*
e-mail la posta elettronica ; l'e-mail *(m)*
   to e-mail s.o. mandare un e-mail a
   qualcuno
e-mail address l'indirizzo di posta
   elettronica *(m)*
embassy l'ambasciata *(f)*
emergency l'emergenza *(f)*
emergency exit l'uscita d'emergenza *(f)*
emery board la limetta per le unghie
empty vuoto(a)
end la fine
engaged *(to be married)* fidanzato(a)
   (phone, toilet, etc) occupato(a)

engine il motore
England l'Inghilterra *(f)*
English inglese
  (language) l'inglese *(m)*
to enjoy divertirsi
  (to like) piacere
  I enjoyed the trip la gita mi è piaciuta
  I enjoy swimming mi piace nuotare
  enjoy your meal! buon appetito!
enough abbastanza
  that's enough basta così
enquiry desk il banco informazioni
to enter entrare
entertainment il divertimento
entrance l'entrata *(f)* ; l'ingresso *(m)*
entrance fee il biglietto d'ingresso
envelope la busta
epileptic epilettico(a)
epileptic fit la crisi epilettica
equal uguale ; pari
equipment l'attrezzatura *(f)*
eraser la gomma da cancellare
error l'errore *(m)*
eruption l'eruzione *(f)*
escalator la scala mobile
to escape fuggire
essential essenziale
estate agent's l'agenzia immobiliare *(f)*
euro l'Euro *(m)*
eurocheque l'eurocheque *(m)*
Europe l'Europa *(f)*
European europeo(a)
European Union l'Unione Europea *(f)*
eve la vigilia
evening la sera
  this evening stasera
  tomorrow evening domani sera
  in the evening la sera
evening dress l'abito da sera *(m)*
evening meal la cena
every ogni ; ciascuno ; tutti
everyone tutti
everything tutto
everywhere dappertutto
examination l'esame *(m)*
example: *for example* per esempio
excellent ottimo(a)
except salvo
excess baggage il bagaglio in eccedenza
to exchange cambiare
exchange rate il cambio
exciting emozionante
excursion l'escursione *(f)*

to excuse scusare
excuse me! *(sorry)* mi scusi!
  (when passing) permesso!
exercise l'esercizio *(m)*
exhaust pipe il tubo di scappamento
exhibition la mostra
exit l'uscita *(f)*
expenses le spese
expensive costoso(a) ; caro(a)
expert l'esperto(a)
to expire *(ticket, etc)* scadere
to explain spiegare
explosion l'esplosione *(f)*
to export esportare
express *(train)* l'espresso *(m)*
express *(parcel, etc)* espresso(a)
extension *(electrical)* la prolunga
extra *(spare)* in più
  (more) supplementare
  an extra bed un letto in più
eye l'occhio *(m)*
eyebrows le sopracciglia
eye drops il collirio
eyelashes le ciglia
eye shadow l'ombretto *(m)*

F

fabric la stoffa
face la faccia
face cloth il guanto di spugna
facial la pulizia del viso
facilities *(leisure facilities)* le atrezzature
factory la fabbrica
to fail fallire
to faint svenire
fainted svenuto(a)
fair *(just)* giusto(a)
  (blond) biondo(a)
fair *(trade)* la fiera
  (funfair) il luna park
fake falso(a)
fall *(autumn)* l'autunno *(m)*
to fall cadere
  he/she has fallen è caduto(a)
false teeth la dentiera
family la famiglia
famous famoso(a)
fan *(hand-held)* il ventaglio
  (electric) il ventilatore
  (football) il/la tifoso(a)

fan belt la cinghia della ventola
fancy dress in costume ; in maschera
far lontano(a)
  is it far? è lontano?
fare la tariffa
farm la fattoria
farmer l'agricoltore *(m)*
farmhouse la fattoria
fashionable alla moda
fast veloce
  too fast troppo veloce
to fasten *(seatbelt, etc)* allacciare
fat grasso(a)
  (noun) il grasso
  saturated fats i grassi saturi
  unsaturated fats i grassi insaturi
father il padre
father-in-law lo suocero
fault *(defect)* il difetto
  it's not my fault non è colpa mia
favour il favore
favourite preferito(a)
fax il fax
  by fax per fax
to fax mandare un fax
February febbraio
to feed dare da mangiare
to feel sentire ; sentirsi
  I don't feel well non mi sento bene
  I feel sick ho la nausea
feet i piedi
felt-tip pen il pennarello
female femmina ; femminile
ferry il traghetto
festival la festa
to fetch *(bring)* portare
  (to go and get) andare a prendere
fever la febbre
few pochi
  a few alcuni
fiancé(e) il/la fidanzato(a)
field il campo
to fight combattere ; lottare
file *(folder)* il raccoglitore
  (computer) l'archivio *(m)*
to fill riempire
to fill in *(form)* compilare
fill it up! *(petrol)* il pieno!
fillet il filetto
filling *(in tooth)* l'otturazione *(f)*
film *(at cinema)* il film
  (for camera) la pellicola

Filofax® l'agenda *(f)*
filter il filtro
to find trovare
fine *(to be paid)* la multa
finger il dito
to finish finire
finished finito(a)
fire il fuoco ; l'incendio *(m)*
  fire! al fuoco!
fire alarm l'allarme antincendio *(m)*
fire brigade i vigili del fuoco
fire engine l'autopompa *(f)*
fire escape la scala antincendio
fire extinguisher l'estintore *(m)*
fireplace il caminetto
fireworks i fuochi d'artificio
firm *(company)* l'azienda *(f)* ; la ditta
first primo(a)
first aid il pronto soccorso
first aid kit la cassetta di pronto soccorso
first class la prima classe
first name il nome di battesimo
fish il pesce
to fish pescare
fisherman il pescatore
fishing permit la licenza di pesca
fishing rod la canna da pesca
fishmonger's la pescheria
to fit *(clothes)* andare bene
  it doesn't fit non va bene
fit *(seizure)* l'attacco *(m)*
to fix riparare ; sistemare
  can you fix it? può ripararlo?
fizzy gassato(a)
flag la bandiera
flame la fiamma
flash *(for camera)* il flash
flashlight la pila
flask *(thermos)* il thermos
flat l'appartamento *(m)*
flat piatto(a)
  flat battery la batteria scarica
  flat tyre la gomma a terra
flavour il gusto
  what flavour? che gusto?
flaw il difetto
fleas le pulci
flesh la carne
flex il filo flessibile
flight il volo
flip flops gli infradito
flippers le pinne

3 flood l'alluvione *(f)*
flash flood l'inondazione *(f)*
floor *(of building)* il piano
(of room) il pavimento
which floor? a che piano?
on the ground floor al pianterreno
on the first floor al primo piano
on the second floor al secondo piano
floorcloth lo straccio per pavimenti
Florence Firenze
florist's shop il fioraio
flour la farina
flowers i fiori
flu l'influenza *(f)*
fly la mosca
to fly volare
flysheet *(tent)* il sopratetto
fog la nebbia
foggy nebbioso(a)
foil *(silver paper)* la carta stagnola
to fold ripiegare
to follow seguire
food il cibo
food poisoning l'intossicazione
alimentare *(f)*
foot il piede
on foot a piedi
football il calcio ; il pallone
football match la partita di calcio
football pitch il campo di calcio
football player il calciatore
footpath il sentiero
for per
for me/us per me/noi
for him/her per lui/lei
for you per te/lei/voi
forbidden proibito(a)
forehead la fronte
foreign straniero(a)
foreigner lo/la straniero(a)
forest la foresta
forever per sempre
to forget dimenticare
fork *(for eating)* la forchetta
(in road) il bivio
form *(document)* il modulo
fortnight quindici giorni
forward avanti
foul *(football)* il fallo
fountain la fontana
four-wheel drive con quattro ruote
motrici
fox la volpe
fracture la frattura

fragile fragile
fragrance la fragranza
frame *(picture)* la cornice
France la Francia
free *(not occupied)* libero(a)
(costing nothing) gratis
freezer il congelatore
French francese
(language) il francese
French fries le patatine fritte
frequent frequente
fresh fresco(a)
fresh water l'acqua dolce *(f)*
Friday il venerdì
fridge il frigorifero
fried fritto(a)
friend l'amico(a)
friendly amichevole
frog la rana
from da
from Scotland dalla Scozia
from England dall'Inghilterra
front davanti
in front of... di fronte a...
front door la porta d'ingresso
frost la brina
frozen *(food)* surgelato(a)
fruit la frutta
dried fruit la frutta secca
fruit juice il succo di frutta
fruit salad la macedonia
to fry friggere
frying-pan la padella
fuel *(petrol)* la benzina
fuel gauge la spia della benzina
fuel pump la pompa
fuel tank il serbatoio della benzina
full pieno(a)
(occupied) completo(a)
full board la pensione completa
fumes *(of car)* i gas di scarico
fun il divertimento
funeral il funerale
funfair il luna park
funny *(amusing)* divertente
fur il pelo
furnished ammobiliato(a)
furniture i mobili
fuse il fusibile
fuse box la scatola dei fusibili
future il futuro

G

gallery la galleria
game il gioco
  (meat) la selvaggina
garage *(private)* il garage
  (for repairs) l'autofficina *(f)*
  (for petrol) la stazione di servizio
garden il giardino
garlic l'aglio *(m)*
gas il gas
gas cooker la cucina a gas
gas cylinder la bombola del gas
gastritis la gastrite
gate il cancello
  (airport) l'uscita *(f)*
gay *(person)* gay
gear *(car)* la marcia
  first gear la prima
  second gear la seconda
  third gear la terza
  fourth gear la quarta
  neutral folle
  reverse la retromarcia
gearbox il cambio
generous generoso(a)
gents' *(toilet)* la toilette (per uomini)
genuine *(leather, silver)* vero(a)
  (antique, picture, etc) autentico(a)
German tedesco(a)
  (language) il tedesco
German measles la rosolia
Germany la Germania
to get *(obtain)* ottenere
  (to receive) ricevere
  (to fetch) prendere
to get in/on *(vehicle)* salire in/su
to get off *(bus, etc)* scendere da
gift il regalo
gift shop il negozio di souvenir
girl *(young child)* la bambina
  (teenage) la ragazza
girlfriend la ragazza
to give dare
to give back restituire
glacier il ghiacciaio
glass *(substance)* il vetro
  (for drinking) il bicchiere
  a glass of water un bicchiere d'acqua
  a glass of wine un bicchiere di vino
glasses *(spectacles)* gli occhiali
glasses case la custodia degli occhiali

gloves i guanti
glue la colla
to go andare
  I'm going to... vado a...
  we're going to... andiamo a...
to go back ritornare
to go in entrare in
to go out *(leave)* uscire
goat la capra
God Dio
goggles gli occhialini
  (for skiing) gli occhiali da sci
gold l'oro *(m)*
golf il golf
golf ball la pallina da golf
golf clubs le mazze da golf
golf course il campo di golf
good buono(a)
  (pleasant) bello(a)
  very good ottimo(a)
good afternoon buon giorno
  (after 5pm) buona sera
goodbye arrivederci
good day buon giorno
good evening buona sera
good morning buon giorno
good night buona notte
goose l'oca *(f)*
gram il grammo
grandchild il/la nipote
granddaughter la nipote
grandfather il nonno
grandmother la nonna
grandparents i nonni
grandson il nipote
grapes l'uva *(f)*
grass l'erba *(f)*
grated grattugiato(a)
grater la grattugia
greasy grasso(a)
great *(big)* grande
  (wonderful) fantastico(a)
Great Britain la Gran Bretagna
green verde
green card *(car insurance)* la carta verde
greengrocer's il fruttivendolo
greetings card il biglietto d'auguri
grey grigio(a)
grill la griglia
to grill cuocere alla griglia
grilled alla griglia
grocer's il negozio di alimentari
ground la terra
ground floor il pianterreno

on the ground floor a pianterreno
groundsheet il telone impermeabile
group il gruppo
guarantee la garanzia
guard (on train) il capotreno
guest (house guest) l'ospite (m/f)
(in hotel) il/la cliente
guesthouse la pensione
guide (tourist) la guida
guidebook la guida
guided tour la visita guidata
guitar la chitarra
gun (pistol) la pistola
(rifle) il fucile
gym (place) la palestra
gym shoes le scarpe da ginnastica

H

haemorrhoids le emorroidi
hail la grandine
hair i capelli
hairbrush la spazzola per capelli
haircut il taglio di capelli
hairdresser il parrucchiere/la
parrucchiera
hair dryer il fon
hair dye la tintura per capelli
hair gel il gel per capelli
hairgrip la molletta per capelli
hair mousse la spuma
hair spray la lacca per capelli
half la metà
a half bottle of... una mezza
bottiglia di...
half an hour mezz'ora
half board mezza pensione
half fare il ridotto
half-price metà prezzo
ham (cooked) il prosciutto cotto
(cured) il prosciutto crudo
hamburger l'hamburger (m)
hammer il martello
hand la mano
handbag la borsa
handicapped disabile ; handicappato(a)
handkerchief il fazzoletto
handle il manico
handlebars il manubrio
hand luggage il bagaglio a mano
hand-made fatto a mano
hands-free phone il telefono per auto
handsome bello(a)
hanger (coat hanger) la gruccia per abiti

hang gliding il volo con deltaplano
hangover i postumi della sbornia
to happen succedere
what happened? cos'è successo?
happy felice
happy birthday! buon compleanno!
harbour il porto
hard duro(a)
(difficult) difficile
hard disk l'hard disk (m)
hardware shop il negozio di
ferramenta
to harm nuocere
harvest il raccolto ; la vendemmia
hat il cappello
to have avere
I have... ho...
I don't have... non ho...
we have... abbiamo...
we don't have... non abbiamo...
do you have...? ha...?
to have to dovere
hay fever il raffreddore da fieno
he egli ; lui
head la testa
headache il mal di testa
I have a headache ho mal di testa
headlights i fari
headphones la cuffia
health la salute
health-food shop l'erboristeria (f)
healthy sano(a)
to hear sentire
hearing aid l'apparecchio acustico (m)
heart il cuore
heart attack l'infarto (m)
heartburn il bruciore di stomaco
to heat up (food) riscaldare
heater il termosifone
heating il riscaldamento
heavy pesante
heel il tallone
heel bar il banco del calzolaio
height l'altezza (f)
helicopter l'elicottero (m)
hello! salve! ; ciao!
(on telephone) pronto
helmet il casco
help! aiuto!
to help aiutare
can you help me? può aiutarmi?
hem l'orlo (m)

hepatitis l'epatite (f)
her il/la suo(a)
  her passport il suo passaporto
  her room la sua camera
herb l'erba aromatica (f)
herbal tea la tisana
here qui
  here is... ecco...
  here is my passport ecco il mio passaporto
hernia l'ernia (f)
hi! ciao!
to hide nascondere
high (price, number, etc) alto(a)
  (speed) forte
high blood pressure la pressione alta
high chair il seggiolone
hill la collina
hill-walking il trekking
him lui ; lo ; gli
hip l'anca (f)
hip replacement la protesi dell'anca
hire il noleggio
  car hire il noleggio auto
  bike hire il noleggio bici
  boat hire il noleggio barche
  ski hire il noleggio sci
to hire noleggiare
hired car la macchina a noleggio
his il/la suo(a)
  his passport il suo passaporto
  his room la sua camera
historic storico(a)
history la storia
to hit colpire
to hitchhike fare l'autostop
hobby il passatempo
to hold tenere
  (to contain) contenere
hold-up (traffic jam) l'ingorgo (m)
hole il buco
holiday la festa
  on holiday in vacanza
holiday rep il/la rappresentante dell'agenzia di viaggio
home la casa
  at home a casa
homesick: to be homesick avere nostalgia di casa
  I'm homesick ho nostalgia di casa
homosexual omosessuale
honest onesto(a)
honey il miele

honeymoon la luna di miele
hood (on jacket) il cappuccio
hook (for fishing) l'amo (m)
to hope sperare
  I hope so/not spero di sì/no
hors d'œuvre l'antipasto (m)
horse il cavallo
horse racing l'ippica (f)
to horse-ride andare a cavallo
hosepipe la canna dell'acqua
hospital l'ospedale (m)
hostel l'ostello (m)
hot caldo(a)
  I'm hot ho caldo
  it's hot (weather) fa caldo
hot-water bottle la borsa dell'acqua calda
hotel l'albergo (m) ; l'hotel (m)
hour l'ora (f)
  half an hour mezz'ora
  1 hour un'ora
  2 hour due ore
house la casa
housewife la casalinga
house wine il vino della casa
housework i lavori di casa
how? (in what way) come?
  how much? quanto(a)?
  how many? quanti(e)?
  how are you? come sta?
hungry: to be hungry avere fame
hunt la caccia
to hunt andare a caccia
hunting permit la licenza di caccia
hurry: I'm in a hurry ho fretta
to hurt fare male
  that hurts fa male
husband il marito
hut (bathing/beach) la cabina
  (mountain) la baita
hydrofoil l'aliscafo (m)
hypodermic needle l'ago ipodermico (m)

I

I io
ice il ghiaccio
  with ice con ghiaccio
  without ice senza ghiaccio
ice box il freezer
ice cream il gelato
iced coffee il caffè freddo
iced tea il tè freddo
ice lolly il ghiacciolo

ice rink la pista di pattinaggio su ghiaccio
to ice skate pattinare sul ghiaccio
ice skates i pattini da ghiaccio
idea l'idea *(f)*
identity card la carta d'identità
if se
ignition l'accensione *(f)*
ignition key la chiave dell'accensione
ill malato(a)
  I'm ill sto male
illness la malattia
immediately subito
immersion heater lo scaldabagno elettrico
immigration l'immigrazione *(f)*
immunisation l'immunizzazione *(f)*
to import importare
important importante
impossible impossibile
to improve migliorare
in in
  in 2 hours in due ore
  in London a Londra
in front of davanti a
included compreso(a) ; incluso(a)
inconvenient scomodo(a)
to increase aumentare
  to increase volume alzare il volume
indicator *(in car)* la freccia
indigestion l'indigestione *(f)*
indigestion tablets le compresse per digerire
indoors dentro
infection l'infezione *(f)*
infectious contagioso(a)
informal *(clothes)* sportivo(a)
information le informazioni
information office l'ufficio informazioni *(m)*
ingredients gli ingredienti
inhaler l'inalatore *(m)*
injection l'iniezione *(f)* ; la puntura
to injure ferire
injured ferito(a)
injury la lesione
ink l'inchiostro *(m)*
inn la locanda
inner tube la camera d'aria
inquiries le informazioni
insect l'insetto *(m)*
insect bite la puntura d'insetto
insect repellent l'insettifugo *(m)*
inside dentro

instant coffee il caffè solubile
instead of invece di
instructor l'istruttore/l'istruttrice
insulin l'insulina *(f)*
insurance l'assicurazione *(f)*
insurance certificate il certificato di assicurazione
to insure assicurare
insured: *to be insured* essere assicurato(a)
to intend to avere intenzione di
interesting interessante
international internazionale
internet l'Internet *(m)*
internet café il cyber-café
interpreter l'interprete *(m/f)*
interval l'intervallo *(m)*
interview l'intervista *(f)*
into in
  into town in città
  into the centre in centro
to introduce someone to presentare qualcuno a
invitation l'invito *(m)*
to invite invitare
invoice la fattura
Ireland l'Irlanda *(f)*
Irish irlandese
iron *(for clothes)* il ferro da stiro
  (metal) il forro
to iron stirare
ironing board l'asse da stiro *(f)*
ironmonger's il negozio di ferramenta
is è
island l'isola *(f)*
it lo/la
Italian italiano(a)
  (language) l'italiano *(m)*
Italy l'Italia *(f)*
to itch prudere
  my leg itches mi prude la gamba
  my eyes itch mi prudono gli occhi
item *(on bill)* la voce
itemised bill il conto dettagliato

J

jack *(for car)* il cric
jacket la giacca
  waterproof jacket il giaccone impermeabile
jam *(food)* la marmellata

jammed bloccato(a)
January gennaio
jar *(honey, jam, etc)* il vaso
jaundice l'itterizia *(f)*
jaw la mascella
jealous geloso(a) ; invidioso(a)
jeans i blue jeans
jelly *(dessert)* la gelatina
jellyfish la medusa
jet ski l'acqua-scooter *(m)*
jetty il molo
jeweller's la gioielleria
jewellery i gioielli
Jewish ebreo(a)
job il lavoro
to jog fare jogging
to join *(club)* iscriversi a
to join in *(game)* partecipare a
joint *(of body)* l'articolazione *(f)*
joke lo scherzo *(m)*
to joke scherzare
journalist il/la giornalista
journey il viaggio
judge il/la giudice *(m/f)*
jug la brocca
juice il succo
  a carton of juice un cartone di succo
  di frutta
July luglio
to jump saltare
jumper il maglione
jump leads *(for car)* i cavi per far partire
  la macchina
junction *(road)* l'incrocio *(m)*
June giugno
just: *just two* solamente due
  I've just arrived sono appena
  arrivato(a)

K

to keep *(retain)* tenere
  keep the change! tenga il resto
kennel il canile
kettle il bollitore
key la chiave
  card key il passe-partout
keyboard la tastiera
keyring il portachiavi
to kick dare calci a
kid *(child)* il bambino

kidneys *(in body)* i reni
to kill uccidere
kilo il chilo
  a kilo of apples un chilo di mele
  2 kilos due chili
kilogram il chilogrammo
kilometre il chilometro
kind *(sort)* il tipo
kind *(person)* gentile
king il re
kiosk l'edicola *(f)*
kiss il bacio
to kiss baciare
kitchen la cucina
kitchen paper la carta assorbente
  da cucina
kite l'aquilone *(m)*
knee il ginocchio
knee highs i gambaletti
knickers le mutandine
knife il coltello
to knit lavorare a maglia
to knock *(on door)* bussare
to knock down *(car)* investire
to knock over *(glass, vase)* rovesciare
knot il nodo
to know *(facts)* sapere
  (to be acquainted with) conoscere
  I don't know non lo so
to know how to sapere
  to know how to swim saper nuotare
kosher kasher

L

label l'etichetta *(f)*
lace il pizzo
laces *(shoe)* i lacci
ladder la scala
ladies' *(toilet)* la toilette (per signore)
lady la signora
lager la birra (bionda)
lake il lago
lamb l'agnello *(m)*
lame zoppo(a)
lamp la lampada
lamppost il lampione
lampshade il paralume
land la terra
to land *(plane)* atterrare
landlady la padrona di casa
landlord il padrone di casa
landslide la frana
lane la stradina

(of motorway) la corsia
language la lingua
language school la scuola di lingue
laptop il laptop
large grande
last ultimo(a) ; scorso(a)
  the last bus l'ultimo autobus
  the last train l'ultimo treno
  last night ieri notte
  last week la settimana scorsa
  last year l'anno scorso
  last time l'ultima volta
late tardi
  the train's late il treno è in ritardo
  sorry we're late scusi il ritardo
later più tardi
to laugh ridere
launderette la lavanderia automatica
laundry il bucato
lavatory la toilette
lavender la lavanda
law la legge
lawn il prato inglese
lawyer *(m/f)* l'avvocato/l'avvocatessa
laxative il lassativo
layby la piazzola di sosta
lazy pigro(a)
lead *(electric)* il filo
lead *(metal)* il piombo
lead-free senza piombo
leaf la foglia
leak *(of gas, liquid)* la perdita
  (in roof) il buco
to leak: it's leaking *(pipe)* perde
to learn imparare
lease *(rental)* l'affitto *(m)*
leather il cuoio ; la pelle
to leave *(leave behind)* lasciare
  (train, bus, etc) partire
  when does the bus leave? quando parte l'autobus?
  when does the train leave? quando parte il treno?
left la sinistra
  on/to the left a sinistra
left-handed mancino(a)
left-luggage il deposito bagagli
left luggage locker l'armadietto per despositare i bagagli *(m)*
leg la gamba
lemon il limone
lemonade la limonata
to lend prestare
length la lunghezza
lens *(camera)* l'obiettivo *(m)*
  (contact lens) la lente a contatto

lenses le lenti
lesbian lesbica
less meno
  less than meno di
lesson la lezione
to let *(allow)* permettere
  (to hire out) affittare
letter la lettera
letterbox la cassetta delle lettere
lettuce la lattuga
level crossing il passaggio a livello
library la biblioteca
licence il permesso
  (driving) la patente
lid il coperchio
lie *(untruth)* la bugia
to lie down sdraiarsi
life belt il salvagente
lifeboat la scialuppa di salvataggio
lifeguard il bagnino
life insurance l'assicurazione sulla vita *(f)*
life jacket il giubbotto salvagente
life raft la zattera di salvataggio
lift *(elevator)* l'ascensore *(m)*
  (in car) il passaggio
lift pass *(on ski slopes)* lo skipass
light *(not heavy)* leggero(a)
  (colour) chiaro(a)
light la luce
  have you a light? ha da accendere?
light bulb la lampadina
lighter l'accendino *(m)*
lighthouse il faro
lightning il fulmine
like come
to like piacere
  I like coffee mi piace il caffè
  I don't like... non mi piace...
  I'd/we'd like... vorrei/vorremmo...
lilo il materassino
lime *(fruit)* la limetta
line *(row, queue)* la fila
  (telephone) la linea
linen il lino
lingerie la biancheria intima da donna
lip reading la labiolettura
lips le labbra
lip salve il burro di cacao
lipstick il rossetto
liqueur il liquore
list l'elenco *(m)* ; la lista

l/m   eng-italian

to listen (to) ascoltare
litre il litro
 a litre of milk un litro di latte
litter *(rubbish)* i rifiuti
little *(small)* piccolino(a)
 a little... un po' di...
to live vivere ; abitare
 I live in London vivo a Londra
 he lives in a flat abita in un
 appartamento
liver il fegato
living room il salotto
loaf of bread la pagnotta
local locale
to lock chiudere a chiave
lock la serratura
 the lock is broken la serratura è rotta
locker l'armadietto *(m)*
locksmith il fabbro
log book *(car)* il libretto di circolazione
logs i ceppi
lollipop il lecca lecca
London Londra
 in/to London a Londra
long lungo(a)
 for a long time molto tempo
long-sighted ipermetrope
to look after prendersi cura di
to look at guardare
to look for cercare
loose *(not fastened)* slegato(a)
 it's come loose (knot) si è allentato(a)
lorry il camion
to lose perdere
lost *(object)* perso(a)
 I've lost my... ho perso il/la...
 I'm lost mi sono smarrito(a)
 we're lost ci siamo smarriti(e)
lost property office l'ufficio oggetti
 smarriti *(m)*
lot: *a lot* molto
lottery la lotteria
loud forte
lounge *(in hotel)* il salone
 (in house) la sala
 (in airport) la sala d'attesa
love l'amore *(m)*
to love *(person)* amare
 I love you ti amo
 I love swimming mi piace nuotare
lovely bellissimo(a)
low basso(a)

 (standard, quality) scadente
low-alcohol a basso contenuto alcolico
to lower volume abbassare il volume
low-fat magro(a)
luck la fortuna
lucky fortunato(a)
luggage i bagagli
luggage rack il portabagagli
luggage tag l'etichetta *(f)*
luggage trolley il carrello
lump *(swelling)* il gonfiore
lunch il pranzo
lunch break l'intervallo del pranzo *(m)*
lung il polmone
luxury di lusso

M

machine la macchina
mad *(insane)* matto(a)
 (angry) arrabbiato(a)
magazine la rivista
maggot il baco
magnet la calamita
magnifying glass la lente
 d'ingrandimento
maid *(in hotel)* la cameriera
maiden name il nome da ragazza
mail la posta
main principale
main course *(meal)* il secondo
main road la strada principale
to make *(generally)* fare
 (meal) preparare
make-up il trucco
male maschio ; maschile
mallet la mazza
man l'uomo *(m)*
to manage *(be in charge of)* dirigere
manager il direttore ; il gerente
manual *(gear change)* manuale
many molti(e)
map *(of country)* la carta geografica
 (city) la piantina
marble il marmo
March marzo
margarine la margarina
marina il porticciolo
mark *(stain)* la macchia ; il segno
 (brand) la marca
market il mercato
 where is the market? dov'è il
 mercato?

when is the market? quando c'è il mercato?

marmalade la marmellata d'arance

married sposato(a)
I'm married sono sposato(a)
are you married? è sposato(a)?

marry: *to get married* sposarsi

marsh la palude

mascara il mascara

mass *(in church)* la messa

mast l'albero *(m)*

masterpiece il capolavoro

match *(game)* la partita

matches i fiammiferi

material il materiale
(cloth) il tessuto

to matter importare
it doesn't matter non importa
what's the matter? cosa c'è?

mattress il materasso

May maggio

mayonnaise la maionese

mayor il/la sindaco(a)

maximum il massimo

me me ; mi

meal il pasto

to mean *(signify)* voler dire
what does it mean? cosa vuol dire?

measles il morbillo

to measure misurare

meat la carne

mechanic il/la meccanico(a)

medical insurance l'assicurazione medica *(f)*

medical treatment le cure mediche

medicine la medicina

Mediterranean il Mediterraneo

medium rare *(steak)* poco cotto(a)

to meet incontrare
pleased to meet you! piacere!

meeting la riunione
(by chance) l'incontro *(m)*

meeting point il meeting point

to melt sciogliere

member *(of club, etc)* il/la socio(a)

membership card la tessera

memory la memoria
(memories) i ricordi

men gli uomini

to mend riparare

meningitis la meningite

menu il menù
set menu il menù a prezzo fisso ; il menù turistico
à la carte menu il menù alla carta

message il messaggio

metal il metallo

meter il contatore

metre il metro

metro *(underground)* la metropolitana

metro station la stazione del metrò

microwave oven il forno a microonde

midday il mezzogiorno
at midday a mezzogiorno

middle il mezzo

middle-aged di mezz'età

midge il moscerino

midnight la mezzanotte
at midnight a mezzanotte

migraine l'emicrania *(f)*
I have a migraine ho l'emicrania

Milan Milano

mild dolce ; mite

milk il latte
fresh milk il latte fresco
hot milk il latte caldo
long-life milk il latte a lunga conservazione
powdered milk il latte in polvere
whole milk il latte intero
semi-skimmed milk il latte parzialmente scremato
soya milk il latte di soia
with/without milk con/senza latte

milkshake il frappé

millimetre il millimetro

mince *(meat)* la carne macinata

mind: *do you mind?* le dà fastidio?
I don't mind non mi dà fastidio

mineral water l'acqua minerale *(f)*

minibar il minibar

minimum il minimo

minister *(church)* il sacerdote
(political) il ministro

minor road la strada secondaria

mint *(herb)* la menta

mint tea il tè alla menta

minute il minuto

mirror lo specchio

to misbehave comportarsi male

miscarriage l'aborto spontaneo *(m)*

to miss *(train, etc)* perdere

Miss Signorina

missing *(thing)* smarrito(a)
(person) scomparso(a)

mistake l'errore *(m)*

misty nebbioso(a)

misunderstanding il malinteso
to mix mescolare
mobile phone il cellulare
modem il modem
modern moderno(a)
moisturizer l'idratante (m)
mole (on skin) il neo
moment: *just a moment* un momento
monastery il monastero
Monday il lunedì
money i soldi
 I have no money non ho soldi
money belt il marsupio
money order il vaglia
month il mese
 this month questo mese
 last month il mese scorso
 next month il mese prossimo
monthly mensilmente
monument il monumento
moon la luna
mooring l'ormeggio (m)
mop il mocio Vileda
moped il motorino
more (than) più (di)
 more than 3 più di tre
 more wine ancora un po' di vino
morning la mattina
 in the morning di mattina
 this morning stamattina
 tomorrow morning domani mattina
morning-after pill la pillola del giorno dopo
mosquito la zanzara
mosquito net la zanzariera
mosquito repellent lo zanzarifugo
most il/la più ; il massimo
moth (clothes) la tarma
mother la madre
mother-in-law la suocera
motor il motore
motorbike la moto
motorboat il motoscafo
motorway l'autostrada (f)
mould la muffa
mountain la montagna
mountain bike la mountain bike
mountain rescue il soccorso alpino
mountaineering l'alpinismo (m)
mouse il topo
 (computer) il mouse
moustache i baffi

mouth la bocca
mouthwash il colluttorio
move muoversi
 it isn't moving non si muove
movie il film
Mr Signor
Mrs Signora
Ms Signora
much molto
 too much troppo
muddy (ground) fangoso(a)
mugging lo scippo
mumps gli orecchioni
muscle il muscolo
museum il museo
mushrooms i funghi
music la musica
musical il musical
mussels le cozze
must (to have to) dovere
 I must devo
 we must dobbiamo
 I mustn't non devo
 we mustn't non dobbiamo
mustard la senape
my il/la mio(a)
 my passport il mio passaporto
 my room la mia camera

N

nail (metal) il chiodo
 (fingernail) l'unghia (f)
nailbrush lo spazzolino per le unghie
nail clipper il tagliaunghie
nail file la limetta per le unghie
nail polish/varnish lo smalto per le unghie
nail polish remover l'acetone (m)
nail scissors le forbicine
name il nome
 my name is... mi chiamo...
 what is your name? come si chiama?
nanny la bambinaia
napkin il tovagliolo
Naples Napoli
nappies i pannolini
narrow stretto(a)
national nazionale
national park il parco nazionale
nationality la nazionalità
natural naturale
nature la natura
nature reserve la riserva naturale

3 navy blue blu marino
near to vicino(a) a
  is it near? è vicino?
  near the bank vicino alla banca
necessary necessario(a)
neck il collo
necklace la collana
nectarine la nocepesca
to need avere bisogno di...
  I need... ho bisogno di...
  we need... abbiamo bisogno di...
needle l'ago *(m)*
  a needle and thread un ago e filo
negative *(photo)* il negativo
neighbour il/la vicino(a)
nephew il nipote
net la rete
  the Net l'Internet *(m)*
never mai
  I never drink wine non bevo mai il vino
new nuovo(a)
news le notizie
  (on television) il telegiornale
newsagent's il giornalaio
newspaper il giornale
newsstand l'edicola *(f)*
New Year il Capodanno
  happy New Year! buon Anno!
New Year's Eve la notte di San
  Silvestro ; l'ultimo dell'anno *(m)*
New Zealand la Nuova Zelanda
next prossimo(a)
  next to accanto(a) a
  next week la settimana prossima
  the next bus il prossimo autobus
  the next train il prossimo treno
  the next stop la prossima fermata
nice piacevole
  (person) simpatico(a)
niece la nipote
night la notte
  at night di notte
  last night ieri notte
  per night a notte
  tomorrow night domani sera
  tonight stasera
nightclub il nightclub
nightdress la camicia da notte
night porter il portiere notturno
no no
  no entry vietato l'ingresso
  no smoking vietato fumare
  no thanks no, grazie
  (without) senza
  no sugar senza zucchero
  no ice senza ghiaccio
  no problem non c'è problema

nobody nessuno
noise il rumore
noisy rumoroso(a)
  it's very noisy è molto
  rumoroso(a)
non-alcoholic analcolico(a)
none nessuno(a)
non-smoker non-fumatore
non-smoking per non-fumatori
north il nord
Northern Ireland l'Irlanda del Nord *(f)*
nose il naso
not non
  I do not know non lo so
note *(bank note)* la banconota
  (letter) il biglietto
note pad il bloc-notes
nothing niente
  nothing else nient'altro
notice l'avviso *(m)*
notice board la bacheca
novel il romanzo
November novembre
now adesso
nowhere da nessuna parte
nuclear nucleare
nudist beach la spiaggia nudista
number il numero
number plate *(car)* la targa
nurse l'infermiera/l'infermiere *(f/m)*
nursery *(for children)* l'asilo *(m)*
  (for plants) il vivaio
nursery slope la pista per principianti
nut *(to eat)* la noce
  (for bolt) il dado

O

oars i remi
oats l'avena *(f)*
to obtain ottenere
occupation *(work)* il lavoro
ocean l'oceano *(m)*
October ottobre
octopus il polpo
odd *(strange)* strano(a)
of di
  a bottle of wine una bottiglia di vino
  a glass of water un bicchiere d'acqua
  made of... fatto di...

off *(machine, etc)* spento(a)
  (milk, food) andato(a) a male
  this meat is off questa carne è
  andata a male
office l'ufficio *(m)*
often spesso
  how often? ogni quanto?
oil l'olio *(m)*
oil filter il filtro dell'olio
oil gauge l'indicatore del livello
  dell'olio *(m)*
ointment la pomata
OK! va bene!
old vecchio(a)
  how old are you? quanti anni ha?
  I'm ... years old ho ... anni
old age pensioner il/la
  pensionato(a)
olive oil l'olio d'oliva *(m)*
olives le olive
on *(light, engine)* acceso(a)
  (tap) aperto(a)
  on the table sulla tavola
  on time in orario
once una volta
  at once subito
one-way *(street)* a senso unico
onions le cipolle
only solo(a)
open aperto(a)
to open aprire
opera l'opera *(f)*
operation *(surgical)* l'operazione *(f)*
operator *(telephone)* il/la
  centralinista
opposite di fronte a
  opposite the hotel di fronte
  all'albergo
  quite the opposite al contrario
optician's l'ottico *(m)*
or o
orange *(colour)* arancione
orange *(fruit)* l'arancia *(f)*
orange juice il succo d'arancia
orchestra l'orchestra *(f)*
order *(in restaurant)* l'ordine *(f)*
  out of order fuori servizio
to order *(in restaurant)* ordinare
oregano l'origano *(m)*
organic biologico(a)
to organize organizzare
ornament il soprammobile

other l'altro(a)
  the other one l'altro
  have you any others? ce ne sono altri?
our il/la nostro(a)
  our car la nostra macchina
  our hotel il nostro albergo
out *(light)* spento(a)
  he/she's out è fuori
  he's gone out è uscito
outdoor *(pool, etc)* all'aperto
outside: *it's outside* è fuori
oven il forno
ovenproof dish la pirofila
over *(on top of)* sopra
to overbook accettare troppe
  prenotazioni
to overcharge far pagare troppo
overdone *(food)* troppo cotto(a)
overdose l'overdose *(f)*
to overheat surriscaldare
to overload sovraccaricare
to oversleep non svegliarsi in tempo
to overtake *(in car)* sorpassare
to owe dovere
  I owe you... le devo...
  you owe me... mi deve
owner il/la proprietario(a)
oxygen l'ossigeno *(m)*

P

pace il passo
pacemaker il pacemaker
to pack *(suitcase)* fare la valigia
package il pacco
package tour il viaggio organizzato
packet il pacchetto
padded envelope la busta imbottita
paddling pool la piscina per bambini
padlock il lucchetto
Padua Padova
page la pagina
paid pagato(a)
  I've paid ho pagato
pain il dolore
painful doloroso(a)
painkiller l'analgesico *(m)*
to paint *(wall, house)* verniciare
  (picture) dipingere
painting *(picture)* il quadro
pair il paio
palace il palazzo
pale pallido(a)
pan *(saucepan)* la pentola
  (frying pan) la padella

pancake la crêpe
panniers (bike) le borse per la bici
panties le mutandine
pants le mutande
panty liner il proteggislip
paper la carta
paper hankies i fazzolettini di carta
paper napkins i tovagliolini di carta
paragliding il parapendio
paralysed paralizzato(a)
parcel il pacco
pardon? scusi?
  I beg your pardon mi scusi
parents i genitori
park il parco
to park parcheggiare
parking disk il disco orario
parking meter il parchimetro
parking ticket (fine) la multa per sosta vietata
parmesan il parmigiano
  grated parmesan il parmigiano grattugiato
part la parte
partner (business) il/la socio(a)
  (boy/girlfriend) il/la compagno(a)
party (celebration) la festa
  (political) il partito
pass (mountain) il valico
  (bus, train) la tessera
passenger il/la passeggero(a)
passport il passaporto
passport control il controllo passaporti
pasta la pasta
pastry la pasta
  (fancy cake) il pasticcino
path il sentiero
patient (in hospital) il/la paziente
pavement il marciapiede
to pay pagare
  I want to pay vorrei pagare
  where do I pay? dove pago?
payment il pagamento
payphone il telefono pubblico
peace la pace
peaches le pesche
peak rate la tariffa ore di punta
peanut allergy l'allergia alle arachidi (f)
pearls le perle
pears le pere
peas i piselli
pedal il pedale
pedal boat/pedalo il pedalò
pedestrian il/la pedone(a)

pedestrian crossing il passaggio pedonale
to pee pisciare
to peel (fruit) sbucciare
peg (for clothes) la molletta
  (for tent) il picchetto
pen la penna
pencil la matita
penfriend l'amico(a) di penna
penicillin la penicillina
penis il pene
penknife il temperino
pension la pensione
pensioner il/la pensionato(a)
people la gente
pepper (spice) il pepe
  (vegetable) il peperone
per per
  per day al giorno
  per hour all'ora
  per week alla settimana
  per person a persona
  100 km per hour 100 km all'ora
perfect perfetto(a)
performance la rappresentazione
perfume il profumo
perhaps forse
period (menstrual) le mestruazioni
perm la permanente
permit il permesso
person la persona
personal organizer l'agenda elettronica (f)
personal stereo il walkman®
pet l'animale domestico (m)
pet food il cibo per gli animali domestici
pet shop il negozio di animali domestici
petrol la benzina
  4-star petrol la super
  unleaded petrol la benzina senza piombo
petrol cap il tappo del serbatoio
petrol tank il serbatoio della benzina
petrol pump la pompa della benzina
petrol station la stazione di servizio
pharmacy la farmacia
phone il telefono
  by phone per telefono
to phone telefonare
phonebook l'elenco telefonico (m)

phonebox la cabina telefonica
phonecard la scheda telefonica
photocopy la fotocopia
  I need a photocopy mi serve una fotocopia
to photocopy fotocopiare
photograph la foto
  to take a photo fare una foto
phrase book il manuale di conversazione
piano il pianoforte
to pick *(fruit, flowers)* cogliere
  (to choose) scegliere
pickpocket il borseggiatore
pickle i sottaceti
picnic il picnic
  to have a picnic fare un picnic
picnic hamper il cestino per il picnic
picnic rug il plaid
picnic table il tavolo da picnic
picture *(painting)* il quadro
  (photo) la foto
pie *(sweet)* la torta
  (savoury) il pasticcio
piece il pezzo
pier il pontile
pig il maiale
pill la pillola
  to be on the pill prendere la pillola
pillow il guanciale ; il cuscino
pillowcase la federa
pilot il pilota
pin lo spillo
pink rosa
pipe *(water, etc)* il tubo
  (smoker's) la pipa
pity: *what a pity!* che peccato!
pizza la pizza
place il luogo
place of birth il luogo di nascità
plain *(obvious)* chiaro(a) ; evidente
  (unflavoured) naturale
plait la treccia
plan il piano
to plan progettare
plane l'aereo *(m)*
plant la pianta
plaster *(sticking)* il cerotto
  (for broken limb) l'ingessatura *(f)*
plastic *(made of)* di plastica
plastic bag il sacchetto di plastica
plate il piatto

platform *(railway)* il binario
  from which platform? da quale binario?
play *(theatre)* la commedia
to play *(games)* giocare
play area l'area giochi *(f)*
playground il parco giochi
play park il parco giochi
playroom la stanza dei giochi
pleasant piacevole
please per favore
pleased: *pleased to meet you* piacere
plenty l'abbondanza *(f)*
pliers le pinze
plug *(electrical)* la spina
  (for sink) il tappo
to plug in *(appliance)* attaccare
plum la prugna ; la susina
plumber l'idraulico *(m)*
plumbing l'impianto idraulico *(m)*
plunger *(to clear sink)* lo sturalavandini
p.m. del pomeriggio
poached *(egg)* in camicia
  (fish) bollito(a)
pocket la tasca
points *(in car)* le puntine
poison il veleno
poisonous velenoso(a)
police la polizia
policeman/woman il poliziotto/la donna poliziotto
police station il commissariato ; la questura
polish *(for shoes)* il lucido
  (for furniture) la cera
pollen il polline
polluted inquinato(a)
pony il pony
pony trekking le escursioni a cavallo
pool *(swimming)* la piscina
pool attendant il bagnino
poor povero(a)
pope il papa
pop socks i gambaletti
popular popolare
pork la carne di maiale
port *(seaport, wine)* il porto
porter il portiere
  (for luggage) il facchino
portion la porzione
Portugal il Portogallo
Portuguese portoghese
possible possibile
post: *by post* per posta

to post *(letters, etc)* imbucare
postbox la buca delle lettere
postcard la cartolina
postcode il codice postale
poster il poster
postman/woman il/la postino(a)
post office la posta ; l'ufficio postale *(m)*
to postpone rimandare
pot *(cooking)* la pentola
potato la patata
  baked potato la patata al forno
  boiled potatoes le patate lesse
  fried potatoes le patate fritte
  mashed potatoes il purè di patate
  roast potatoes le patate arrosto
potato masher lo schiacciapatate
potato peeler il pelapatate
potato salad l'insalata di patate *(f)*
pothole la buca
pottery la terracotta
pound *(money)* la sterlina
to pour versare
powder: *in powder form* in polvere
powdered milk il latte in polvere
power *(electricity)* l'elettricità *(f)*
power cut l'interruzione di corrente *(f)*
pram la carrozzina
to pray pregare
to prefer preferire
pregnant incinta
  I'm pregnant sono incinta
to prepare preparare
to prescribe ordinare
prescription la ricetta
present *(gift)* il regalo
preservative il conservante
president il presidente
pressure: *tyre pressure* la
  pressione dei pneumatici
  blood pressure la pressione del sangue
pretty carino(a)
price il prezzo
price list il listino prezzi
priest il prete
print *(photo)* la foto
printer lo stampante
prison il carcere ; la prigione
private privato(a)
prize il premio
probably probabilmente
problem il problema
professor il professore/la
  professoressa
programme il programma

prohibited proibito(a)
promise la promessa
to promise promettere
to pronounce pronunciare
  how's it pronounced? come si
  pronuncia?
protein la proteina
Protestant protestante
to provide fornire
public pubblico(a)
public holiday la festa nazionale
pudding il dessert
to pull tirare
to pull over *(car)* accostare
pullover il pullover
pump la pompa
puncture la gomma a terra
puncture repair kit il kit per riparare le
  gomme
puppet il burattino
puppet show lo spettacolo di burattini
purple viola
purse il borsellino
to push spingere
pushchair il passeggino
to put *(to place)* mettere
to put back rimettere
pyjamas il pigiama

Q

quality la qualità
quantity la quantità
quarantine la quarantena
to quarrel litigare
quarter: *a quarter* un quarto
quay il molo
queen la regina
question la domanda
queue la coda
to queue fare la coda
quick veloce
quickly velocemente
quiet *(place)* tranquillo(a)
  a quiet room una stanza tranquilla
quilt la trapunta
quite *(rather)* abbastanza
  it's quite expensive è abbastanza
  caro(a)
  quite the opposite al contrario
quiz show il gioco a quiz

R

rabbit il coniglio
rabies la rabbia
race (sport) la gara
race course l'ippodromo (m)
racket (tennis, etc) la racchetta
radiator (car) il radiatore
  (heater) il termosifone
radio la radio
railcard la tessera di riduzione
  ferroviaria
railway station la stazione dei treni
rain la pioggia
to rain piovere
  it's raining piove
raincoat l'impermeabile (m)
rake il rastrello
rape lo stupro
raped violentata
  I've been raped sono stata violentata
rare (unique) raro(a)
  (steak) al sangue
rash (skin) l'orticaria (f)
rate (cost) la tariffa
rate of exchange il cambio
raw crudo(a)
razor il rasoio
razor blades le lamette
to read leggere
ready pronto(a)
  to get ready prepararsi
real vero(a)
to realize rendersi conto di
rearview mirror lo specchietto
  retrovisore
receipt la ricevuta
receiver (phone) il ricevitore
reception (desk) la reception
receptionist il/la receptionist
to recharge (battery) ricaricare
recipe la ricetta
to recognize riconoscere
to recommend raccomandare
to record (programme) registrare
to recover (from illness) rimettersi
to recycle riciclare
red rosso(a)
to reduce ridurre
reduction la riduzione

to refer to (for information) rivolgersi a
refill (pen) il ricambio
  (lighter) la bomboletta di gas
refund il rimborso
to refuse rifiutare
regarding riguardo a
region la regione
register il registro
to register (letter) assicurare
  (car) immatricolare
  (for class) iscriversi
registered letter la lettera

registration form il modulo d'iscrizione
to reimburse rimborsare
relation (family) il/la parente
relationship il rapporto
to remain restare ; rimanere
to remember ricordare
  I don't remember non mi ricordo
remote control il telecomando
removal firm la ditta di traslochi
to remove togliere
rent l'affitto (m)
to rent (house) affittare
  (car) noleggiare
rental (house) l'affitto (m)
  (car) il nolo
repair la riparazione
to repair riparare
to repeat ripetere
to reply rispondere
report il resoconto
to report (crime) denunciare
request la richiesta
to request richiedere
to rescue salvare
reservation la prenotazione
to reserve prenotare
reserved prenotato(a)
resident residente
resort la località di vacanza
rest (repose) il riposo
  (remainder) il resto
to rest riposarsi
restaurant il ristorante
restaurant car il vagone ristorante
retired: *I'm retired* sono in pensione
to return (go back) ritornare
  (to give back) restituire
return ticket il biglietto di andata e
  ritorno
to reverse fare marcia indietro
to reverse the charges fare una
  telefonata al carico del destinatario

reverse charge call la chiamata a carico del destinatario
reverse gear la retromarcia
rheumatism il reumatismo
rib la costola
rice il riso
rich ricco(a)
ride *(in a car)* il giro in macchina
to ride a horse andare a cavallo
right *(correct)* giusto(a)
right la destra
  at/to the right a destra
  on the right sulla destra
right of way la precedenza
to ring *(bell)* suonare
  (phone) squillare
  it's ringing suona
ring l'anello *(m)*
ring road la circonvallazione
ripe maturo(a)
river il fiume
road la strada
road map la carta stradale
road sign il cartello stradale
roadworks i lavori stradali
roast arrosto(a)
roll *(bread)* il panino
rollerblades i pattini in linea
romantic romantico(a)
roof il tetto
roof-rack il portabagagli
room *(hotel)* la camera
  (space) lo spazio
  double room la camera doppia
  family room la camera per famiglia
  single room la camera singola
room number il numero di camera
room service il servizio in camera
root la radice
rope la corda
rose la rosa
rosé wine il vino rosato
rotten *(food)* marcio(a)
rough *(sea)* mosso(a)
round rotondo(a)
roundabout la rotatoria
row *(in theatre, etc)* la fila
to row *(boat)* remare
rowing boat la barca a remi
rubber *(eraser)* la gomma da cancellare
  (material) la gomma
rubber band l'elastico *(m)*
rubber gloves i guanti di gomma
rubbish la spazzatura

rubella la rosolia
rucksack lo zaino
rug *(carpet)* il tappeto
ruins le rovine
ruler *(for measuring)* il righello
to run correre
rush hour l'ora di punta *(f)*
rusty arrugginito(a)

S

sad triste
saddle la sella
safe *(for valuables)* la cassaforte
safe *(medicine, etc)* senza pericolo
  is it safe? è senza pericolo?
safety la sicurezza
safetybelt la cintura di sicurezza
safety pin la spilla di sicurezza
to sail andare in barca
sailboard la tavola da windsurf
sailing la vela
sailing boat la barca a vela
saint il/la santo(a)
salad l'insalata *(f)*
  green salad l'insalata verde
  mixed salad l'insalata mista
  potato salad l'insalata di patate
  tomato salad l'insalata di pomodori
salad dressing il condimento per l'insalata
salami il salame
salary lol stipendio
sales *(reductions)* i saldi
salesman/woman il/la commesso(a)
sales rep il/la rappresentante
salt il sale
salt water l'acqua salata *(f)*
salty salato(a)
same stesso(a)
sample il campione
sand la sabbia
sandals i sandali
sandwich il panino ; il tramezzino
  toasted sandwich il toast
sanitary towels gli assorbenti
Sardinia la Sardegna
satellite dish l'antenna parabolica *(f)*
satellite TV la televisione via satellite
Saturday il sabato

sauce la salsa
  tomato sauce la salsa di pomodoro
saucepan la pentola
saucer il piattino
sauna la sauna
sausage la salsiccia
to save (life) salvare
  (money) risparmiare
savoury (not sweet) salato(a)
to say dire
scales (weighing) la bilancia
scarf la sciarpa
  (headscarf) il foulard
scenery il paesaggio
schedule il programma
  (timetable) l'orario (m)
school la scuola
  primary school la scuola elementare
  secondary school il liceo
scissors le forbici
score il punteggio
to score (goal) segnare
Scot lo/la scozzese
Scotland la Scozia
Scottish scozzese
scouring pad la paglietta
screen (computer, TV) lo schermo
screen wash il liquido lavavetri
screw la vite
screwdriver il cacciavite
  phillips screwdriver il cacciavite a
  stella
scuba diving le immersioni subacquee
sculpture la scultura
sea il mare
seacat il catamarano
seafood i frutti di mare
seam (of dress) la cucitura
to search cercare
sea sickness il mal di mare
seaside: at the seaside al mare
season (of year) la stagione
  (holiday) il periodo delle vacanze
  in season di stagione
seasonal stagionale
seasoning il condimento
season ticket l'abbonamento (m)
seat (chair) la sedia
  (in theatre, plane, etc) il posto
seatbelt la cintura di sicurezza
seaweed le alghe
second (time) il secondo

second secondo(a)
second class la seconda classe
second-hand di seconda mano
secretary la segretaria
security guard la guardia giurata
sedative il sedativo
to see vedere
to seize afferrare
self-catering con uso di cucina
self-employed autonomo(a)
self-service il self-service
to sell vendere
  do you sell...? vende...?
sell-by date la data di scadenza
Sellotape® lo Scotch®
to send mandare ; spedire ; inviare
senior citizen l'anziano(a)
sensible pratico(a)
separated separato(a)
separately: to pay separately pagare
  separatamente
September settembre
septic tank la fossa settica
serious grave
  (not funny) serio(a)
to serve servire
service (in church) la funzione
  (in restaurant) il servizio
  is service included? il servizio è
  incluso?
service charge il servizio
service station la stazione di servizio
set menu il menù turistico
settee il divano
several alcuni(e)
to sew cucire
sewerage la fognatura
sex (gender) il sesso
  (intercourse) i rapporti sessuali
shade l'ombra (f)
  in the shade all'ombra
to shake (bottle) agitare
shallow basso(a)
shampoo lo shampoo
shampoo and set lo shampoo e messa
  in piega
to share dividere
sharp (razor, blade) affilato(a)
to shave farsi la barba
shaving cream la crema da barba
shawl lo scialle
she ella ; lei
sheep la pecora
sheet (bed) il lenzuolo

1

shelf la mensola
shell *(seashell)* la conchiglia
shellfish i frutti di mare
sheltered riparato(a)
to shine brillare
shingles *(illness)* il fuoco di sant'Antonio
ship la nave
shirt la camicia
shock *(mental)* lo shock
(electric) la scossa
shock absorber l'ammortizzatore *(m)*
shoe la scarpa
shoelaces i lacci delle scarpe
shoe polish il lucido per scarpe
shoe repairer il calzolaio
shoe shop il negozio di calzature
shop il negozio
to shop andare a fare compere
shop assistant il/la commesso(a)
shop window la vetrina
shopping: *to go shopping* fare
compere ; fare la spesa
shopping centre il centro commerciale
shore la riva
short corto(a)
(person) basso(a)
short circuit il corto circuito
short cut la scorciatoia
shortage la carenza
shorts i calzoncini corti
short-sighted miope
shoulder la spalla
to shout gridare
show *(at theatre)* lo spettacolo
to show mostrare
shower la doccia
(rain) il rovescio
to take a shower fare la doccia
shower cap la cuffia da doccia
shower gel il bagnoschiuma
to shrink restringersi
shrub l'arbusto *(m)*
shut *(closed)* chiuso(a)
shutter l'imposta *(f)*
shuttle service la navetta
Sicily la Sicilia
sick *(ill)* malato(a)
(nauseous) nauseato(a)
I feel sick mi sento male
side il lato
side dish il contorno
sidelight la luce di posizione
sidewalk il marciapiede
sieve il setaccio

sightseeing tour il giro turistico
sign il segno
(on road) il segnale
to sign firmare
signature la firma
signpost il segnale
silk la seta
silver l'argento *(m)*
similar to simile a
since *(time)* da
to sing cantare
single *(unmarried)* non sposato(a)
(not double) singolo(a)
(ticket) di (sola) andata
single bed il letto a una piazza
single room la camera singola
sink il lavandino
sir Signore
sister la sorella
sister-in-law la cognata
to sit sedersi
please, sit down prego, si accomodi
size *(of clothes)* la taglia
(of shoes) il numero
to skate *(on ice)* pattinare sul ghiaccio
skateboard lo skateboard
skates *(ice)* i pattini da ghiaccio
(roller) i pattini a rotelle
to ski sciare
ski lo sci
skis gli sci
ski boots gli scarponi da sci
ski instructor il/la maestro(a) di sci
ski jump il trampolino
ski lift lo ski-lift
ski pass lo skipass
ski pole/stick la racchetta da sci
ski run la pista
ski suit la tuta da sci
skin la pelle
skirt la gonna
sky il cielo
sledge la slitta
to sleep dormire
to sleep in dormire fino a tardi
sleeper *(on train)* la cuccetta
sleeping bag il sacco a pelo
sleeping car il vagone letto
sleeping pill il sonnifero
slice *(piece of)* la fetta
sliced bread il pancarrè

slide (photo) la diapositiva
to slip scivolare
slippers le pantofole
slow lento(a)
to slow down rallentare
slowly lentamente
small piccolo(a)
  smaller (than) più piccolo (di)
smell l'odore (m)
  bad smell il puzzo
  nice smell il profumo
to smell (bad) puzzare
  to smell of avere odore di
smile il sorriso
to smile sorridere
smoke il fumo
to smoke fumare
  I don't smoke non fumo
  can I smoke? posso fumare?
smoke alarm l'allarme antincendio (m)
smoked (food) affumicato(a)
smokers (sign) fumatori
smooth liscio(a)
snack lo spuntino
  to have a snack fare lo spuntino
snake il serpente
  (grass) la biscia
snake bite il morso di vipera
to sneeze starnutire
snorkel il boccaglio
snow la neve
to snow: *it's snowing* nevica
snowboard lo snowboard
snowboarding: *to go snowboarding* andare a fare lo snowboard
snow chains le catene da neve
snow tyres i pneumatici da neve
snow plough lo spazzaneve
snowed up isolato(a) a causa della neve
soap il sapone
soap powder il detersivo in polvere
sober sobrio(a)
socket (electric) la presa
socks i calzini
soda water l'acqua di selz (f)
sofa il divano
sofa bed il divano letto
soft soffice ; morbido(a)
soft drink la bibita
software lo software

soldier il soldato
sole (of foot, shoe) la suola
soluble solubile
some di (del/della)
  (a few) alcuni/alcune
someone qualcuno
something qualcosa
sometimes qualche volta
son il figlio
son-in-law il genero
song la canzone
soon presto
  as soon as possible il più presto possibile
sore throat il mal di gola
sorry: *I'm sorry!* mi scusi!
sort il tipo
  what sort? che tipo?
soup la minestra
sour aspro(a) ; agro(a)
soured cream la panna acida
south il sud
souvenir il souvenir
spa la stazione termale
space lo spazio
  (parking) il posteggio
spade il badile
Spain la Spagna
Spanish spagnolo(a)
spanner la chiave inglese
spare parts i pezzi di ricambio
spare room la stanza degli ospiti
spare tyre la gomma di scorta
spare wheel la ruota di scorta
sparkling frizzante
  sparkling water l'acqua gassata
  sparkling wine il vino frizzante
spark plugs le candele
to speak parlare
  do you speak English? parla inglese?
special speciale
specialist lo/la specialista
speciality la specialità
speech il discorso
speed la velocità
speedboat il motoscafo
speed limit il limite di velocità
  to exceed the speed limit superare il limite di velocità
speeding l'eccesso di velocità (m)
speeding ticket la multa per eccesso di velocità
speedometer il tachimetro
to spell scrivere
  how is it spelt? come si scrive?

to spend spendere
spice le spezie
spicy piccante
spider il ragno
to spill rovesciare
spin-dryer la centrifuga
spine la spina dorsale
spirits *(alcohol)* i liquori
splinter la scheggia
spoke *(of wheel)* il raggio
sponge la spugna
spoon il cucchiaio
sport lo sport
sports centre il centro sportivo
sports shop il negozio di articoli sportivi
spot *(stain)* la macchia
  (place) il posto
sprain la slogatura
spring *(season)* la primavera
  (metal) la molla
square *(in town)* la piazza
squash *(game)* lo squash
to squeeze premere ; stringere
squid il calamaro
stadium lo stadio
staff il personale
stage *(theatre)* il palcoscenico
stain la macchia
stained glass il vetro colorato
stain remover lo smacchiatore
stairs le scale
stale *(bread)* raffermo(a)
stalls *(in theatre)* la platea
stamp il francobollo
to stand stare in piedi
star la stella
starfish la stella marina
to start cominciare
starter *(in meal)* l'antipasto *(m)*
  (in car) il motorino d'avviamento
station la stazione
stationer's la cartoleria
statue la statua
stay il soggiorno
  enjoy your stay! buona permanenza!
to stay *(remain)* rimanere
  I'm staying at the Grand Hotel sono
  al Grand Hotel
steak la bistecca
to steal rubare
steamed al vapore
to steam cuocere a vapore
steel l'acciaio *(m)*
steep: *is it steep?* è in salita?

steeple il campanile
steering wheel il volante
step *(stair)* il gradino
stepdaughter la figliastra
stepfather il patrigno
stepmother la matrigna
stepson il figliastro
stereo lo stereo
sterling la sterlina
steward lo steward
stewardess la hostess
to stick *(with glue)* incollare
  (door) incepparsi
sticking plaster il cerotto
still *(motionless)* fermo(a)
  (water) naturale
  (yet) ancora
sting la puntura
to sting pungere
stitches i punti
stockings le calze
stolen rubato(a)
stomach lo stomaco ; la pancia
stomachache il mal di pancia
stone la pietra
to stop *(come to a halt)* fermarsi
  (stop doing something) smettere
stop sign lo stop
store *(shop)* il negozio
storey il piano
storm la tempesta ; il temporale
story il racconto
straightaway subito
straight on diritto
strange strano(a)
straw *(for drinking)* la cannuccia
strawberries le fragole
stream il ruscello
street la strada
street map la piantina
strength *(of person)* la forza
  (of wine) la gradazione alcolica
stress lo stress
strike *(of workers)* lo sciopero
string lo spago
striped a strisce
stroke *(medical)* l'ictus *(m)*
  to have a stroke avere un ictus
strong forte
  strong coffee il caffè ristretto
  strong tea il tè forte

stuck bloccato(a)
student lo studente/la studentessa
student discount lo sconto per studenti
stuffed farcito(a)
stung punto(a)
stupid stupido(a)
subscription l'abbonamento *(m)*
subtitles i sottotitoli
subway *(train)* la metropolitana *(passage)* il sottopassaggio
suddenly all'improvviso
suede il camoscio
sugar lo zucchero
sugar-free senza zucchero
to suggest proporre
suit *(man's)* l'abito *(m)* *(woman's)* il tailleur
suitcase la valigia
sum *(of money)* la somma
summer l'estate *(f)*
summer holidays le vacanze estive
summit il vertice
sun il sole
to sunbathe prendere il sole
sunblock la protezione solare totale
sunburn la scottatura solare
Sunday la domenica
sunglasses gli occhiali da sole
sunny: *it's sunny* c'è il sole
sunrise l'alba *(f)*
sunroof *(car)* il tettuccio apribile
sunscreen la crema solare protettiva
sunset il tramonto
sunshade l'ombrellone *(m)*
sunstroke l'insolazione *(f)*
suntan l'abbronzatura *(f)*
suntan lotion la crema abbronzante
supermarket il supermercato
supper *(dinner)* la cena
supplement il supplemento
to supply fornire
sure sicuro(a) ; certo(a)
  I'm sure sono sicuro(a)
to surf fare il surf
  to surf the net navigare in internet
surfboard la tavola da surf
surgery *(surgical treatment)* la chirurgia
surname il cognome
  my surname is... di cognome mi chiamo...

surprise la sorpresa
suspension *(in car)* la sospensione
to survive sopravvivere
to swallow inghiottire
to swear *(bad language)* dire le parolacce
to sweat sudare
sweater il maglione
sweatshirt la felpa
sweet *(not savoury)* dolce
sweetener il dolcificante
sweets le caramelle
to swell gonfiare
to swim nuotare
swimming pool la piscina
swimsuit il costume da bagno
swing *(for children)* l'altalena *(f)*
Swiss svizzero(a)
switch l'interruttore *(m)*
to switch off spegnere
to switch on accendere
Switzerland la Svizzera
swollen gonfio(a)
synagogue la sinagoga
syringe la siringa

T

table la tavola
tablecloth la tovaglia
tablet *(pill)* la pastiglia
table tennis il ping pong
table wine il vino da tavola
tailor il sarto
to take *(carry)* portare
  (to grab, seize) prendere
  (to take someone to) portare a
  how long does it take? quanto tempo ci vuole?
take-away *(food)* da asporto
to take off decollare
to take out *(of bag)* tirar fuori
talc il borotalco
to talk parlare
tall alto(a)
tampons gli assorbenti interni
tangerine il mandarino
tank la cisterna
  (car) il serbatoio
  (fish) l'acquario *(m)*
tap il rubinetto
tap water l'acqua del rubinetto *(f)*
tape il nastro
tape measure il metro a nastro

5

tape recorder il registratore
target lo scopo
tart la crostata
taste il sapore
to taste assaggiare ; provare
  can I taste some? ne posso
  assaggiare un pò?
tax la tassa ; l'imposta *(f)*
taxi il taxi
taxi driver il/la tassista
taxi rank il posteggio dei taxi
tea il tè
  herbal tea la tisana
  fruit tea il tè alla frutta
  lemon tea il tè al limone
  tea with milk il tè al latte
tea bag la bustina di tè
tea pot la teiera
to teach insegnare
teacher l'insegnante *(m/f)*
team la squadra
tear *(in material)* lo strappo
teaspoon il cucchiaino
teat *(on bottle)* la tettarella
tea towel lo strofinaccio per i piatti
teenager il/la teenager
teeth i denti
telegram il telegramma
telephone il telefono
to telephone telefonare
telephone box la cabina telefonica
telephone call la telefonata
telephone card la scheda telefonica
telephone directory l'elenco
  telefonico *(m)*
telephone number il numero di
  telefono
television la televisione
to tell dire
temperature la temperatura
  to have a temperature avere la febbre
temporary provvisorio(a)
tenant l'inquilino(a)
tendon il tendine
tennis il tennis
tennis ball la pallina da tennis
tennis court il campo da tennis
tennis racket la racchetta da tennis
tent la tenda
tent peg il picchetto
terminal *(airport)* il terminal
terrace la terrazza
terracotta la terracotta
to test *(try out)* provare

testicles i testicoli
tetanus injection l'antitetanica *(f)*
than di
to thank ringraziare
thank you grazie
  thanks very much molte grazie
that quel/quella/quello
  that one quello là
the *(sing)* il/lo/la
  (plural) i/gli/le
theatre il teatro
theft il furto
their il/la loro
them loro ; li ; le
there *(over there)* lì
there is/there are c'è/ci sono
thermometer il termometro
these questi/queste
  these ones questi qui
they loro ; essi/esse
thick spesso(a)
thief il/la ladro(a)
thigh la coscia
thin sottile
  (person) magro(a)
thing la cosa
  my things la mia roba
to think pensare
thirsty: to be thirsty avere sete
this questo/questa
  this one questo(a)
those quei/quelle/quegli
  those ones quelli(e)
thread il filo
throat la gola
throat lozenges le pastiglie per la gola
through attraverso
to throw away buttare via
thumb il pollice
thunder il tuono
thunderstorm il temporale
Thursday il giovedì
thyme il timo
ticket *(bus, train, etc)* il biglietto
  (entry fee) il biglietto d'ingresso
  a single ticket un biglietto di (sola)
  andata
  a return ticket un biglietto di andata
  e ritorno
  tourist ticket il biglietto turistico
  book of tickets il blocchetto di
  biglietti

ticket inspector il controllore
ticket office la biglietteria
tidy ordinato(a)
to tidy up fare ordine
tie la cravatta
tight stretto(a)
tights i collant ; la calzamaglia
tile (floor) la piastrella
till (cash desk) la cassa
till (until) fino a
 till 2 o'clock fino alle due
time il tempo
 (of day) l'ora (f)
 this time questa volta
 what time is it? che ore sono?
 do you have the time? ha l'ora?
timetable l'orario (m)
tin (can) la scatola ; la lattina
tinfoil la carta stagnola
tin-opener l'apriscatole (m)
tip (to waiter, etc) la mancia
to tip (waiter, etc) dare la mancia
tired stanco(a)
tissues i fazzoletti di carta
to a
 to London a Londra
 to the airport all'aeroporto
toadstool il fungo velenoso
toast (to eat) il pane tostato
 (raising glass) il brindisi
tobacco il tabacco
tobacconist's il tabaccaio
today oggi
toe il dito del piede
together insieme
toilet la toilette
 toilet for disabled la toilette per i
 disabili
toilet brush lo spazzolino del
 gabinetto
toilet paper la carta igienica
toiletries gli articoli per l'igiene
token (for phone, etc) il gettone
toll (motorway) il pedaggio
tomato il pomodoro
 tinned tomatoes i pelati
tomato juice il succo di pomodoro
tomato purée il concentrato di
 pomodoro
tomato sauce la salsa di pomodoro
tomorrow domani
 tomorrow morning domani mattina

tomorrow afternoon domani
 pomeriggio
 tomorrow evening domani sera
tongue la lingua
tonic water l'acqua tonica (f)
tonight stasera
tonsilitis la tonsillite
too (also) anche
 too big troppo grande
 too small troppo piccolo(a)
 too hot troppo caldo(a)
 too noisy troppo rumoroso(a)
tool l'attrezzo (m)
toolkit gli attrezzi
tooth il dente
toothache il mal di denti
toothbrush lo spazzolino da denti
toothpaste il dentifricio
toothpick lo stuzzicadenti
top: the top floor l'ultimo piano (m)
top la cima
 (clothing) la maglietta
 on top of sopra di
topless topless
torch (flashlight) la pila
torn strappato(a)
total il totale
to touch toccare
tough (meat) duro(a)
tour il giro
 guided tour la visita guidata
tour guide la guida turistica (m/f)
tour operator l'operatore turistico (m)
tourist il/la turista
tourist information le informazioni
 turistiche
tourist office l'ufficio turistico (m)
tourist route l'itinerario turistico (m)
tourist ticket il biglietto turistico
to tow rimorchiare
towbar la barra di rimorchio
tow rope il cavo da rimorchio
towel l'asciugamano (m)
tower la torre
town la città
town centre il centro città
town hall il municipio
town plan la piantina
toxic tossico(a)
toy il giocattolo
toy shop il negozio di giocattoli
tracksuit la tuta sportiva
traditional tradizionale
traffic il traffico

7 **traffic jam** l'ingorgo *(m)*
traffic lights il semaforo
traffic warden il vigile
trailer il rimorchio
train il treno
  the next train il prossimo treno
  the first train il primo treno
  the last train l'ultimo treno
trainers le scarpe da ginnastica
tram il tram
tranquillizer il tranquillante
to transfer trasferire
to translate tradurre
translation la traduzione
to travel viaggiare
travel agent's l'agenzia di viaggi *(f)*
travel documents i documenti di viaggio
travel guide la guida
travel insurance l'assicurazione di viaggio *(f)*
travel sickness *(sea)* il mal di mare
  (air) il mal d'aria
  (car) il mal d'auto
traveller's cheques i traveller's (cheque)
tray il vassoio
tree l'albero *(m)*
trip la gita ; il viaggio
trolley il carrello
trouble i problemi
  to be in trouble avere qualche problema
trousers i pantaloni
truck il camion
true vero(a)
trunk *(luggage)* il baule
trunks *(swimming)* i calzoncini da bagno
to try provare
to try on *(clothes, shoes)* provare
t-shirt la maglietta
Tuesday il martedì
tumble dryer l'asciugatrice *(f)*
tunnel la galleria
Turin Torino
to turn *(handle, wheel)* girare
  to turn around girarsi
to turn off *(light, etc)* spegnere
  (tap) chiudere
to turn on *(light, etc)* accendere
  (tap) aprire
turquoise *(colour)* turchese
tweezers le pinzette
twice due volte ; il doppio
twin beds i letti gemelli
twins i gemelli

to type battere a macchina
typical tipico(a)
tyre la gomma ; il pneumatico
tyre pressure la pressione delle gomme

U

ugly brutto(a)
ulcer *(stomach)* l'ulcera *(f)*
  (mouth) l'afta *(f)*
umbrella l'ombrello *(m)*
  (sunshade) l'ombrellone *(m)*
uncle lo zio
uncomfortable scomodo(a)
unconscious svenuto(a)
under sotto
undercooked poco cotto(a)
underground *(metro)* la metropolitana
underpants le mutande
underpass il sottopassaggio
to understand capire
  I don't understand non capisco
  do you understand? capisce?
underwear la biancheria intima
to undress spogliarsi
unemployed disoccupato(a)
to unfasten slacciare
United Kingdom il Regno Unito
United States gli Stati Uniti
university l'università *(f)*
unleaded petrol la benzina senza piombo ; la benzina verde
unlikely improbabile
to unlock aprire
to unpack disfare la valigia
unpleasant sgradevole
to unplug staccare
to unscrew svitare
until fino a
unusual raro(a)
up: to get up alzarsi
upside down sottosopra
upstairs di sopra
urgent urgente
urine l'orina *(f)*
us ci ; noi
to use usare
useful utile
usual solito(a)
usually di solito
U-turn l'inversione a U *(f)*

V

vacancy *(in hotel)* la camera libera
vacant libero(a)
vacation la vacanza
vaccination la vaccinazione
vacuum cleaner l'aspirapolvere *(m)*
vagina la vagina
valid valido(a)
valley la valle
valuable di valore
valuables gli oggetti di valori
value il valore
valve la valvola
van il furgone
vase il vaso
VAT l'IVA *(f)*
vegan vegetaliano(a)
 I'm vegan sono vegetaliano(a)
vegetables le verdure
vegetarian vegetariano(a)
 I'm vegetarian sono vegetariano(a)
vehicle il veicolo
vein la vena
Velcro® il velcro®
vending machine il distributore automatico
venereal disease la malattia venerea
Venice Venezia
ventilator il ventilatore
very molto
vest la canottiera
vet il/la veterinario(a)
via passando per
to video *(from TV)* registrare su videocassetta
video il video
video camera la videocamera
video cassette/tape la videocassetta
video game il videogioco
video recorder il videoregistratore
view la vista
villa la villa
village il paese
vinegar l'aceto *(m)*
vineyard la vigna
viper la vipera
virus il virus
visa il visto
visit la visita

to visit visitare
visiting hours l'orario delle visite *(m)*
visitor il visitatore/la visitatrice
vitamin la vitamina
voice la voce
volcano il vulcano
volleyball la pallavolo
voltage il voltaggio
to vomit vomitare
voucher il buono

W

wage il salario
waist la vita
waistcoat il gilè
to wait (for) aspettare
waiter/waitress il cameriere/la cameriera
waiting room la sala d'aspetto
to wake up svegliare
Wales il Galles
walk la passeggiata
to walk andare a piedi
walking boots gli scarponcini
walking stick il bastone
Walkman® il walkman®
wall il muro ; la parete
wallet il portafoglio
to want volere
 I want... voglio...
 we want... vogliamo...
war la guerra
ward *(hospital)* il reparto
wardrobe l'armadio *(m)*
warm caldo(a)
 it's warm fa caldo
to warm up *(milk, etc)* riscaldare
warning triangle il triangolo d'emergenza
to wash lavare
 (to wash oneself) lavarsi
wash and blow dry lo shampoo e messa in piega
washbasin il lavandino
washing machine la lavatrice
washing powder il detersivo in polvere
washing-up bowl la bacinella
washing-up liquid il detersivo per i piatti
wasp la vespa
wasp sting la puntura di vespa
waste bin il bidone della spazzatura

watch l'orologio (m)
to watch guardare
watchstrap il cinturino dell'orologio
water l'acqua (f)
   bottled water l'acqua in bottiglia (f)
   drinking water l'acqua potabile
   mineral water l'acqua minerale
   sparkling water l'acqua gassata
   still water l'acqua naturale
water heater lo scaldabagno
watermelon l'anguria (f)
waterproof impermeabile
to water-ski fare lo sci nautico
watersports gli sport acquatici
waterwings i braccioli salvagente
waves (on sea) le onde
waxing (hair removal) la ceretta
way in l'entrata (f) ; l'ingresso (m)
way out l'uscita (f)
we noi
weak (person) debole
   (tea, coffee, etc) leggero(a)
to wear portare
weather il tempo
weather forecast le previsioni del
   tempo
website il sito web
wedding il matrimonio
wedding anniversary l'anniversario di
   matrimonio (m)
wedding present il regalo di
   matrimonio
wedding ring la fede
Wednesday mercoledì
week la settimana
   last week la settimana scorsa
   next week la prossima settimana
   per week alla settimana
   this week questa settimana
   during the week durante la settimana
weekday il giorno feriale
weekend il fine settimana
   next weekend il prossimo fine
   settimana
   this weekend questo fine settimana
weekly settimanale
   weekly ticket l'abbonamento
   settimanale (m)
to weigh pesare
weight il peso
welcome benvenuto
well bene
well (for water) il pozzo
well-done (steak) ben cotto(a)
wellington boots gli stivale di gomma
Welsh gallese

west ovest
wet bagnato(a)
wetsuit la muta
what cosa
   what is it? cos'è?
wheat il grano
wheel la ruota
wheelchair la sedia a rotelle
wheel clamp il ceppo bloccaruote
when quando
where dove
which qual/quale
while mentre
   in a while fra poco
whipped cream la panna montata
whisky l'whisky (m)
white bianco(a)
who chi
whole tutto
wholemeal bread il pane integrale
whose: whose is it? di chi è?
why perché
wide largo(a) ; ampio(a)
widow la vedova
widower il vedovo
width la larghezza
wife la moglie
wig la parrucca
to win vincere
wind il vento
windbreak (camping) il frangivento
windmill il mulino a vento
window la finestra
   (shop) la vetrina
   (car) il finestrino
windscreen il parabrezza
windscreen wiper il tergicristallo
to windsurf fare il windsurf
windy: it's windy c'è vento
wine il vino
   red wine il vino rosso
   white wine il vino bianco
   dry wine il vino secco
   sweet wine il vino dolce
   rosé wine il vino rosato
   sparkling wine il vino frizzante
   house wine il vino della casa
wine list la lista dei vini
wing (of bird) l'ala (f)
   (of car) la fiancata
wing mirror lo specchietto laterale
winter l'inverno (m)

w/x/y/z eng–italian

wire il filo
with con
  with ice con ghiaccio
  with milk con latte
  with sugar con zucchero
without senza
  without ice senza ghiaccio
  without milk senza latte
  without sugar senza zucchero
witness il/la testimone
woman la donna
wonderful meraviglioso(a)
wood *(material)* il legno
  (forest) il bosco
wooden di legno
wool la lana
word la parola
work il lavoro
to work *(person)* lavorare
  (machine, car, etc) funzionare
  it doesn't work non funziona
work permit il premesso di lavoro
world il mondo
worried preoccupato(a)
worse peggio
worth *(value)* il valore
  it's worth £5 vale cinque sterline
to wrap up *(parcel)* incartare
wrapping paper la carta di regalo
wrinkles le rughe
wrist il polso
to write scrivere
  please write it down lo scriva per favore
writing paper la carta da lettere
wrong sbagliato(a)
  what's wrong? cosa c'è?
wrought iron il ferro battuto

X

x-ray la radiografia
to x-ray radiografare

Y

yacht lo yacht
year l'anno *(m)*
  this year quest'anno
  next year l'anno prossimo
  last year l'anno scorso
yearly *(every year)* annualmente

yellow giallo(a)
Yellow Pages le pagine gialle®
yes sì
yesterday ieri
yet: *not yet* non ancora
yoghurt lo yogurt
  plain yoghurt lo yogurt naturale
yolk il tuorlo
you lei ; tu ; voi
young giovane
your il/la suo(a) ; il/la tuo(a) ; il/la vostro(a)
  your passport il suo passaporto
  your room la sua camera
youth hostel l'ostello della gioventù *(m)*

Z

zebra crossing le strisce pedonali
zero lo zero
zip la cerniera
zone la zona
zoo lo zoo
zoom lens lo zoom

a at ; in
abbaglianti *mpl* full-beam headlights
abbiamo... we have...
  non abbiamo... we don't have...
abbigliamento *m* clothes
abbonamento *m* subscription ; season ticket
abbronzatura *f* suntan
abito *m* dress ; man's suit
aborto *m* abortion
  aborto spontaneo miscarriage
abuso *m* misuse
a.C. B.C.
accamparsi to camp
accanto (a) beside ; next (to)
acceleratore *m* accelerator
accendere to turn on ; to light
  accendere i fari switch on your headlights
accendino *m* cigarette lighter
accensione *f* ignition
accento *m* accent *(pronunciation)*
acceso(a) on *(light, engine)*
accesso *m* access
  divieto di accesso no access
accettazione *f* reception
  accettazione bagagli check-in
accomodarsi to make oneself comfortable
  si accomodi do take a seat
accompagnare to accompany
accordo *m* agreement
acetone *m* nail polish remover
ACI *m* = Automobile Association
acqua *f* water
  acqua calda hot water
  acqua corrente running water
  acqua distillata distilled water
  acqua gassata sparkling water
  acqua minerale mineral water
  acqua naturale still water
  acqua potabile drinking water
acquisto *m* purchase
addetto(a) authorized
adesso now
adulto(a) adult
aereo *m* plane ; aircraft
aeroplano *m* airplane
aeroporto *m* airport
affari *mpl* business
  per affari on business

affittare to rent ; to let
  affitasi for rent
affitto *m* lease ; rent
affogare to drown
agenda *f* diary
agenzia *f* agency
  agenzia di viaggi travel agent
  agenzia immobiliare estate agent
aggredire to attack
aglio *m* garlic
ago *m* needle
  ago ipodermico hypodermic needle
agosto *m* August
AIDS *m* AIDS
aiutare to help
aiuto! help!
alba *f* dawn
albergo *m* hotel
albero *m* tree ; mast
albicocca *f* apricot
alcolici *mpl* alcoholic drinks
alcolico(a) alcoholic
alcool *m* alcohol
alcuni(e) some ; a few
alcuno(a) any ; some
alimentari *mpl* groceries
allacciare to fasten *(seatbelt, etc)*
allarme *m* alarm
  allarmo antincendio fire alarm
allergia *f* allergy
allergico(a) a allergic to
alloggio *m* accommodation
alluvione *f* flood
Alpi *fpl* Alps
alpinismo *m* climbing
alt stop
altezza *f* height
alto(a) high ; tall
  alta stagione high season
  alta marea high tide
altro(a) other
  altri passaporti other passports
alzarsi to get up ; to stand up
amabile sweet *(wine)*
amare to love *(person)*
amarena *f* bitter cherry
amaro(a) bitter *(taste)*
ambasciata *f* embassy
ambiente *m* environment
ambulanza *f* ambulance

ambulatorio m surgery ; out-patients
America f America
americano(a) American
amico(a) m/f friend
ammalato(a) ill
amministratore delegato m managing director
ammontare m total amount
ammortizzatore m shock absorber
amo m bait
amore m love
analisi del sangue f blood test
analcolico m soft drink
analcolico(a) non-alcoholic
analgesico m painkiller
ananas m pineapple
anatra f duck
anca f hip
anche too ; also ; even
ancora still ; yet ; again
  ancora un po'? a little more?
  non ancora not yet
ancora f anchor
andare to go
  andare a cavallo to ride a horse
  andare a piedi to go on foot
  andare bene to fit *(clothes)*
  andare in macchina to go by car
andata: *andata e ritorno* return *(ticket)*
  di (sola) andata single *(ticket)*
andiamo! let's go!
  andiamo a... we're going to...
anestetico m anaesthetic
angina pectoris f angina
anguria f watermelon
anice m aniseed
animale m animal
  animale domestico pet
annata f vintage ; year
  vino d'annata vintage wine
anniversario m anniversary
anno m year
  buon anno! happy New Year!
annuale annual
annullamento m cancellation
annullare to cancel
annuncio m announcement ; advert
antibiotico m antibiotic
anticipo m advance *(loan)*
  in anticipo in advance ; early

anticoncezionale m contraceptive
antifurto m burglar alarm
antigelo m antifreeze ; de-icer
antipasto m starter ; hors d'œuvre
antisettico m antiseptic
antistaminico m anihistamine
anziano(a) m/f senior citizen
ape f bee
aperitivo m apéritif
aperto(a) open
  all'aperto open-air
appartamento m flat ; apartment
appendicite f appendicitis
appuntamento m appointment ; date
apribottiglie m bottle opener
aprile m April
aprire to open ; to turn on *(tap)*
apriscatole m tin-opener
arachide f peanut
arancia f orange
aranciata f orange squash
arancione orange *(colour)*
area f area
  area di servizio service area
argento m silver
aria condizionata f air-conditioning
armadio m cupboard ; wardrobe
arrabbiato(a) angry
arredato(a) furnished
arrestare to arrest
arrivare to arrive
arrivederci goodbye
arrivo m arrival
  arrivi nazionali domestic arrivals
  arrivi internazionali international arrivals
arrosto m roast
arte f art ; craft
articolo m article
  articoli da dichiarare goods to declare
  articoli da regalo gifts
artigiano(a) m/f craftsperson
artista m/f artist
artrite f arthritis
ascensore m lift ; elevator
ascesso m abscess
asciugamano m towel
asciugare to dry
asciugatrice f tumble dryer
ascoltare to listen (to)
asma f asthma
aspettare to wait (for) ; to expect
aspirapolvere m vacuum cleaner

aspirina *f* aspirin
assaggiare to taste
asse *m* axle *(car)*
  asse da stiro ironing board
assegno *m* cheque
assicurato(a) insured
assicurazione *f* insurance
assistente *m/f* assistant
assistenza *f* assistance ; aid
associazione *f* society
assorbenti *mpl* sanitary towels
  assorbenti interni tampons
ATM public transport service
attaccare to attach ; to attack ; to fasten
attacco *m* fit *(seizure)*
  attacco cardiaco heart attack
attendere to wait for
attento(a) careful
attenzione *f* caution
  fare attenzione to be careful
atterraggio *m* landing *(of plane)*
atterrare to land *(plane)*
attestare to declare
attore *m* actor
attracco *m* mooring ; berth
attraente attractive
attraversare to cross
attraverso through
attrazione *f* attraction
attrezzatura *f* equipment
attrezzo *m* tool
attrice *f* actress
auguri! happy birthday! ; best wishes!
aumentare to increase
Australia *f* Australia
australiano(a) Australian
austriaco(a) Austrian
autentico(a) genuine
autista *m/f* driver
auto *f* car
autobus *m* bus
autofficina *f* garage *(for repairs)*
autoforniture *fpl* car parts and accessories
autonoleggio *m* car hire
autore *m* author
autorimessa *f* garage
autorizzazione *f* authorization
autostop *m* hitchhiking
autostrada *f* motorway
autunno *m* autumn

avanti in front ; forward(s)
  avanti! come in!
avere to have
  avere bisogno di to need
  avere fame to be hungry
  avere sete to be thirsty
avvertire to warn
avvisare to inform ; to warn
avviso *m* notice ; advertisement
azienda *f* business ; firm
  azienda di soggiorno local tourist board
azzardo *m* risk ; hazard
azzurro(a) light blue

B

babbo *m* daddy
  Babbo Natale Father Christmas
baciare to kiss
bacinella *f* washing-up bowl
bacio *m* kiss
baci! love and kisses *(in letter)*
baffi *mpl* moustache
bagagli *mpl* luggage
bagagliaio *m* boot *(of car)*
bagaglio *m* luggage
  bagaglio a mano hand luggage
bagnarsi to bathe ; to get wet
bagnino *m* lifeguard
bagno *m* bath ; bathroom
balcone *m* balcony
ballare to dance
balletto *m* ballet
ballo *m* dance
balneazione *f* bathing
  divieto di balneazione no swimming
balsamo *m* hair conditioner
bambino(a) *m/f* child ; baby
bambini *mpl* children
  per bambini for children
bambola *f* doll
banana *f* banana
banca *f* bank
bancarella *f* stall ; stand
banchina *f* platform ; quay
banco *m* counter ; desk
  banco informazioni enquiry desk
Bancomat® *m* cash dispenser
banconota *f* banknote

bandiera f flag
bar m bar ; café
barattolo m tin ; jar
barba f beard
barbiere m barber
barca f boat
barista m/f barman/barmaid
basso(a) low ; short
  bassa marea low tide
basta that's enough
battello m boat
batteria f battery (car)
  batteria scarica flat battery
baule m trunk (luggage)
bavaglino m bib
bello(a) beautiful ; fine ; lovely
benda f bandage
bene well ; all right ; OK
benvenuto welcome
benzina f petrol
  fare benzina to get petrol
bere to drink
bevanda f drink
biancheria f linen (for beds, table)
  biancheria intima underwear
bianco(a) white ; blank
  lasciate in bianco leave blank
biberon m baby's bottle
bibita f soft drink
  bibite soft drinks
bicchiere m glass (for drinking)
bici f bike (pushbike)
bicicletta f bicycle
bidet m bidet
bidone m bin ; dustbin ; can
biglietteria f ticket office
biglietto m ticket ; note ; card
  biglietto d'auguri greetings card
  biglietto da visita business card
bin. abbreviation of **binario**
binario m platform
biologico(a) organic
biondo(a) blond (person)
biro f biro
birra f beer
  birra alla spina draught beer
  birra bionda lager
  birra chiara lager
birreria f bar ; pub
biscotto m biscuit
bisogno m need

avere bisogno di to need
bistecca f steak
bloccare to block
  bloccare un assegno to stop a cheque
blocchetto di biglietti m book of tickets
blocco m block ; notepad
blu blue
blue jeans mpl jeans
boa f buoy
bocca f mouth
boccaglio m snorkel
bocce fpl bowls (game)
bolletta f bill
bollire to boil
bollitore m kettle
bomba f bomb
bombola del gas f gas cylinder
bombolone m doughnut
borotalco m talc
borsa f bag ; handbag ; briefcase
  borsa della spazzatura bin liner
  borsa termica cool-box (for picnic)
borseggiatore m pickpocket
borsellino m purse
bosco m wood ; forest
bottega f shop
botteghino m box office
bottiglia f bottle
bottone m button
boxer mpl boxer shorts
braccialetto m bracelet
braccio m arm
braccioli mpl armbands (swimming)
braciola f steak ; chop
brindisi m toast (raising glass)
brioche f croissant
britannico(a) f British
bronchite f bronchitis
bruciare to burn
bruciore di stomaco m heartburn
brutto(a) bad (weather, news) ; ugly
buca delle lettere f postbox
bucato m washing ; laundry
  bucato in lavatrice machine wash
  bucato a mano hand washing
buco m hole ; leak
buono(a) good
  buon appetito! enjoy your meal!
  buon compleanno! happy birthday!
  buon giorno good morning/afternoon
  buona notte good night

57

buona sera good afternoon/ evening
a buon mercato cheap
buono *m* voucher ; coupon ; token
burattino *m* puppet
burrasca *f* storm
burro *m* butter
burro di cacao *m* lip salve
bussare to knock *(on door)*
busta *f* envelope
bustina di tè *f* tea bag
buttare via to throw away

C

cabina *f* beach hut ; cabin
cabina telefonica phonebox
cacciavite *m* screwdriver
cadere to fall
caffè *m* coffee *(espresso)*
caffè corretto espresso with spirit
such as grappa
caffè macchiato espresso with a
little warm milk
caffè solubile instant coffee
caffellatte milky coffee
caffettiera *f* espresso-maker
calamita *f* magnet
calciatore *m* football player
calcio *m* football ; kick
calcolatrice *f* calculator
caldo(a) hot
calendario *m* calendar
calle *f* street *(in Venice dialect)*
callo *m* corn *(on foot)*
calmante *m* painkiller
calmo(a) calm
calpestare to tread on
calvo(a) bald
calza *f* stocking ; sock
calzamaglia *f* tights
calzature *fpl* shoeshop
calze *fpl* stockings
calzini *mpl* socks
calzolaio *m* shoe mender's
calzoleria *f* shoeshop
calzoncini corti *mpl* shorts
calzoncini da bagno swimming trunks
cambiamento *m* change
cambiare to change
cambiare autobus/treno to change
bus/train
cambiare soldi to change money
cambiarsi to change one's clothes

italian–eng b/c

cambio *m* exchange ; gear
camera *f* room *(in house, hotel)*
camera da letto bedroom
camera doppia double room
camera libera vacancy *(in hotel)*
camera per famiglia family room
camera singola single room
camere vacancies
cameriera *f* chambermaid
cameriere *m* waiter
camiceria *f* shirt shop
camicetta *f* blouse
camicia *f* shirt
camicia da notte nightdress
camion *m* lorry
camminare to walk
camoscio *m* suede
campagna *f* countryside ; campaign
campanello *m* bell
campeggiare to camp
campeggio *m* camping ; campsite
campeggio libero free campsite
camping gas *m* camping gas
campione *m* sample ; champion
campo *m* field ; court
campo da tennis tennis court
campo di calcio football pitch
campo di golf golf course
campo sportivo sports ground
camposanto *m* cemetery
Canada *m* Canada
canadese Canadian
canale *m* canal ; channel
cancellare to erase ; to cancel
cancellazione *f* cancellation
cancro *m* cancer
candeggina *f* bleach
candela *f* candle ; spark plug
candida *f* thrush *(candida)*
cane *m* dog
canile *m* kennel
canna da pesca *f* fishing rod
cannuccia *f* straw *(for drinking)*
canoa *f* canoe
canottaggio *m* rowing
canottiera *f* vest
canotto *m* dinghy *(rubber)*
cantante *m/f* singer
cantare to sing
cantiere *m* building site

cantina f cellar ; wine cellar
canzone f song
capelli mpl hair
capire to understand
  capisce? do you understand?
  non capisco I don't understand
capitale f capital *(city)*
capitolo m chapter
capo m head ; leader ; boss
Capodanno m New Year's day
capogruppo m group leader
capolavoro m masterpiece
capolinea m terminus
capoluogo m county town
capotreno m guard *(on train)*
cappella f chapel
cappello m hat
cappotto m overcoat
cappuccino m cappuccino
capra f goat
carabiniere m policeman
caraffa f carafe
caramelle fpl sweets
carbone m coal ; charcoal
carburante m fuel
carburatore m carburettor
carcere m prison
caricare to charge *(battery)*
carico m load ; shipment ; cargo
carino(a) pretty ; lovely ; nice
carne f meat
carnevale m carnival
caro(a) dear ; expensive
carote fpl carrots
carrello m trolley
carriera f career
carro m cart
  carro attrezzi breakdown van
carrozza f carriage
  carrozze cuccette couchettes
  carrozza letto sleeper
carrozzeria f bodywork
carrozzina f pram
carta f paper ; card ; map
  carta assegni cheque card
  alla carta à la carte
  carta d'argento senior citizen's rail card
  carta di credito credit card
  carta famiglia family rail card

  carta d'identità identity card
  carta igienica toilet paper
  carta d'imbarco boarding card
  carta stradale road map
  carta verde green card
carte da gioco fpl playing cards
cartella f briefcase ; folder
cartello m sign ; signpost
cartine fpl cigarette papers
cartoccio m paper bag
cartoleria f stationer's
cartolina f postcard
casa f house ; home
  a casa at home
casalinga f housewife
casalinghi mpl household articles
cascata f waterfall
casco m helmet
casella postale f post-office box
casinò m casino
caso: in caso di in case of
cassa f vacancies
  cassa chiusa position closed
cassaforte f safe *(for valuables)*
cassetta f cassette
  cassetta delle lettere letterbox
cassetto m drawer
cassiere(a) m/f cashier ; teller
castello m castle
catena f chain ; mountain range
  catene (da neve) snow chains
cattedrale f cathedral
cattivo(a) bad ; nasty ; naughty
cattolico(a) Catholic
causa f cause ; case *(lawsuit)*
  a causa di because of
cavalcare to ride *(horse)*
cavallo m horse
cavatappi m corkscrew
cavo m cable
  cavo da rimorchio tow rope
cavolfiore m cauliflower
CD m CD
c'è there is
cedro m cedar ; lime *(fruit)*
CE f EC
celibe single *(not married)*
cellulare m mobile phone
cena f dinner *(evening meal)*
cenare to have dinner
cenone m New Year's Eve dinner
centimetro m centimetre
cento hundred

centrale central
centralino m switchboard
centro m centre
  centro città city centre
  centro commerciale shopping centre
  centro storico old town
ceppo bloccaruote m wheel clamp
cera f wax *(for furniture)*
ceramica f ceramics ; pottery
cercare to look for
ceretta f waxing *(hair removal)*
cerini mpl matches
cerniera f zip
cerotto m sticking plaster
certificato m certificate
  certificato di nascita birth
  certificate
cervello m brain
cestino m basket ; waste paper bin
che what ; who ; which
  che gusto? what flavour?
  che ore sono? what time is it?
cherosene m paraffin
chi? who?
  di chi è? whose is it?
chiamare to call
  chiamare per telefono to phone
chiamarsi to be called *(name)*
  come si chiama? what's your name?
chiamata f call *(telephone)*
chiave f key
  chiave inglese spanner
chiedere to ask ; to ask for
chiesa f church
chilo m kilo
chilogrammo m kilogram
chilometraggio m mileage *(in km)*
chilometro m kilometre
chiodo m nail *(metal)*
chirurgia f surgery *(operations)*
chitarra f guitar
chiudere to close ; to turn off *(tap)*
  chiudere a chiave to lock
chiuso(a) closed
  chiuso per turno closed for weekly
  day off
  chiuso per ferie closed for holidays
chiusura centralizzata f central
  locking *(car)*
ciabatta f flat bread ; slipper
ciao! hi! ; bye!
cibo m food
cielo m sky
ciliegia f cherry

cinghia della ventola f fan belt
cintura f belt
  cintura di sicurezza seatbelt
cinturino dell'orologio m watchstrap
cioccolato m chocolate
cipolla f onion
circo m circus
circolare to move *(traffic)*
circolazione f traffic
circonvallazione f ring road
cisterna f cistern ; tank
cisti f cyst
cistite f cystitis
CIT f Italian Tourist Agency
citofono m intercom
città f city ; town
cittadino(a) citizen
classe f class
clavicola f collar bone
cliente m/f customer
climatizzato(a) air-conditioned
clinica f clinic
cocco m coconut
cocomero m watermelon
coda f tail ; queue
codice m code
  codice a barra barcode
  codice postale postcode
cofano m bonnet *(car)*
cognata f sister-in-law
cognato m brother-in-law
cognome m surname
  di cognome mi chiamo... my
  surname is...
coincidenza f connection *(train, etc)*
colazione f breakfast ; lunch
collana f necklace
collant mpl tights
collega m/f colleague
colletto m collar
collina f hill
collo m neck ; package
colluttorio m mouthwash
colomba f dove ; Easter cake
colore m colour
Colosseo m Coliseum
colpa f fault
  non è colpa mia it's not my fault
coltello m knife

combustibile m fuel
come like ; as ; how
  come? how? *(in what way)*
  come si chiama? what's your name?
  come si pronuncia? how is it
  pronounced?
  come si scrive? how is it spelt?
  come sta? how are you?
cominciare to begin
commesso(a) m/f assistant ; clerk
commissariato m police station
commozione cerebrale f concussion
comodo(a) comfortable
compagnia f company
  compagnia aerea airline
compilare to fill in *(form)*
compleanno m birthday
completo(a) no vacancies ; full
comporre to dial *(number)*
comprare to buy
compreso(a) included
compressa f tablet
computer m computer
comune m town hall ; commune
con with
  con bagno with bathroom
  con filtro filter-tipped
  con ghiaccio with ice
concerto m concert
conchiglia f seashell
condimento m seasoning ;
  dressing *(for food)*
conducente m/f driver *(taxi, bus)*
confermare to confirm
confine m boundary ; border
congelatore m freezer
congratulazioni! congratulations!
congresso m conference
cono m cone
  cono gelato ice-cream cone
conoscere to know *(to be acquainted
  with)*
consegna f consignment ; delivery
conservante m preservative
consigliare to advise
consiglio m advice
consumare to use up
  da consumarsi entro best before
consumazione f drink
contanti mpl cash
  pagare in contanti to pay cash

contatore m electricity meter
contento(a) happy
continuare to continue
conto m account ; bill
  conto dettagliato itemised bill
  conto in banca bank account
contorno m vegetable side dish
contrabbando m smuggling
contratto m contract
contravvenzione f fine
contro against ; versus
controllare to check
controllo m check ; control
  controllo passaporti passport control
controllore m ticket collector
convalida f date stamp
convalidare to validate *(ticket)*
convincere to persuade
coperta f blanket
coperto m place setting ; cover charge
copertura f cover *(insurance)*
coppa gelato f ice cream served in
  goblet/tub
coppia f couple *(two people)*
copriletto m bedspread
coraggioso(a) brave
corda f rope
cornetto m ice cream cone
corpo m body
corrente f current *(electric, water)*
  corrente d'aria draught
correre to run
corridoio m corridor
corriere m courier
corsa f race ; journey
  corsa semplice single fare
corsia f lane ; hospital ward ; route
  corsia di emergenza hard
  shoulder
  corsia di sorpasso outside lane
corso m course ; avenue
  corso dei cambi exchange rates
  corso intensivo crash course
cortile m courtyard
corto(a) short
cos'è? what is it?
  cos'è successo? what happened?
cosa f thing
  cosa? what?
coscia f thigh
così so ; thus *(in this way)*
cosmetici mpl cosmetics
costa f coast
  Costa Azzurra French Riviera

costare to cost
costoletta f chop
costoso(a) expensive
costruire to build
costume m custom ; costume
  costume da bagno swimsuit
cotone m cotton
  cotone idrofilo cotton wool
cotto(a) cooked
  poco cotto(a) medium rare *(steak)*
cotton fioc® m cotton bud
crampi mpl cramps
cravatta f tie
credere to believe
credito m credit
  non si fa credito no credit given
crema f cream ; custard
  crema da barba shaving cream
crescere to grow
crespella f fried pastry twist
cric m jack *(for car)*
crisi epilettica f epileptic fit
cristallo m crystal
  di cristallo made of crystal
croccante f crisp
croce f cross
crocevia m crossroads
crociera f cruise
crollo m collapse
cronaca f news
cruciverba m crossword puzzle
crudo(a) raw
cuccetta f couchette ; sleeper
cucchiaino m teaspoon
cucchiaio m spoon ; tablespoon
cucina f cooker ; kitchen ; cooking
  cucina a gas gas cooker
cucinare to cook
cucire to sew
cuffia f bathing cap
cuffie fpl earphones
cugino(a) m/f cousin
culla f cradle
cuocere to cook
  cuocere a vapore to steam
  cuocere alla griglia to grill
cuoco m chef
cuoio m leather
cuore m heart
cupola f dome
curva f bend ; corner
cuscino m cushion
custode m caretaker

custodia f case ; holder
cyber-café m internet cafe

D

da from ; by ; with
  da asporto take away *(food)*
  dall'Inghilterra from England
  dalla Scozia from Scotland
danneggiare to spoil ; to damage
danno m damage
dappertutto everywhere
dare to give
  dare su to overlook ; to give onto
  dare la precedenza give way
  dare da mangiare to feed
  dare la mancia to tip *(waiter, etc)*
data f date
  data di nascita date of birth
  data di scadenza sell-by date
dati mpl data
dattero m date *(fruit)*
davanti a in front of ; opposite
dazio m customs duty
d.C. A.D.
debito m debt
decaffeinato(a) decaffeinated
decollare to take-off
decollo m takeoff
delizioso(a) delicious
dente m tooth
dentiera f dentures
dentifricio m toothpaste
dentro in ; indoors ; inside
deodorante m deodorant
  deodorante per ambienti air
  freshener
deposito bagagli m left-luggage
descrivere to describe
descrizione f description
desiderare to want ; to desire
destinazione f destination
destra f right
detergente m cleanser
detersivo m detergent
  detersivo in polvere soap powder
  detersivo per i piatti washing-up
  liquid
detrazione f deduction
dettagli mpl details

deviazione f detour ; diversion
di of ; some
  di cristallo/plastica made of crystal/plastic
  di lusso luxury (hotel, etc)
  di mattina in the morning
  di pomeriggio in the afternoon
  di notte at night
  di stagione in season
  di valore of value ; valuable
diabete m diabetes
diabetico(a) diabetic
diaframma m cap (diaphragm)
dialetto m dialect
diamante m diamond
diapositiva f slide (photo)
diarrea f diarrhoea
dicembre m December
dichiarare to declare
dichiarazione f declaration
dieta f diet
  essere a dieta to be on a diet
dietro behind ; after
  dietro di behind
difetto m fault
difficile difficult
diga f dam ; dyke
digerire to digest
digestivo m after-dinner liqueur
dimenticare to forget
Dio m God
dipinto(a) painted
diramazione f fork (in road)
dire to say ; to tell
diretto(a) direct
  treno diretto through train
direttore m manager ; director
direzione f management ; direction
dirigere to manage (be in charge of)
diritto(a) straight
  sempre diritto straight on
disabile disabled (person)
disastro m disaster
dischetto m floppy disk ; diskette
disco m disk ; record
  disco orario parking disk
discoteca f disco
disdire to cancel
disegno m drawing
disfare la valigia to unpack

disinfettante m disinfectant
disoccupato(a) unemployed
dispiacere: mi dispiace I'm sorry
disponibile available
distaccare to detach ; to unplug
distante far ; distant
distanza f distance
distorsione f sprain
distributore m dispenser
  distributore di benzina petrol station
disturbare to disturb
disturbo m trouble
dito m finger
  dito del piede toe
ditta f firm ; company
diurno(a) day(time)
divano m sofa ; divan
  divano letto sofa bed
diversi(e) several ; various
diverso(a) different
divertente funny (amusing)
divertimento m entertainment ; fun
divertirsi to enjoy oneself
dividere to share
divieto forbidden
  divieto di sorpasso no overtaking
  divieto di sosta no parking
divisa f uniform
divorziato(a) divorced
dizionario m dictionary
DOC abbreviation of **denominazione di origine controllata** (guarantee of wine quality)
doccia f shower
docente m/f lecturer
DOCG abbreviation of **denominazione di origine controllata e garantita** (guarantee of wine quality)
documenti mpl papers (passport)
dogana f customs
dolce sweet (not savoury) ; mild
dolce m sweet ; dessert ; cake
dolcelatte m creamy blue cheese
dolcificante m sweetener
dolciumi mpl sweets
dollari mpl dollars
dolore m pain ; grief
doloroso(a) painful
domanda f question
domandare to ask (a question)
domani tomorrow
  domani mattina tomorrow morning
  domani pomeriggio tomorrow

afternoon
domani sera tomorrow evening/night
domattina tomorrow morning
domenica Sunday
donna f woman
donne Ladies
dopo after ; afterward(s)
dopobarba m aftershave
doppio(a) double
dormire to sleep
dove? where?
dovere to have to
droga f drugs *(narcotics)*
drogheria f grocery shop
duepezzi m bikini
duomo m cathedral
durante during
durare to last
duro(a) hard ; tough ; harsh

E

e and
E east *(abbreviation)*
è is (to be)
ebreo(a) Jewish
ecc. etc.
eccedenza f excess ; surplus
eccesso m excess
eccesso di velocità speeding
eccezionale exceptional
eccezione f exception
ecco here is/are
economico(a) cheap
edicola f newsstand ; kiosk
edificio m building
effetto m effect
effetti personali belongings
egregio(a) dear *(in formal letter)*
elastico m rubber band
elenco m list
elenco telefonico phone directory
elettricista m/f electrician
elettricità f electricity
elettrico(a) electric(al)
elettrodomestici mpl electrical goods
emergenza f emergency
emicrania f migraine
emorroidi fpl haemorrhoids
enoteca f stock of vintage wines

ente m corporation ; body
entrambi(e) both
entrare to come/go in ; to enter
entrata f entrance
entrata abbonati season ticket holders' entrance
entrata libera free admission
epatite f hepatitis
epilessia f epilepsy
epilettico(a) epileptic
equitazione f horse-riding
erba f grass
ernia f hernia
errore m mistake
esame m examination
esatto(a) exact ; accurate
esaurimento nervoso m nervous breakdown
esaurito(a) exhausted ; out of print
tutto esaurito sold out
esca m fishing bait
escluso(a) excluding
escursione f excursion
esente exempt
esente da dogana duty-free
esempio example
per esempio for example
esercizio m exercise ; business
esigenza f requirement
esperto(a) expert ; experienced
esplosione f explosion
esportare to export
esposto(a) exposed
esposto(a) a nord north-facing
espresso m express train ; coffee
espresso(a) express *(parcel, etc)*
essere to be
essere assicurato(a) to be insured
essere capace (di) to be able (to)
essere d'accordo to agree
essere nato(a) to be born
est m east
estate f summer
esterno(a) outside ; external
estero(a) foreign
all'estero abroad
estintore m fire extinguisher
estivo(a) summer
età f age
etichetta f luggage tag ; label

eurocheque m Eurocheque
Europa f Europe
eventuale possible
evitare to avoid

F

fa ago
fabbrica f factory
fabbricare to manufacture
facchino m porter (for luggage)
faccia f face
facile easy
fagiano m pheasant
fallire to fail
fallito(a) bankrupt
fallo m foul (football)
falso(a) fake
fame f hunger
  avere fame to be hungry
famiglia f family
familiare family ; familiar
famoso(a) famous
fanale m light
fanalino dello stop m brake light
fango m mud
farcito(a) stuffed ; filled
fare to do ; to make
  fare attenzione to be careful
  fare la spesa to go shopping
farfalla f butterfly
fari mpl headlights
farina f flour
farmacia f chemist's ; pharmacy
  farmacie di turno duty chemists
farmaco m drug (medicine)
faro m headlight ; lighthouse
fascia f band ; bandage
fastidio: *non mi dà fastidio* I don't
  mind
fatelo da voi m DIY
fatto a mano hand-made
fatto di ... made of ...
fattoria f farm ; farmhouse
fattura f invoice
favore m favour
  per favore please
fax m fax
fazzoletto m handkerchief

fazzoletto di carta tissue
febbraio February
febbre f fever
  avere la febbre to have a
  temperature
  febbre da fieno hay fever
fede f wedding ring
federa f pillowcase
fegato m liver
felice happy
felpa f sweatshirt
femmina f female
feriale workday (Monday-Saturday)
ferie fpl holiday(s)
  essere in ferie to be on holiday
ferire to injure
ferita f wound ; injury ; cut
ferito(a) injured
fermare to stop
fermata f stop
  fermata dell'autobus bus stop
fermo(a) still ; off (machine)
  stare fermo to stay still
ferro da stiro m iron (for clothes)
ferrovia f railway
festa f festival ; holiday ; party
  festa nazionale public holiday
festivo(a) sundays/public holiday
fetta f slice
fiamma f flame
fiammifero m match
fico m fig
fidanzato(a) engaged (to marry)
fieno m hay
fiera f fair (trade)
figlia f daughter
figlio m son
fila f line (row, queue)
  fare la fila to queue
filiale f branch ; subsidiary
film m film (at cinema)
filo m thread ; wire
  filo interdentale dental floss
filtro m filter
  filtro dell'olio oil filter
finanza f finance
  Guardia di finanza Customs and
  Excise
fine f end
  fine settimana weekend
  fine stagione end of season
finestra f window
finestrino m window (car, train)
finire to finish

finito(a) finished
fino(a) fine ; elegant
fino a until ; as far as
  fino alle due till 2 o'clock
fioraio *m* florist's shop
fior di latte *m* cream *(ice cream flavour)*
fiori *mpl* flowers
fiorista *m/f* florist
Firenze Florence
firma *f* signature
firmare to sign
  firmare il registro to sign register
fiume *m* river
focaccia *f* flat salted bread
foglia *f* leaf *(of tree, etc)*
fogna *f* sewer ; drain
folla *f* crowd
folle mad
  in folle in neutral *(car)*
fon *m* hairdryer
fondo *m* back *(of room)* ; bottom
fontana *f* fountain
fonte *f* source
foratura *f* puncture
forbici *fpl* scissors
  forbicine nail scissors
forchetta *f* fork *(for eating)*
foresta *f* forest
forfora *f* dandruff
formaggio *m* cheese
fornaio *m* baker
fornello *m* stove ; hotplate
fornitore *m* supplier
forno *m* oven
  forno a microonde microwave
forse perhaps
forte strong ; loud ; high *(speed)*
fortunato(a) lucky
forza *f* strength ; force
foto *f* photo
fotocopia *f* photocopy
fotocopiare to photocopy
fototessera *f* passport-type photo
foulard *m* headscarf
fra between ; among(st)
  fra 2 giorni in 2 days
  fra poco in a while
fragile breakable
fragola *f* strawberry
frana *f* landslide
francese French
francese *m* French *(language)*
Francia *f* France

francobollo *m* stamp
frappé *m* milk shake
fratello *m* brother
frattura *f* fracture
frazione *f* village
freccia *f* indicator *(car)* ; arrow
freddo(a) cold
frenare to brake
freno *m* brake
  freno a mano handbrake
frequente frequent
fretta *f* hurry
  avere fretta to be in a hurry
friggere to fry
frigorifero *m* refrigerator
frittata *f* omelette
fritto(a) fried
frizione *f* clutch *(car)*
frizzante fizzy ; sparkling
fronte *f* forehead ; front
  di fronte a facing ; opposite
frontiera *f* frontier ; border
frullato *m* milkshake
frutta *f* fruit
  frutta secca dried fruit
frutti di mare *mpl* seafood
fruttivendolo *m* greengrocer
FS Italian State Railways
fuga *f* escape ; leak *(gas)*
fuggire to escape
fulmine *m* lightning
fumare to smoke
  non fumo I don't smoke
fumatori smokers
fumo *m* smoke
funerale *m* funeral
funghi *mpl* mushrooms
  funghi porcini boletus mushrooms
  funghi secchi dried mushrooms
funicolare *f* funicular railway
funzionare to work *(mechanism)*
  non funziona it doesn't work
fuoco *m* fire ; focus
  fuochi d'artificio fireworks
fuori outside ; out
  fuori servizio out of order
furgone *m* van
furto *m* theft
fuseaux *mpl* leggings
fusibile *m* fuse
futuro *m* future

G

gabinetto *m* lavatory
  gabinetto biologico chemical toilet
  gabinetto medico doctor's surgery
galleria *f* tunnel ; gallery ; arcade ;
  circle *(theatre)*
  galleria d'arte art gallery
Galles *m* Wales
gallese Welsh
gamba *f* leg
gara *f* race *(sport)*
garanzia *f* guarantee ; warranty
gas *m* gas
gasolio *m* diesel
gassato(a) fizzy
gassosa *f* lemonade
gastrite *f* gastritis
gatto *m* cat
gay gay *(person)*
gel per capelli *m* hair gel
gelateria *f* ice-cream shop
gelatina *f* jelly
gelato *m* ice cream
gelo *m* frost
geloso(a) jealous
gemelli *mpl* twins ; cufflinks
genere *m* kind *(type)* ; gender
genero *m* son-in-law
genitori *mpl* parents
Genova *f* Genoa
gentile kind *(person)*
Germania *f* Germany
gesso *m* chalk ; plaster *(for limb)*
gettare to throw
  non gettare rifiuti no dumping
gettone *m* token *(for phone)*
ghiaccio *m* ice
ghiacciolo *m* ice lolly
giacca *f* jacket
giallo *m* thriller *(book or film)*
giallo(a) yellow ; amber *(light)*
giardiniere *m* gardener
giardino *m* garden
gilè *m* waistcoat
gin *m* gin
  gin tonic gin and tonic
ginocchio *m* knee
giocare to play ; to gamble

giocattolo *m* toy
gioco *m* game
  gioco a quiz quiz show
gioielleria *f* jeweller's
gioielli *mpl* jewellery
gioielliere *m* jeweller
giornalaio *m* newsagent
giornale *m* newspaper
giornalista *m/f* journalist
giornata *f* day
giorno *m* day
  giorni feriali Monday-Saturday
  giorni festivi Sundays/holidays
giovane young
giovedì *m* Thursday
girare to turn ; to spin
  girarsi to turn around
girasole *m* sunflower
girella *f* scrunchie
giro *m* tour ; turn
  fare un giro a piedi to go for a stroll
  giro turistico sightseeing tour
gita *f* trip ; excursion
  gita in barca boat trip
  gita in pullman coach trip
giù down ; downstairs
giubbotto salvagente *m* life jacket
giudice *m* judge
giugno *m* June
giusto(a) fair ; right *(correct)*
gli the ; to him/it
globale inclusive *(costs)*
goccia *f* drop *(of liquid)* ; drip
gola *f* throat ; gorge
golfo *m* gulf
gomito *m* elbow
gomma *f* rubber ; tyre
  gomma a terra flat tyre
  gomma da cancellare eraser
gommone *m* dinghy *(inflatable)*
gonfiare to inflate
gonfio(a) swollen
gonfiore *m* lump *(swelling)*
gonna *f* skirt
gradazione *f* content *(of alcohol)*
gradevole pleasant
gradino *m* step ; stair
Gran Bretagna *f* Great Britain
grana *f* parmesan cheese
granaio *m* barn
granchio *m* crab
grande large ; great ; big
grande magazzino *m* department store

grandine f hail

granita f water ice *(flavoured)*

grappa f strong spirit *(often drunk with coffee)*

grasso(a) fat ; greasy

gratis free of charge

grattacielo m skyscraper

grattugia f grater

grattugiato(a) grated

gratuito(a) free of charge
  il servizio è gratuito service included

grave serious

grazie thank you

gridare to shout

grigio(a) grey

griglia f grill
  alla griglia grilled

grissini mpl breadsticks

grosso(a) big ; thick

grucce fpl crutches

gruccia f coat hanger

gruppo m group
  gruppo sanguigno blood group

guadagnare to earn

guanciale m pillow

guanto m glove
  guanto da forno oven glove
  guanto di spugna facecloth
  guanti di gomma rubber gloves

guardacoste m coastguard

guardare to look (at) ; to watch

guardaroba m cloakroom

guardia f guard
  Guardia di finanza Customs and Excise

guasto out of order

guerra f war

guida f guide *(person or book)* ; directory
  guida a sinistra left-hand drive
  guida telefonica telephone directory
  guida turistica tour guide

guidare to drive ; to steer

guidatore m driver

guinzaglio m lead *(for dog)*

gustare to taste ; to enjoy

gusto m flavour

H

ha...? do you have...?
  ha l'ora? do you have the time?

hamburger m burger

herpes m cold sore ; herpes

ho... I have...
  ho ... anni I'm ... years old
  ho bisogno di... I need...
  ho fame I'm hungry
  ho fretta I'm in a hurry
  ho sete I'm thirsty

hostess f stewardess

I

i the

identificare to identify

idratante m moisturizer

idraulico m plumber

ieri yesterday

il the

imbarcarsi to embark

imbarcazione f boat

imbarco m boarding
  carta d'imbarco boarding card

imbottigliato(a) bottled

imbucare to post *(letters, etc)*

immediatamente at once

immergere to dip *(into liquid)*

immersioni subacquee fpl scuba diving

immondizie fpl rubbish

immunizzazione f immunisation

impanato coated in breadcrumbs

imparare to learn

impasto m mixture

imperatore m emperor

impermeabile m raincoat

impero m empire

impiego m use ; employment

impiegato(a) m/f employee ; white-collar worker

importante important

importare to import ; to matter
  non importa it doesn't matter

importo m (total) amount

impossibile impossible

imposta f tax *(on income)* ; shutter
  imposta sul valore aggiunto (IVA) value-added tax (VAT)

improbabile unlikely

in in ; to
  in Spagna to Spain
  in vacanza on holiday

inalatore m inhaler

inadempienza f negligence
incantevole charming
incaricarsi di to take charge of
incartare to wrap up (parcel)
incassare to cash (cheque)
incendio m fire
inchiostro m ink
incidente m accident
incinta pregnant
incluso(a) included ; enclosed
incontrare to meet
incontro m meeting (by chance)
incrocio m crossroads ; junction
indicatore m indicator ; gauge
  indicatore del livello dell'olio oil gauge
indicazioni fpl directions
indice m index ; contents
indietro backwards ; behind
indirizzo m address
infarto m heart attack
infatti in fact ; actually
infermeria f infirmary
infermiera f nurse
infezione infection
infiammabile inflammable
infiammazione f inflammation
influenza f flu
informare to inform
  informarsi (di) to inquire (about)
informazioni fpl information
ingessatura f plaster cast
Inghilterra f England
inghiottire to swallow
inglese English
ingorgato(a) blocked (pipe, sink)
ingorgo m blockage ; hold-up
  ingorgo stradale traffic jam
ingresso m entry/entrance
  ingresso gratuito free entry
iniezione f injection
inizio m start
innocuo(a) harmless
inondazione m flood
inoltre besides
inquinato(a) polluted
insalata f salad
  insalata di patate potato salad
  insalata di pomodori tomato salad
  insalata mista mixed salad

insalata verde green salad
insegnante m/f teacher
insegnare to teach
inserire to insert
  inserire le banconote una per volta insert banknotes one at a time
insettifugo m insect repellent
insetto m insect
insieme together
insieme m outfit
insolazione f sunstroke
insulina f insulin
interessante interesting
internazionale international
Internet m Internet
interno m inside ; extension (phone)
intero(a) whole
interpretazione f interpretation
interprete m/f interpreter
interruttore m switch
intervallo m half-time ; interval
intervento m operation
inversione f U-turn
intervista f interview
intestato(a) a registered in the name of
intimi donna mpl ladies' underwear
intorno around
intossicazione alimentare f food-poisoning
introdurre to introduce
inutile unnecessary ; useless
invalido(a) disabled ; invalid
invece di instead of
invernale winter
inverno m winter
investire to knock down (car)
inviare to send
invitare to invite
invito m invitation
io I
ipermercato m hypermarket
ipermetrope long-sighted
Irlanda f Ireland
  Irlanda del Nord Northern Ireland
irlandese Irish
iscritto m member
  per iscritto in writing
iscriversi a to join (club)
iscrizione f inscription ; enrolment
isola f island
istituto m institute

istruttore(trice) m/f instructor
istruzioni fpl instructions
Italia f Italy
italiano(a) Italian
itinerario m route
  itinerario turistico scenic route
itterizia f jaundice
IVA f VAT

J

jolly m joker (cards)

L

l' the ; him ; her ; it ; you
la the ; her ; it ; you
là there
  per di là that way
labbra fpl lips
lacca f lacquer ; hair spray
ladro m thief
lago m lake
lamette fpl razor blades
lampada f lamp
lampadina f lightbulb
lampone m raspberry
lana f wool
largo(a) wide ; broad
lasciare to leave ; to let (allow)
lassativo m laxative
lassù up there
latte m milk
  latte a lunga conservazione long-life milk
  latte di soia soya milk
  latte fresco fresh milk
  latte in polvere powdered milk
  latte intero whole milk
  latte scremato skimmed milk
  latte parzialmente scremato semi-skimmed milk
lattuga f lettuce
lavabile washable
lavaggio m washing
  lavaggio auto car wash
  per lavaggi frequenti for frequent use
lavanderia f laundry (place)
  lavanderia automatica launderette
lavandino m sink
lavare to wash
  lavare a secco to dry-clean
lavarsi to wash (oneself)

lavasecco m dry-cleaner's
lavastoviglie f dishwasher
lavatrice f washing machine
lavorare to work (person)
lavoro m job ; occupation ; work
  lavori stradali road works
  lavori in corso road works
le the ; them ; to her/it ; to you
legge f law
leggere to read
leggero(a) light (not heavy) ; weak
legno m wood (material)
lei she ; her ; you
lentamente slowly
lente f lens (of glasses)
  lente d'ingrandimento magnifying glass
  lenti a contatto contact lenses
lento slow
lenzuolo m sheet (bed)
lesbica lesbian
lesione f injury
lettera f letter
  lettera raccomandata registered letter
lettino m cot
letto m bed
  letto a una piazza single bed
  letto matrimoniale double bed
  letti gemelli twin beds
  letti a castello bunk beds
lettore CD m CD player
lì there (over there)
libero(a) free/vacant
libreria f bookshop
libretto m booklet
  libretto degli assegni cheque book
libro m book
licenza f licence ; permit
  licenza di caccia hunting permit
  licenza di pesca fishing permit
limetta per le unghie f nail file
limite m limit ; boundary
  limite di velocità speed limit
limone m lemon
linea f line ; route
  linea aerea airline
lingua f language ; tongue
lino m linen
liquido m liquid
  liquido dei freni brake fluid

liquido lavavetri screen wash
liquido per lenti a contatto contact lens solution
liquore *m* liqueur
liquori *mpl* spirits *(alcohol)*
liscio(a) straight ; smooth
lista *f* list
lista dei vini wine list
listino prezzi *m* price list
litro *m* litre
livello *m* level
lo him ; it
locale local
locale *m* room ; place ; local train
locale notturno nightclub
località di vacanza *f* resort
locanda *f* inn
Londra *f* London
lontano(a) far
lozione *f* lotion
lozione solare suntan lotion
lucchetto *m* padlock
lucchetto della bici bike lock
luce *f* light
lucertola *f* lizard
luglio *m* July
lui him
lumaca *f* snail
luna *f* moon
luna di miele honeymoon
luna park *m* funfair
lunedì *m* Monday
lunghezza *f* length
lungo(a) long
lungo la strada along the street
a lungo for a long time
lungomare *m* promenade ; seafront
luogo *m* place
luogo di nascita place of birth
lupo *m* wolf
lusso *m* luxury
di lusso luxury *(hotel, etc)*

M

ma but
macchia *f* stain ; mark
macchina *f* car ; machine
macchina a noleggio hire car
macchina fotografica camera

macchina sportiva sports car
macedonia *f* fruit salad
macellaio *m* butcher's
macinato(a) ground *(coffee, meat)*
madre *f* mother
magazzino *m* warehouse
maggio *m* May
maggiore larger ; greater ; largest ; older ; oldest
maglietta *f* t-shirt
maglione *m* jumper ; sweater
magro(a) thin *(person)* ; low-fat ; lean *(meat)*
mai never ; ever
maiale *m* pig ; pork
mal *see* **male**
malato(a) ill ; sick
malattia *f* disease
malattia venerea venereal disease
male badly *(not well)*
male *m* pain ; ache
mal d'aria air sickness
mal d'auto car sickness
mal d'orecchi earache
mal di denti toothache
mal di gola sore throat
mal di mare sea sickness
mal di pancia stomachache
mal di testa headache
maltempo *m* bad weather
mamma *f* mum(my)
mancia *f* tip *(to waiter, etc)*
mandare to send
mandare per fax to fax
mangiare to eat
mangiare fuori to eat out
manica *f* sleeve
la Manica the English Channel
mano *f* hand
fatto(a) a mano handmade
Mantova *f* Mantua
manuale di conversazione *m* phrase book
manzo *m* beef
marca *f* brand *(make)*
marcia *f* gear *(car)* ; march
marciapiede *m* pavement
mare *m* sea ; seaside
Mare del Nord North Sea
margarina *f* margarine
margherita *f* daisy
marina *f* navy
marito *m* husband

1

marmellata f jam
  marmellata d'arance marmalade
marrone m brown ; chestnut
marsupio m bumbag ; money belt
martedì m Tuesday
  martedì grasso Shrove Tuesday
martello m hammer
marzo m March
maschera f mask ; fancy dress
maschile masculine ; male
massimo(a) maximum
masticare to chew
materassino m airbed ; lilo
materasso m mattress
materiale m material
matrigna f stepmother
matrimonio m wedding
mattina f morning
  di mattina in the morning
matto(a) mad
mazza f mallet
  mazze da golf golf clubs
meccanico m mechanic ; repair shop
medicina f medicine
medico m doctor
Mediterraneo m Mediterranean
medusa f jellyfish
meglio better ; best
  meglio di better than
mela f apple
melanzana f aubergine ; eggplant
melone m melon
membro m member
meningite f meningitis
meno less ; minus
mensa f canteen
mensile monthly
mensilmente monthly
mensola f shelf
menta f mint
mento m chin
mentre while ; whereas
menù m menu
  menù alla carta à la carte menu
  menù a prezzo fisso set-price menu
  menù turistico set menu
meraviglioso(a) wonderful
mercatino dell'usato m flea market
mercato m market
merce f goods
merci fpl freight ; goods
mercoledì m Wednesday
merenda f snack

meridionale southern
mese m month
messa f mass *(in church)*
messaggio m message
mestruazioni fpl period *(menstrual)*
metà f half
  metà prezzo half-price
metro m metre
  metro a nastro tape measure
metropolitana f underground ; metro
mettere to put ; to put on *(clothes)*
  mettersi in contatto con to contact
mezzanotte f midnight
mezzi mpl means ; transport
mezzo m middle
mezzo(a) half
  mezza pensione half board
mezzogiorno m midday ; noon
  il Mezzogiorno the south of Italy
mezz'ora f half an hour
mi me ; to me ; myself
mia my
miele m honey
migliorare to improve
migliore better ; best
Milano Milan
miliardo m billion
milione m million
mille thousand
millimetro m millimetre
minestra f soup
minimo m minimum
ministro m minister *(political)*
minorenne underage
minori mpl minors
minuto m minute
mio my
miscela f blend
misto(a) mixed
mittente m/f sender
MM metro ; underground
mobili mpl furniture
moda f fashion
moderno(a) modern
modo m way ; manner
modulo m form *(document)*
  modulo d'iscrizione registration form
moglie f wife
molletta f clothes peg
  molletta per capelli hairgrip

molo m jetty ; quay ; pier
molti(e) many
  molte grazie thanks very much
molto much ; a lot ; very
  molto tempo for a long time
  molta gente lots of people
monastero m monastery
moneta f coin ; currency
montagna f mountain
monumento m monument
mordere to bite *(animal)*
morire to die
morsicare to bite *(insect)*
morsicato(a) bite *(from insect)*
morso(a) bitten
morto(a) dead
mosca f fly
moscerino m midge ; gnat
moschea f mosque
mosso(a) rough *(sea)* ; ruffled
mostra f exhibition
mostrare to show
moto f motorbike
motore m engine ; motor
motorino m moped
motorino d'avviamento m
  starter motor
multa f fine *(to be paid)*
municipio m town hall
muro m wall
museo m museum
musica f music
muta f wetsuit
mutande fpl underpants
mutandine fpl knickers ; panties

N

N north *(abbreviation)*
nafta f diesel
Napoli Naples
nascita f birth
naso m nose
nastro m tape ; ribbon
nato(a) born
nauseato(a) nauseous
nave f ship
nave-traghetto f ferry
nazionale national ; domestic *(flight)*

nazionalità f nationality
nazione f nation
né … né neither … nor
nebbia f fog
necessario(a) necessary
negativo m negative *(photo)*
negozio m shop
nero(a) black
nessuno(a) no ; nobody ; none
netto m net
  al netto di IVA net of VAT
neve f snow
nevicare to snow
niente nothing
  niente da dichiarare nothing to
  declare
nipote f granddaughter ; niece
nipote m grandson ; nephew
noce f walnut
nocivo(a) harmful
nodo m knot ; bow
  nodo ferroviario junction *(railway)*
noi we
noleggiare to hire
noleggio m hire
  noleggio auto car hire
  noleggio barche boat hire
  noleggio bici bike hire
  noleggio sci ski hire
nolo m hire
nome m name ; first name ;
  nome da ragazza maiden name
non not
  non ancora not yet
  non funziona it doesn't work
  non capisco I don't understand
  non pericoloso(a) safe
non-fumatore m/f non-smoker
nonna f grandmother
nonno m grandfather
nord m north
nostro(a) our
notare to notice
notizie fpl news
notte f night
  notte di San Silvestro New Year's Eve
  di notte at night
novembre m November
nubile single *(woman)*
nulla nothing ; anything
nullo(a) void *(contract)*
numero m number ; size *(of shoe)*
  numero di camera room number
  numero del conto account number
  numero di telefono phone number

nuora f daughter-in-law
nuotare to swim
Nuova Zelanda f New Zealand
nuovo(a) new
  di nuovo again
nuvoloso(a) cloudy

O

o or
O west (*abbreviation*)
obbligatorio(a) compulsory
oceano m ocean
occasione f opportunity ; bargain
occhiali mpl glasses
  occhiali da sci skiing goggles
  occhiali da sole sunglasses
occhio m eye
occupato(a) busy/engaged
odore m smell
offerta f offer
officina f workshop ; repair shop
oggetto m object
oggi today
ogni each ; every
  ogni giorno every day ; daily
  ogni quanto? how often?
  ogni tanto occasionally
olio m oil
  olio solare suntan oil
  olio di girasole sunflower oil
  olio d'oliva olive oil
olive fpl olives
oltre beyond ; besides
ombra f shade
  all'ombra in the shade
ombrello m umbrella
ombrellone m sun umbrella
ombretto m eye shadow
omogemeizzati mpl baby food
omosessuale homosexual
onde fpl waves
onestà f honesty
onesto(a) honest
opera f opera
operatore turistico m tour operator
operazione f operation (*surgical*)
opuscolo m brochure
ora now
ora f hour
  ora di punta rush hour
  che ore sono? what's the time?
orario m timetable

in orario on time
orario di apertura opening hours
orario di cassa banking hours
orario visite visiting hours
ordinare to order ; to prescribe
ordine f order (*in restaurant*)
ordinato(a) tidy
orecchini mpl earrings
orecchio m ear
orecchioni mpl mumps
oreficeria f jeweller's
orina f urine
ormeggiare to moor
ormeggio m mooring
oro m gold
  placcato oro gold-plated
orologeria m watchmaker's
orologio m clock ; watch
orticaria f rash (*skin*)
ortografia f spelling
ospedale m hospital
ospite m/f guest ; host/hostess
osso m bone
ostello m hostel
  ostello della gioventù youth hostel
osteria f inn
ottenere to get ; obtain
  ottenere la linea to get through (*on phone*)
ottimo(a) excellent
ottobre m October
otturazione f filling (*in tooth*)
ovest m west

P

pacchetto m packet
pacco m package ; parcel
padella f frying-pan
Padova Padua
padre m father
padrone(a) m/f owner
paesaggio m scenery ; countryside
paese m country (*nation*) ; village
pagare to pay ; to pay for
pagato(a) paid
pagina f page
paio m pair
palazzo m building ; block of flats ; palace

palestra f gym
palla f ball
pallina f ball (small)
  pallina da golf golf ball
  pallina da tennis tennis ball
pallone m football
pandoro m Italian Christmas cake
pane m bread ; loaf
  pane integrale wholemeal bread
  pane carré sandwich bread
  pane e coperto cover charge
  pane di segale rye bread
pannettone m Italian Christmas cake
panetteria f baker's
pangrattato m breadcrumbs
panificio m bakery
panino m bread roll
  panino imbottito sandwich
paninoteca f sandwich bar
panna f cream
panno m cloth ; fabric
pannolini mpl nappies
pantaloni mpl trousers
  pantaloni corti shorts
pantofole fpl slippers
papa m pope
papà m daddy
parabrezza m windscreen
paraurti m bumper (on car)
parcheggiare to park
parcheggio m car park
  parcheggio custodito supervised car-park
  parcheggio libero free parking
  parcheggio sotterraneo underground car park
parchimetro m parking meter
parco m park
  parco nazionale national park
parente m/f relation ; relative
Parigi f Paris
parlare to speak ; to talk
parmigiano m parmesan
  parmigiano grattugiato grated parmesan
parola f word
parolaccia f swear word
parrucchiere(a) m/f hairdresser
parte f share ; part ; side
partenza f departures
  partenze internazionali international departures
  partenze nazionali domestic departures

partire to depart ; to leave
partita f match ; game
  partita di calcio football match
passaggio m passage ; lift (in car)
  dare un passaggio to give a lift
passaporto m passport
passeggiata f walk ; stroll
passeggino m pushchair
passo m pace ; pass (mountain)
  passo carrabile keep clear
  passo chiuso pass closed
pasticcino m cake (small, fancy)
pastiglia f tablet (pill)
pasto m meal
pastorizzato pasteurised
patata f potato
patatine fpl crisps
  patatine frite chips
patente f permit ; driving licence
patrigno m stepfather
pavimento m floor
paziente m/f patient
pecora f sheep
pedaggio m toll (motorway)
pedale m pedal
pedalò m pedalboat
pedicure m chiropodist
pedoni mpl pedestrians
peggio worse
pelati mpl tinned tomatoes
pelle f skin ; hide ; leather
pellegrino m pilgrim
pelletterie fpl leather goods
pellicola f film (for camera)
  pellicola a colori colour film
  pellicola in bianco e nero black and white film
pelo m fur
pene m penis
penicillina f penicillin
penisola f peninsula
penna f pen
pensare to think
pensione f guesthouse
  pensione completa full board
  mezza pensione half board
  pensione familiare bed and breakfast
pentola f saucepan
pepe m pepper (spice)
per for ; per ; in order to
  per esempio for example
  per favore please
  per via aerea air mail
pera f pear

perché why ; because ; so that
percorso *m* walk ; journey ; route
 percorso panoramico scenic route
perdere to lose ; to miss *(train, etc)*
perdita *f* leak *(of gas, liquid)*
pericolante unsafe
pericolo *m* danger
pericoloso(a) dangerous
 non pericoloso(a) safe
periferia *f* outskirts ; suburbs
permanente continua parking
 restrictions still apply
permanenza *f* stay ; residency
permesso *m* licence ; permit
 permesso! excuse me! *(to get by)*
 permesso di soggiorno
 residence permit
permettere to allow
perso(a) lost *(object)* ; missed *(train, plane, etc)*
persona *f* person
personale *m* staff
pesante heavy
pesare to weigh
pesca *f* angling ; fishing ; peach
 divieto di pesca no fishing
pescare to fish
pesce *m* fish
pescivendolo *m* fishmonger's
peso *m* weight
pettine *m* comb
petto *m* chest ; breast
 petto di pollo chicken breast
pezzo *m* piece ; bit ; cut *(of meat)*
piacere to please
 le piace? do you like it?
 piacere! pleased to meet you!
piangere to cry *(weep)*
piano slowly ; quietly
piano *m* floor *(of building)* ; plan
pianta *f* map ; plan ; plant
pianterreno *m* ground floor
piantina *f* street map
piatto *m* dish ; course ; plate
 primo piatto first course
piazza *f* square *(in town)*
piazzale *m* large square
piazzola (di sosta) *f* lay-by
piccante spicy ; hot
picchetto *m* tent peg
piccolo(a) little ; small
piede *m* foot
 a piedi on foot

pieno(a) full
pietra *f* stone
pigiama *m* pyjamas
pigro(a) lazy
pila *f* battery ; torch
pillola *f* pill
pinne *fpl* flippers
pino *m* pine
pinze *fpl* pliers
pinzette *fpl* tweezers
pioggia *f* rain
piombo *m* lead *(metal)*
piovere to rain
piscina *f* swimming pool
 piscina per bambini paddling pool
pista *f* track ; race track
 pista da ballo dance floor
 pista da sci ski run
più more ; most ; plus
 più di more than
 più economico(a) cheaper
 più tardi later
piumino *m* duvet
pizzeria *m* pizza restaurant
pizzico *m* pinch ; sting
pizzo *m* lace
plastica *f* plastic
 di plastica made of plastic
pneumatico *m* tyre
po' a little *(shortened form of **poco**)*
pochi(e) few
poco(a) little ; not much
 un po' a little
poi then
polizia *f* police
 polizia stradale traffic police
poliziotto *m* policeman
polizza *f* policy
pollo *m* chicken
polmone *m* lung
poltrona *f* armchair ; seat in stalls
pomata *f* ointment
pomeriggio *m* afternoon
 di pomeriggio in the afternoon
pomodoro *m* tomato
pompa *f* pump
pompelmo *m* grapefruit
ponte *m* bridge ; deck
 ponte macchine car deck
pontile *m* jetty ; pier

porcellana f china

porta f door ; gate ; goal
porta di sicurezza emergency exit

portabagagli m luggage rack ;
porter *(at airport, station, etc)*

portacenere m ashtray

portafoglio m wallet

portare to carry/bring ; to wear

portiere m porter *(doorkeeper)* ; goal-keeper

portineria f caretaker's lodge

porto m port ; harbour
porto di scalo port of call

Portogallo m Portugal

porzione f portion ; helping

posate fpl cutlery

posologia f dosage

possiamo we can
non possiamo we cannot

posso I can
non posso I cannot

posta f post office ; mail
posta elettronica e-mail
posta raccomandata registered mail

posteggio m car park
posteggio taxi taxi rank

posto m place ; job ; seat
posti in piedi standing room
posti a sedere seating capacity
posti prenotati reserved seats

potabile ok to drink

potere to be able

pranzo m lunch

pré-maman m maternity dress

preavviso m advance notice

precotto(a) ready-cooked

predeterminare l'importo desiderato
select required amount

preferire to prefer

preferito(a) favourite

prefisso m prefix ; area code
prefisso telefonico dialling code

pregare to pray
si prega... please...

prego don't mention it!

prelievo m collection ; sample

premere to push ; to press

premio m prize

prendere to take ; to catch *(bus, etc)*
prendere il sole to sunbathe
prendere in prestito to borrow

prenome m first name

prenotare to book ; to reserve

prenotato(a) reserved

prenotazione f reservation

preoccupato(a) worried

preparare to prepare ; to get ready

presa f socket *(electric)*

preservativo m condom

pressione del sangue f blood pressure

prestare to lend

presto early ; soon

prete m priest

previsione f forecast
previsioni del tempo weather forecast

previsto(a) scheduled ; expected
come previsto as expected

prezzo m price
prezzo al dettaglio retail price
prezzo fisso set price
prezzo di catalogo list price
prezzo al minuto retail price
prezzo d'ingresso entrance fee

prima di before

primavera f spring *(season)*

primo(a) first ; top ; early
primo piano first floor
primo piatto first course

principale main

principiante m/f beginner

privato(a) private

problema m problem

professione f profession

professore m/f teacher ; professor

profondità f depth

profondo(a) deep

profumeria f perfume shop

progettare to plan

programma m programme ;
syllabus ; schedule

proibire to ban ; to prohibit

proibito(a) forbidden ; prohibited

prolunga f extension *(electrical)*

promettere to promise

pronto(a) ready
pronto! hello! *(on telephone)*
pronto soccorso casualty

proprietario(a) m/f owner

proprio(a) own

prossimamente coming soon

prossimo(a) next

proteggislip m panty liner

protesi dell'anca f hip replacement

protestante Protestant
provare to try ; to test *(try out)* ; to try on *(clothes)*
provvisorio(a) temporary
prugna f plum
PTP *abbreviation of* **Posto Telefonico Pubblico**
pubblicità f advertisement
pubblico m audience ; public
pulce f flea
pulito(a) clean
pulizia f cleaning
pulizia del viso facial
pullman m coach
pulmino m minibus
punteggio m score
puntine fpl points
punto m point ; stitch ; full stop
punto d'incontro meeting place
puntura f bite ; sting ; injection
puzzle m jigsaw
puzzo m bad smell

Q

qua here
quaderno m exercise book
quadro m picture ; painting
qual(e) what ; which ; which one
qualche some
qualche volta sometimes
qualcosa something ; anything
qualcuno someone ; somebody
qualificato(a) qualified
qualità f quality
qualsiasi any
qualunque any
quando? when?
quanto(a)? how much?
quanti(e)? how many?
quartiere m district
quarto m quarter
quarto d'ora quarter of an hour
quattro four
quei those ; those ones
quel(la) that ; that one
quelli(e) those ; those ones
quello(a) that ; that one
questi(e) these ; these ones
questo(a) this ; this one
questura f police station
qui here

quindi then ; therefore
quindici giorni fortnight
quotidiano m daily (paper)
quotidiano(a) daily

R

rabarbaro m rhubarb
rabbia f anger ; rabies
racchetta f racket ; bat
racchetta da neve snowshoe
racchetta da sci ski pole
raccomandare to recommend
racconto m story
radiatore m radiator
radio f radio
radiografia f x-ray
raffreddore m cold *(illness)*
raffreddore da fieno hay fever
ragazza f girl ; girlfriend
ragazza alla pari au pair
ragazzo m boy ; boyfriend
RAI f Italian State Broadcasting
rallentare to slow down
rapido m express train
rapido(a) high-speed ; quick
rasoio m razor
rasoio elettrico electric razor
reato m crime
recarsi alla cassa pay at cash desk
recentemente recently
reclamo m complaint
recupero monete returned coins
regalo m present ; gift
reggiseno m bra
regione f region ; district ; area
registrare to record
registratore m cassette player
registro m register
Regno Unito m United Kingdom
regolamento m regulation
regolare regular ; steady
remare to row *(boat)*
rendersi conto di to realize
rene m kidney
reparto m department ; ward
restare to stay ; to remain
restituire to return ; to give back
restituzione f return ; repayment

r italian-eng

resto m remainder ; change *(money)*
restringersi to shrink
rete f net ; goal
  rete portabagagli rack *(luggage)*
retro m back
  vedi retro please turn over
retromarcia f reverse gear
reumatismo m rheumatism
ricambio m spare part ; refill
ricaricare to recharge *(battery)*
ricetta f prescription ; recipe
ricevere to receive ; to welcome
ricevitore m receiver *(phone)*
ricevuta f receipt
richiedere to require
richiesta f request
riciclare to recycle
riconoscere to recognize
riconoscimento m identification
ricordare to remember
  non mi ricordo I don't remember
ricordo m souvenir ; memory
ricorrere a to resort to
ricoverare to admit *(to hospital)*
ridere to laugh
ridurre to reduce
riduttore m adaptor
riduzione f reduction
riempire to fill
rientro m return ; return home
rifare to do again ; to repair
rifiutare to refuse
rifiuti mpl rubbish ; waste
rifugio m mountain inn ; shelter
righello m ruler *(for measuring)*
rigore m penalty *(football)*
riguardo m care ; respect
  riguardo a... regarding...
rilasciato(a) a issued at
rimandare to postpone
rimanere to stay ; to remain
rimborsare to reimburse
rimborso m refund
rimessa f remittance ; garage
rimettere to put back
rimettersi to recover *(from illness)*
rimorchiare to tow
rimorchio m trailer
  a rimorchio on tow

rimozione f removal ; towing away
Rinascimento m Renaissance
rinfreschi mpl refreshments
ringraziare to thank
rinnovare to renew
rinunciare to give up
riparare to repair
riparato(a) sheltered
riparazione f repair
ripetere to repeat
ripido(a) abrupt ; steep
ripiegare to fold
ripieno m stuffing
riposarsi to rest
riposo m rest *(repose)*
risalita f reascent
risarcimento m compensation
riscaldamento m heating
riscaldare to heat up *(food)*
rischio m risk
risciacquare to rinse
riscuotere to collect ; to cash
riserva f reserve ; reservation
  riserva di caccia private hunting
  riserva naturale nature reserve
riservare to reserve
riservato(a) reserved
riso m rice ; laugh
risotto m rice cooked in stock
risparmiare to save *(money)*
rispondere to answer ; to reply
risposta f answer
ristorante m restaurant
ritardo m delay
ritirare to withdraw
ritiro m retirement ; withdrawal
  ritiro bagagli baggage reclaim
ritornare to return *(go back)*
ritorno m return
riunione f meeting
riuscita f result ; outcome
riva f bank ; shore
riviera f riviera
rivista f magazine ; revue
rivolgersi a to refer to *(for info)*
roba f stuff ; belongings
roccia f rock
rognoni mpl kidneys
romanico(a) Romanesque
romanzo m novel
  romanzo rosa romantic novel
rompere to break

rondine f swallow *(bird)*
rosa pink
rosa f rose
rosmarino m rosemary
rosolia f German measles ; rubella
rossetto m lipstick
rosso(a) red
rosticceria f shop selling cooked food
rotonda f roundabout
rotondo(a) round
rotto(a) broken
roulotte f caravan
rovesciare to spill ; to knock over
rovine fpl ruins
rtd delay
rubare to steal
rubinetto m tap
rubrica f address book
ruggine f rust
rughe fpl wrinkles
rullino m roll of film
rum m rum
rumore m noise
rumoroso(a) noisy
ruota f wheel
   ruota di scorta spare wheel
rupe f mountain cliff
ruscello m stream
russare to snore

S

S south *(abbreviation)*
sabato Saturday
sabbia f sand
saccarina f saccharin
sacchetto m small bag
   sacchetto di carta paper bag
   sacchetto di plastica plastic bag
sacco a pelo m sleeping bag
sacerdote m priest
sagra f local food festival
sala f hall ; auditorium
   sala da pranzo dining room
   sala d'aspetto waiting room
   sala partenze departure lounge
salame m salami
salario m wage
salato(a) salted ; savoury
saldare to settle *(bill)* ; to weld
saldi sale
saldo m payment ; balance

sale m salt
salire to rise ; to go up
   salire in to get in *(vehicle)*
salita f climb ; slope
   in salita uphill
salmone m salmon
   salmone affumicato smoked salmon
salone m lounge ; salon
salotto m living room ; lounge
salsa f sauce
salsiccia f sausage
saltare to jump
saltato(a) sautéed
salumeria f delicatessen
salumi mpl cured pork meats
salute f health
   salute! cheers!
saluto m greeting
salvagente m life belt
salvare to rescue ; to save *(life)*
salvavita m circuit breaker
salve! hello!
salvia f sage *(herb)*
salvietta f serviette
salviettine per bambini fpl baby wipes
salvo except ; unless
sandali mpl sandals
sangue m blood
   al sangue rare *(steak)*
sanguinare to bleed
sapere to know
sapone m soap
sapore m flavour ; taste
saporito(a) tasty
Sardegna f Sardinia
sarto m tailor
sartoria f tailor's ; dressmaker's
sasso m stone
sauna f sauna
sbagliato(a) wrong
sbaglio m mistake
sbarco m landing *(boat)*
sbrigare to hurry
scadente low *(standard, quality)*
scadenza f expiry
scadere to expire *(ticket, etc)*
scaduto(a) out-of-date ; expired
scala f scale ; ladder ; staircase
   scala anticendio fire escape
   scala mobile escalator

scalare to climb
scaldabagno m water heater
scaldare to heat up
scale fpl stairs
scalino m step
scalo m stopover
scaloppina f veal escalope
scarico(a) flat (battery)
scarpa f shoe
  scarpe da ginnastica trainers
scarponcini mpl walking boots
scarponi da sci mpl ski boots
scatola f box ; tin
scegliere to choose
scelta f range ; selection ; choice
scendere to go down
  scendere da to get off (bus, etc)
scheda f slip (of paper) ; card
  scheda telefonica phonecard
schiena f back (of body)
sci m ski ; skiing
  sci di fondo cross-country skiing
  sci nautico water-skiing
scialuppa di salvataggio f lifeboat
sciare to ski
sciarpa f scarf
sciogliere to melt
sciopero m strike
sciovia f ski-lift
scivolare to slip
scomodo(a) inconvenient ; uncomfortable
scomparire to disappear
scompartimento m compartment
scongelare to defrost
sconto m discount
  sconti reductions
scontrino m ticket ; receipt ; chit
scopa f broom (brush)
scorso(a) last
scossa f shock (electric)
scottatura f burn
  scottatura solare sunburn
Scozia f Scotland
scozzese Scottish
scrivania f desk
scrivere to write ; to spell
scultura f sculpture
scuola f school
  scuola di sci ski school
  scuola materna nursery school

scuro(a) dark (colour)
scusare to excuse ; to forgive
scusarsi to apologise
scusi? pardon?
se if ; whether
sé oneself
seconda f second gear
secondo m second (time) ; main course (meal)
secondo(a) second ; according to
  seconda classe second class
  di seconda mano secondhand
sede f seat ; head office
sedersi to sit down
sedia f chair
  sedia a rotelle wheelchair
  sedia a sdraio deckchair
sedile per bambini m babyseat (car)
seggiolone m highchair
seggiovia f chair-lift
segnale m signal ; road sign
segnare to score (goal)
segreteria telefonica f answering machine
seguente following
seguire to follow ; to continue
sella f saddle
selvatico(a) wild
semaforo m traffic lights
semifreddo m dessert made with ice cream
seminterrato basement
semplice plain ; simple
sempre always ; ever
senso unico one-way street
  senso vietato no entry
sentiero m path ; footpath
sentire to hear
sentirsi to feel
senza without
separato(a) separated
sera f evening
serbatoio m tank (car)
  serbatoio dell'acqua cistern
serio serious (not funny)
serpente m snake
serratura f lock
servire to serve
servizio m service ; report (in press)
  servizio al tavolo waiter service
  servizio compreso service included
servizi mpl facilities ; bathroom
sesso m sex

181

seta f silk

sete f thirst
avere sete to be thirsty

settembre m September

settentrionale northern

settimana f week
settimana bianca week's skiing holiday

settimanale weekly

sfida f challenge

sfuso(a) loose ; on tap *(wine)*

sganciare to lift receiver

sì yes

Sicilia f Sicily

sicurezza f safety ; security

sicuro(a) sure

sidro m cider

Sig. Mr *abbreviation of* Signor

Sig.a Mrs/Ms *abbreviation of* Signora

sigaretta f cigarette

sigaro m cigar

Sig.na Miss *abbreviation. of* Signorina

Signor: *il Signor Grandi* Mr Grandi

signora f lady ; madam ; Mrs ; Ms
signore ladies

signore m gentleman ; sir
signori gents

signorina f young woman ; Miss

silenzio m silence

simile a similar to

simpatico(a) pleasant ; nice

sindaco m mayor

singolo(a) single

sinistra f left

sistemare to arrange

sito m site
sito web website

skipass m skipass

slacciare to unfasten ; to undo

slavina f snowslide ; landslide

slegato(a) loose *(not fastened)*

slogatura f sprain

smarrito(a) missing *(thing)*

smettere to stop doing something

soccorso m assistance ; help
soccorso alpino mountain rescue

socio m associate ; member

soggiorno m stay ; sitting room

soldi mpl money

sole m sun ; sunshine

solito: *di solito* usually

sollevare to raise ; to relieve

sollievo m relief

solo(a) alone ; only

solubile soluble
caffè solubile instant coffee

sonnifero m sleeping pill

sono I am (to be)

sopra on ; above ; over
di sopra upstairs

sopracciglia fpl eyebrows

sopravvivere to survive

sorella f sister

sorpassare to overtake *(in car)*

sorpresa f surprise

sorridere to smile

sorriso m smile

sospeso(a) suspended ; postponed

sosta f stop
divieto di sosta no parking

sott'acqua underwater

sotterraneo(a) underground

sotto underneath ; under ; below

Spagna f Spain

spagnolo(a) Spanish

spalla f shoulder

sparire to disappear

spazzatura f rubbish

spazzola f brush
spazzola per capelli hairbrush
spazzolino da denti toothbrush

speciale special

specialità f speciality

specialmente especially

spedire to send ; to dispatch

spegnere to turn off ; to put out

spendere to spend *(money)*

spento(a) turned off ; out *(light, etc)*

sperare to hope

spese fpl shopping ; expenses

spesso often

spettacolo m show ; performance

spezzatino m stew

spiaggia f beach ; shore
spiaggia privata private beach

spiccioli mpl small coins ; change
non ho spiccioli I've no change

spiegare to explain

spina f bone *(of fish)* ; plug *(electric)*

spingere to push

spirale f coil *(IUD)*

spogliatoio m dressing room

sporco(a) dirty

sportello *m* counter ; window

sportivo(a) informal *(clothes)*

sposarsi to get married

sposato(a) married
 non sposato(a) single

spugna *f* sponge

spuma *f* hair mousse

spumante *m* sparkling wine

spuntino *m* snack

squadra *f* team

squillare to ring *(phone)*

Srl Ltd

stabilimento *m* factory

stadio *m* stadium

stagione *f* season
 di stagione in season

stalla *f* stable

stampatello *m* block letters

stanco(a) tired

stanza *f* room
 stanza da bagno bathroom
 stanza dei giochi playroom

stare to be
 stare attento(a) a... beware of..
 stare in piedi to stand

stasera tonight ; this evening

Stati Uniti *mpl* United States

stazione *f* station ; resort
 stazione balneare seaside resort
 stazione dell'autobus bus station
 stazione di servizio petrol station
 stazione ferroviaria train station

stella *f* star

sterlina *f* sterling ; pound

stesso(a) same

stirare to iron

stitichezza *f* constipation

stitico(a) constipated

stivali *mpl* boots

storia *f* history

storico(a) historic(al)
 centro storico old town

strada *f* road ; street
 strada chiusa road closed
 strada panoramica scenic route
 strada sbarrata road closed
 strada statale main road
 strada senza uscita no through road

stradina *f* lane

straniero(a) foreign ; foreigner

strano(a) strange

stupido(a) stupid

su on ; onto ; over ; about ; up

sua his ; her(s) ; its ; your(s)

subito at once ; immediately

succedere to happen

succo *m* juice
 succo d'arancia orange juice
 succo di frutta fruit juice
 succo di mela apple juice
 succo di pomodoro tomato juice

succursale *m* branch *(of bank, etc)*

sud *m* south

sue his ; her(s) ; its ; your(s)

suo(i) his ; her(s) ; its ; your(s)

suocera *f* mother-in-law

suocero *m* father-in-law

suola *f* sole *(of foot, shoe)*

suonare to ring ; to play

suono *m* sound

superare to exceed ; to overtake

supermercato *m* supermarket

supplemento *m* supplement

supposta *f* suppository

surf *m* surf

surgelato(a) frozen

sveglia *f* alarm clock

svegliare to wake up

svenire to faint

sviluppare to develop *(photos)*

Svizzera *f* Switzerland

svizzero(a) Swiss

svolta *f* turn

T

tabaccaio *m* tobacconist's

tacco *m* heel

tachimetro *m* speedometer

taglia *f* size *(of clothes)*

tagliare to cut

tailleur *m* women's suit

tallone *m* heel

tangenziale *f* by-pass

tanti(e) so many

tanto(a) so much ; so

tappo *m* cork ; plug ; cap
 tappo del serbatoio petrol cap

tardi late

targa *f* numberplate *(car)*

tariffa *f* tariff ; rate
 tariffa economica cheap rate
 tariffa festiva rate on holidays
 tariffa ore di punta peak rate

183

tartuffo m truffle
tasca f pocket
tassa f tax
tasso m rate
   tasso di cambio exchange rate
tavola f table ; plank ; board
   tavola calda hot snacks
   tavola da surf surfboard
   tavola a vela windsurfing board
taxi m taxi
tazza f cup
tè m tea
   tè al latte tea with milk
   tè al limone lemon tea
   tè freddo iced tea
teatro m theatre ; drama
tedesco(a) German
telecomando m remote control
telefonare to (tele)phone
telefonata f phone call
telefonino m mobile phone
telefono m telephone
   telefono pubblico payphone
televisione f television
telone impermeabile m groundsheet
temperatura f temperature
temperino m penknife
tempesta f storm
tempio m temple
tempo m weather ; time
temporale m thunderstorm
tenda f curtain ; tent
tendine m tendon
tenere to keep ; to hold
tenore m tenor *(singer)*
tenore alcolico m alcohol content
tergicristallo m windscreen wiper
terminal m terminal *(airport)*
termometro m thermometer
termosifone m heater
terra f earth ; ground
terrazza f terrace
terremoto m earthquake
terza f third gear
terzi mpl third party
terzo(a) third
tessera f pass ; season ticket
tesserino m pass *(bus, train)*
tessuto m fabric
testa f head
testicoli mpl testicles
tettarella f dummy *(for baby)*
tetto m roof

tettuccio apribile m sunroof *(car)*
Tevere m Tiber
thermos m thermos flask
thriller m thriller
timone m rudder
tirare to pull
toccare to touch ; to feel
   non toccare do not touch
togliere to remove ; to take away
toilette f toilet
tonno m tuna
topo m mouse
Torino f Turin
tornare to return ; to come/go back
torneo m tournament
toro m bull
torre f tower
torrone m nougat
torta f cake ; tart ; pie
Toscana f Tuscany
tosse f cough
tossico(a) toxic
tossire to cough
totale m total *(amount)*
tovaglia f tablecloth
tovagliolo m napkin
tra between ; among(st) ; in
tradizionale traditional
tradurre to translate
traduzione f translation
traffico m traffic
traghetto m ferry
tramezzino m sandwich
trampolino m diving board ; ski jump
tranquillante m tranquillizer
tranquillo(a) quiet *(place)*
trasferire to transfer
trasporto m transport
trattoria f restaurant
traveller's cheque mpl traveller's cheque
traversata f crossing ; flight
treno m train
   treno merci goods train
triangolo d'emergenza m warning triangle
tribuna f stand (stadium)
tribunale m law court
trimestre m term *(school)*

triste sad

tritare to mince ; to chop

troppi(e) too many

troppo too much ; too

trovare to find

trucco m make-up

tu you (familiar)

tubo m pipe ; tube
  tubo di scappamento exhaust

tuffarsi to dive

turno m turn ; shift
  di turno on duty

tuta sportiva f tracksuit

tutti (e) all ; everybody
  tutte le direzioni all routes

tutto everything ; all

U

ubriaco(a) drunk

uccello m bird

uccidere to kill

UE European Union

ufficio m office ; church service
  ufficio informazioni information bureau
  ufficio oggetti smarriti lost property office
  ufficio postale post office

ufficio turistico tourist office

uguale equal ; even

ulcera f ulcer

ultimo(a) last

un a ; an ; one

unghia f nail (finger, toe)

unione f union
  Unione Europea European Union

Unità Sanitaria Locale local health centre

università f university

uno(a) a ; an ; one

uomo m man
  uomini gents

uova mpl eggs

uovo m egg
  uovo di Pasqua Easter egg
  uovo sodo hard-boiled egg

uragano m hurricane

urgente urgent

usare to use

uscire to go/come out

uscita f exit/gate
  uscita di sicurezza emergency exit

USL abbreviation of **Unità Sanitaria Locale**

uso m use

utile useful

uva f grapes

V

va bene all right (agreed)

vacanza f holiday(s)
  vacanze estive summer holidays

vaccinazione f vaccination

vagina f vagina

vaglia m money order

vagone m carriage ; wagon
  vagone letto sleeper
  vagone ristorante restaurant car

valanga f avalanche

valico m pass (mountain)

valido(a) valid
  valido fino a... valid until...

valigia f suitcase

valore m value; worth
  di valore valuable

valuta f currency

valvola f valve

varicella f chickenpox

vasetto m jar

vaso m vase

vassoio m tray

vecchio(a) old

vedere to see

vedova f widow

vedovo m widower

vegetaliano(a) vegan

vegetariano(a) vegetarian

veicolo m vehicle

vela f sail ; sailing

veleno m poison

velenoso(a) poisonous

veloce quick

velocemente quickly

velocità f speed

vena f vein

vendere to sell
  vendesi for sale

vendita f sale
  vendita al minuto retail
  vendita a rate hire purchase

venerdì m Friday

venerdì santo *m* Good Friday
Venezia *f* Venice
venire to come
ventaglio *m* fan *(hand-held)*
ventilatore *m* electric fan
vento *m* wind
verde green
verdura *f* vegetables
verità *f* truth
vermut *m* vermouth
vernice *f* paint
verniciare to paint
vero(a) true ; real ; genuine
versamento *m* payment ; deposit
versare to pour
vertice *m* summit
vescica *f* blister
vespa *f* wasp
vestaglia *f* dressing gown
vestirsi to get dressed
vestiti *mpl* clothes
vestito *m* dress
vetrina *f* shop window
vetro *m* glass *(substance)*
via *f* street ; by *(via)*
 per via aerea by air mail
viaggiare to travel
viaggiatore *m* traveller
viaggio *m* journey ; trip ; drive
 viaggio d'affari business trip
 viaggio organizzato package tour
viale *m* avenue
vicino (a) near ; close by
vicolo *m* alley ; lane
 vicolo cieco cul-de-sac
videocamera *f* videocamera
videocassetta *f* videocassette
videogioco *m* computer game
videoregistratore *m* video recorder
vietato forbidden
 vietato accendere fuochi do not
 light fires
 vietato fumare no smoking
 vietato l'ingresso no entry
 vietato ingresso veicoli no entry for
 vehicles
 vietato scendere no exit
vigili del fuoco fire brigade
vigilia *f* eve
 Vigilia di Natale Christmas Eve
vigna *f* vineyard
vincere to win
vino *m* wine

italian–eng v/z

 vino bianco white wine
 vini da pasto table wines
 vino da tavola table wine
 vini pregiati quality wines
 vino rosso red wine
violentare to rape
virus *m* virus
visita *f* visit
 visite guidate guided tours
visitare to visit
vista *f* view
visto *m* visa
vita *f* life ; waist
 vita notturna night life
vitamina *f* vitamin
vite *f* vine ; screw
vivere to live
vivo(a) live ; alive
voce *f* voice
volante *m* steering wheel
volare to fly
voler dire to mean *(signify)*
volere to want
volo *m* flight
 volo di linea scheduled flight
 volo charter charter flight
volta *f* time
 una volta once
 due volte twice
voltaggio *m* voltage
vomitare to vomit
vongola *f* clam
vostro(a) your ; yours
vulcano *m* volcano
vuoto(a) empty

Z

zanzara *f* mosquito
zanzaria *f* mosquito net
zia *f* aunt
zio *m* uncle
zona *f* zone
 zona blu restricted parking zone
 zona pedonale pedestrian
zucchero *m* sugar
zucchini *mpl* courgettes
zuppa *f* soup
 zuppa inglese type of trifle

HOW ITALIAN WORKS

NOUNS

*A **noun** is word such as **car**, **horse** or **Mary** which is used to refer to a person or thing.*

Unlike English, Italian nouns have a gender: they are either *masculine* (**il**) or *feminine* (**la**). Therefore words for *the* and *a(n)* must agree with the noun they accompany – whether *masculine*, *feminine* or *plural*:

	masculine	*feminine*	*plural*
the	**il gato, l'anno**	**la strada, l'alba**	**i gati, le strade, le albe**
a(n)	**un gato, un anno**	**una strada un'alba**	**dei gati, delle strade, dell'albe**

NOTE: you will come across the articles **lo** and **gli** for masculine nouns beginning with s+consonant

	masculine	*plural*
the	**lo stato, lo spallo**	**gli stati, gli spalli**
a, an	**uno stato, uno spallo**	**degli stati, degli spalli**

PLURALS

For most nouns, the singular ending changes as follows:

masc. sing.	*masc. plur.*	*example*
-**o**	-**i**	**il libro → i libri**
-**e**	-**i**	**il padre → i padri**

fem. sing.	*fem. plur.*	*example*
-**a**	-**e**	**la mela → le mele**
-**e**	-**i**	**le madre → le madri**

NOTE: nouns ending in **e** can be either *masculine* or *feminine*. In the plural they all end in -**i**, e.g.

la televisione	**le televisioni**
il mare	**i mari**

NOTE: most nouns ending in -**co** and -**go** become -**chi** and -**ghi** in the plural to keep the **c** and **g** hard sounding. Some exceptions occur in the masculine, e.g. **amico – amici**

NOTE: nouns ending in -**ca** and -**ga** become -**che** and -**ghe** in the plural to keep the **c** and **g** hard sounding. Nouns ending in -**cia** and -**gia** often becomes -**ce** and **ge** to keep the **c** and **g** soft sounding.

NOTE: definite articles (**il**, **la**, **i**, **le**, *etc.*) used after the prepositions **a** (**to**, **at**), **da** (**by**, **from**), **su** (**on**), **di** (**of**, **some**) and **in** (**in**, **into**) contract as follows:

a + il = al	**da + il = dal**	**su + il = sul**
a + lo = allo	**da + lo = dallo**	**su + lo = sullo**
a + l' = all'	**da + l' = dall'**	**su + l' = sull'**
a + la = alla	**da + la = dalla**	**su + la = sulla**
a + i = ai	**da + i = dai**	**su + i = sui**
a + gli = agli	**da + gli = dagli**	**su + gli = sugli**
a + le = alle	**da + le = dalle**	**su + le = sulle**

di + il = del	in + il = nel
di + lo = dello	in + lo = nello
di + l' = dell'	in + l' = nell'
di + la = della	in + la = nella
di + i = dei	in + i = nei
di + gli= degli	in + gli = negli
di + le = delle	in + le = nelle

e.g. **alla** casa (**to the** house)   **sul** tavolo (**on the** table)

ADJECTIVES

*An **adjective** is word such as **small**, **pretty** or **practical** that
describes a person or thing, or gives extra information about them.*

Adjectives normally follow the noun they describe in Italian,
e.g. la mela **rossa** (the red apple)
Some common exceptions which go before the noun are:
bello beautiful, **breve** short, **brutto** ugly, **buono** good, **cattivo** bad, **giovane**
young, **grande** big, **lungo** long, **nuovo** new, **piccolo** small, **vecchio** old
e.g. una **bella** giornata (a beautiful day)

Italian adjectives have to reflect the gender of the noun they describe. To
make an adjective feminine, an **a** replaces the **o** of the masculine, e.g. ross**o** –
ross**a**. Adjectives ending in **e**, e.g. **giovane**, can be either masculine or
feminine. The plural forms of the adjective change in the way described for
nouns (above).

MY, YOUR, HIS, HER, OUR, THEIR

These words also depend on the gender and number of the noun they
accompany, and not on the sex of the 'owner'.

	with masc. sing. noun	*with fem. sing. noun*	*with masc. plur. noun*	*with fem. plur. noun*
my	**il mio**	**la mia**	**i miei**	**le mie**
your *(polite)*	**il suo**	**la sua**	**i suoi**	**le sue**
your *(familiar)*	**il tuo**	**la tua**	**i tuoi**	**le tue**
your *(plural)*	**il vostro**	**la vostra**	**i vostri**	**le vostre**
his/her	**il suo**	**la sua**	**i suoi**	**le sue**
our	**il nostro**	**la nostra**	**i nostri**	**le nostre**
their	**il loro**	**la loro**	**i loro**	**le loro**

*A **pronoun** is word that you use to refer to someone or something when you do not need to use a noun, often because the person or thing has been mentioned earlier. Examples are **it**, **she**, **something** and **myself**.*

SUBJECT		OBJECT	
I		io	me **mi**
you	**lei**	you	**la**
he	**lui/egli**	him	**lo/l'** (+vowel)
she	**lei/ella**	her	**la/l'** (+vowel)
it (masc.)	**esso**	it (masc.)	**lo/l'** (+vowel)
it (fem.)	**essa**	it (fem.)	**la/l'** (+vowel)
we	**noi**	us	**ci**
you	**voi**	you	**vi**
they	**loro**	them (masc.)	**li**
(things:masc)	**essi**	them (fem.)	**le**
(things:fem.)	**esse**		

The object pronouns shown above are also used to mean **to me, to us**, etc., except:

> to him/to it = **gli**
> to her/to it/to you = **le**
> to them = **loro**

Object pronouns (other than **loro**) usually go before the verb:

> **lo vedo** but **scriverò loro**
> I see him I will write to them

When used with an infinitive (the verb form given in the dictionary), the pronoun follows and is attached to the infinitive less its final *e*:

> **voglio comprarlo** I want to buy it

Subject pronouns (**io, tu, egli**, etc.) are often omitted in Italian, since the verb ending generally distinguishes the person:

> **parlo** I speak
> **parliamo** we speak
> **parlano** they speak

In Italian there are two forms for *you* – **Lei** (singular) and **voi** (plural). **Tu**, the familiar form for **you**, should only be used with people you know well, or children.

VERBS

*A **verb** is a word such as **sing**, **walk** or **cry** which is used with a subject to say what someone or something does or what happens to them. **Regular verbs** follow the same pattern of endings. **Irregular verbs** do not follow a regular pattern so you need to learn the different endings.*

There are three main patterns of endings for verbs in Italian – those ending **-are**, **-ere** and **-ire** in the dictionary. Two examples of the **-ire** verbs are shown, since two distinct groups of endings exist. Subject pronouns are shown in brackets because these are often not used:

	PARLARE	TO SPEAK
(io)	**parlo**	I speak
(tu)	**parli**	you speak
(lui/lei)	**parla**	(s)he speaks
(noi)	**parliamo**	we speak
(voi)	**parlate**	you speak
(loro)	**parlano**	they speak

past participle: **parlato** (with **avere**)

	VENDERE	TO SELL
(io)	**vendo**	I sell
(tu)	**vendi**	you sell
(lui/lei)	**vende**	(s)he sells
(noi)	**vendiamo**	we sell
(voi)	**vendete**	you sell
(loro)	**vendono**	they sell

past participle: **venduto** (with **avere**)

	DORMIRE	TO SLEEP
(io)	**dormo**	I sleep
(tu)	**dormi**	you sleep
(lui/lei)	**dorme**	(s)he sleeps
(noi)	**dormiamo**	we sleep
(voi)	**dormite**	you sleep
(loro)	**dormono**	they sleep

past participle: **dormito** (with **avere**)

	FINIRE	TO FINISH
(io)	**finisco**	I finish
(tu)	**finisci**	you finish
(lui/lei)	**finisce**	(s)he finishes
(noi)	**finiamo**	we finish
(voi)	**finite**	you finish
(loro)	**finiscono**	they finish

past participle: **finito** (with **avere**)

IRREGULAR VERBS

Among the most important irregular verbs are the following:

	ESSERE	TO BE	**AVERE**	TO HAVE
(io)	**sono**	I am	**ho**	I have
(tu)	**sei**	you are	**hai**	you have
(lui/lei)	**è**	(s)he is	**ha**	(s)he has
(noi)	**siamo**	we are	**abbiamo**	we have
(voi)	**siete**	you are	**avete**	you have
(loro)	**sono**	they are	**hanno**	they have

past participle: **stato** (with **essere**) past participle: **avuto** (with **avere**)

	ANDARE	TO GO	**FARE**	TO DO
(io)	**vado**	I go	**faccio**	I do
(tu)	**vai**	you go	**fai**	you do
(lui/lei)	**va**	(s)he goes	**fa**	(s)he does
(noi)	**andiamo**	we go	**facciamo**	we do
(voi)	**andate**	you go	**fate**	you do
(loro)	**vanno**	they go	**fanno**	they do

past participle: **andato** (with **essere**) past participle: **fatto** (with **avere**)

	POTERE	TO BE ABLE	**VOLERE**	TO WANT
(io)	**posso**	I can	**voglio**	I want
(tu)	**puoi**	you can	**vuoi**	you want
(lui/lei)	**può**	(s)he can	**vuole**	(s)he wants
(noi)	**possiamo**	we can	**vogliamo**	we want
(voi)	**potete**	you can	**volete**	you want
(loro)	**possono**	they can	**vogliono**	they want

past participle: **potuto** (with **avere**) past participle: **voluto** (with **avere**)

	DOVERE	TO HAVE TO (MUST)
(io)	**devo**	I must
(tu)	**devi**	you must
(lui/lei)	**deve**	he/she must
(noi)	**dobbiamo**	we must
(voi)	**dovete**	you must
(loro)	**devono**	they must

past participle: **dovuto** (with **avere**)

PAST TENSE

*To make a simple past tense you need an **auxiliary verb** with the past participle of the main verb, e.g. **I have** (auxiliary) **been** (past participle), **I have** (auxiliary) **eaten** (past participle). In Italian the basic auxiliary verbs are **avere** (to have) and **essere** (to be). A **reflexive verb** is one where the subject and object are the same e.g. **to enjoy yourself, to dress yourself**. These verbs take **essere** as their auxiliary verb.*

To form the simple past tense, I spoke/I have spoken, I sold/I have sold, etc. combine the present tense of the verb **avere** – to have with the past participle of the verb, e.g.

ho parlato	I spoke/I have spoken
ho venduto	I sold/I have sold

PARLARE (past)

ho parlato	I spoke
hai parlato	you spoke
ha parlato	(s)he spoke
abbiamo parlato	we spoke
avete parlato	you spoke
hanno parlato	they spoke

VENDERE (past)

ho venduto	I sold
hai venduto	you sold
ha venduto	(s)he sold
abbiamo venduto	we sold
avete venduto	you sold
hanno venduto	they sold

DORMIRE (past)

ho dormito	I slept
hai dormito	you slept
ha dormito	(s)he slept
abbiamo dormito	we slept
avete dormito	you slept
hanno dormito	they slept

FINIRE (past)

ho finito	I finished
hai finito	you finished
ha finito	(s)he finished
abbiamo finito	we finished
avete finito	you finished
hanno finito	they finished

NOTE: not all verbs take **avere** (**ho, hai**, etc.) as their auxiliary verb, some take **essere** (**sono, sei**, etc.). These are mainly verbs of motion or staying, e.g. **andare–to go, stare–to be** (located at):

e.g. **sono andato**   I went
     sono stato a Roma   I was in Rome

When the auxiliary verb **essere** is used, the past particple (**andato, stato**) becomes an adjective and should agree with the subject of the verb, e.g.

sono andata	I went *(fem. sing.)*
siamo stati	we went *(masc. plural)*

To make a sentence negative e. g. I am not eating, you use **non** before the verb.

e.g.   **non mangio**   I am not eating
          non sono andato   I did not go